NEW MEXICO

. . .Very nice, the great South-West, put on a sombrero and knot a red kerchief round your neck, to go out in the great free spaces!

That is New Mexico wrapped in the absolutely hygienic and shiny mucous-paper of our trite civilization. That is the New Mexico known to most of the Americans who know it at all. But break through the shiny sterilized wrapping, and actually *touch* the country, and you will never be the same again.

D. H. LAWRENCE

NEW MEXICO
The Shining Land

JOHN L. SINCLAIR

UNIVERSITY OF NEW MEXICO PRESS

Albuquerque

Library of Congress Cataloging in Publication Data

Sinclair, John L   1902-
    New Mexico, the shining land.

      1. New Mexico—History—Addresses, essays,
lectures. 2. Indians of North America—New
Mexico—History—Addresses, essays, lectures.
3. New Mexico—Description and travel—Addresses,
essays, lectures. I. Title.
F796.5.S56   978.9   80-52271
ISBN O-8263-0548-2

Acknowledgment is here given the editors of
Westways of Los Angeles,
and to the *New Mexico Magazine* of Santa Fe,
in whose pages some of these chapters first appeared.

Designed by CHARLES E. SKAGGS.
Jacket Watercolor by DAN STOUFFER.
Manufactured in the United States of America
Library of Congress Catalog Card Number 80-52271
International Standard Book Number 0-8263-0548-2
FIRST EDITION

CONTENTS

ACKNOWLEDGMENTS

The contents of this book have been written with the help of a number of people over a great period of time. And now, in my twilight years, after fifty-seven spent living and earning and loving in this blessed Land of the Sun, I write in gratitude for the inspiration they gave me, the stories they told, and the things they did.

I give special thanks to the editors of *Westways* magazine of Los Angeles, namely Patrice Manahan, Larry L. Meyer, Davis Dutton; and the current lady at the helm, Frances Ring. And to the editorial staff of the *New Mexico Magazine* of Santa Fe, to Sheila Tryk, who is not only my editor there but a staunch friend, and who likes what I strive to do. Several chapters of this book had first-time publication in the periodicals named.

I give most special gratitude to George Fitzpatrick, now retired but long-time editor of the *New Mexico Magazine*, who purchased my first story in 1937 and put me into print, and to whom I owe my literary career, for without his help it likely would not have been.

I humble myself in the memory of the cattlemen and sheepmen who employed me on their ranches in Chaves and Lincoln counties from the early 1920s to the mid-1930s, and the cowboys, sheep *caporales*, and herders I worked with. And the homesteaders settled on their claims out of Texas, Oklahoma, and the Ozarks, who through my admiration of their veracity, homespun honesty, and life-style, and especially their poetic vernacular, in later years urged me to write novels based on their daily lives, humorous or tragic.

I wish to thank William Lumpkins, noted architect of Santa Fe, who insisted in the mid-1930s that I come out of the Lincoln County "cow pasture" and take up residence in the more literary atmosphere of Santa Fe. With affection I remember the years when Santa Fe, the town with a 15,000 population, was perfection in adobe, with the incense of piñon smoke drifting over the rooftops, when the wood-venders drove their loaded burros through the streets selling the pitchy fuel at *dos reales* a packsaddle-load. And when Canyon Road and the Camino del Monte Sol were unpaved and rustic, and great works of art and literature were made along their separate ways, by the great artists and writers of the day—Randall Davey, Will Shuster, Josef Bakos, Lynn Riggs, Olive Rush, Alfred Morang, Witter Bynner, Raymond Jonson—and a score of others. When Brian Boru Dunne was "Mr. Santa Fe" himself, voicing his philosophies with Irish wit in the lobby of La Fonda, slouch-hatted and garbed to match the color the town shared with Taos, distinguished then as the most colorful in the West.

I think back with pleasure to the staff of the Museum of New Mexico when I started in the Palace of the Governors as a research assistant in 1938— Wayne Mauzy, Helen Dorman, Bertha Dutton, Dr. Reginald Fisher, Jean Cady, Hulda Hobbs, Ruth Rambo, Hester Jones, Mary Van Stone—and Dr. Edgar L. Hewett, the director and founder of the Museum, as well as the Anthropology Department at the University of New Mexico, who gave generously of his great knowledge during my first two years at Kuaua on the Coronado State Monument.

I wish to thank the excavators of Kuaua not only for the great Monument they created but for my pleasure in having them for friends—Marjorie Lambert, now retired, Curator of Archaeology of the Museum of New Mexico; Wesley Bliss for his masterly handling in the preservation of the Kuaua Murals; and Albert Ely, Gordon Vivian, Dorothy Luhrs, now departed far too soon in view of their tremendous worth to Southwestern archaeology.

Thanks go to Edward Penfield, of Lincoln Town, and to his mother, the late Ruth Martin, proprietors of the old and historic Tunstall-McSween store, for their help and friendship throughout my two years of tenure at the Lincoln Museum. And Bert and Clark Phingsten, Roman and Theodora Maez, the late Bill Hale and Felix Ramey.

I think back now to the many visits to my home on the Coronado State Monument, through my eighteen years of living there, of Dr. Stephen Borhegy of the Museum of Natural History in New York, researcher and writer, the world's foremost authority on facts concerning the Valley of Chimayó and the Santuario de Potrero. To Adlai Feather, of Mesilla Park, historian of all

Southwestern New Mexico. To the editors of my books, who though not of New Mexico became fast friends and long-time correspondents—Harold S. Latham of Macmillan, noted for his discovery of Margaret Mitchell and publication of *Gone With the Wind*; Erd Brandt of the *Saturday Evening Post*; Alan Swallow of Sage Books; and, although he published none of my own, a great friend and Westerner, Thayer Hobson of Morrow.

I thank for their help and friendship some of the most esteemed of New Mexico writers of the day—Dr. T.M. Pearce, retired professor of English of the University of New Mexico, who knew me from the very beginning; William Buchanan of Albuquerque, who settled in New Mexico to give of his mighty talent; Howard Bryan of the Albuquerque *Tribune*, researcher-historian extraordinary, tireless writer of every phase of life possible in New Mexico, past and present; and to Frank Waters of Taos, dean of Southwestern writers, long-time friend and source of inspiration.

And finally, and above all, my love and gratitude goes to my wife, Evelyn, who in our long years together has given trust and encouragement to every word come off my typewriter, and whose research and criticisms, and countless excursions to the Xerox machine, made this and all my work possible.

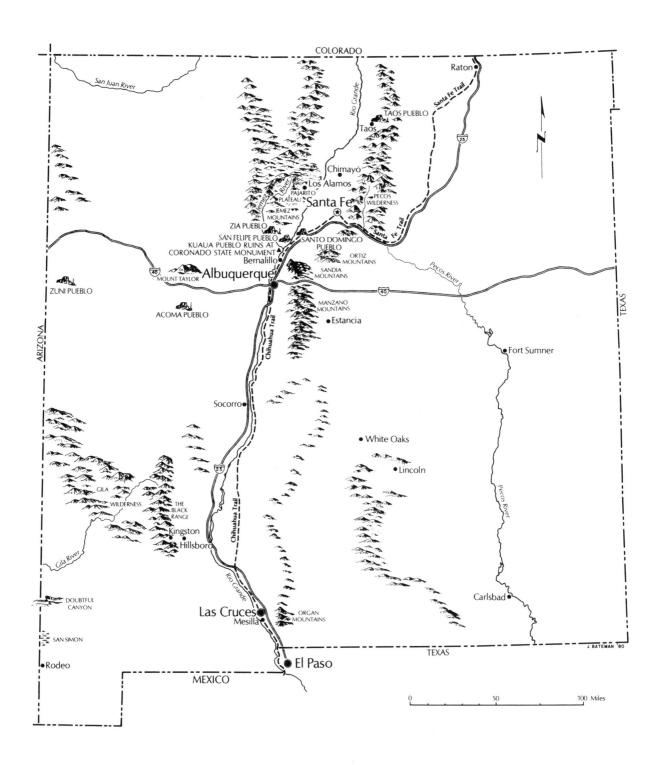

1

A TOUCH OF ALL THE WORLD

I WAS TALKING with Hans Lembourn, the Danish novelist, beside the Rio Grande and looking to the Sandia Mountains. We were at my home at the Coronado State Monument, near Bernalillo, in the autumn of 1957. Lembourn spread a hand against the superb panorama.

He said, "You are aware, of course, that this view has a twin."

Aware? How could I help but be aware? Ten twins! A hundred twins!

Ahead of us was the narrow strip of the river flowing south; beyond was *bosque,* a green of almost tropical density on the opposite bank. Further east lay the hidden farmlands, the irrigated valley, then the bench that rises to the mountain's base—and at last the majestic mountain itself. Above it all was the magnificent blue New Mexican sky, the only one of its kind in America.

In my fourteen eventful years superintending the Coronado Monument, I would feast my eyes daily on that same view, and almost as often listen to tourists compare the scene with spots familiar to them. And the places they described were exotic and far away.

Aware?

Yes, indeed, I was thoroughly aware.

"Surely," I said, "the twin can't be found in Denmark!"

He shook his head. "No," he replied. "In Tanganyika. The scene is decidedly African. I've looked upon this many, many times."

He went on to say how the mountain could be one of many in Kenya, and the river—happily flowing and full from bank to bank at the time—is one that shouldn't be in the northern hemisphere at all. The wooded bosque beyond the stream is far too lush not to be tropical. In fact, all that is missing from this New Mexican landscape to make it Tanganyikan is the animal and bird life, not to

1

forget the reptiles. Giraffes, Lembourn told me then, would be slaking their long-necked thirsts at the bank; hippopotami of sundry sex and kinship would be wallowing in the silt; lions and leopards would slink about; all manner of African game would be in congress; lengthy snakes would drape themselves around the tree limbs; and birds of gay plumage would be quite deafening.

"Yes," said Hans Lembourn. "I have beheld this view before. And not only in Africa. . . ."

And at Corrales, directly south of where I lived, a lady brought up in South Africa built an *adobe* home among some cottonwoods. She loved it, her husband explained to me, because "it gives her a feeling of the *veldt*."

New Mexico is blessed by its diverse terrain which often rises abruptly from desert to tundra, from altitudes of 2,500 to 13,000 feet. Everywhere, because of its suddenly changing elevations, the landscape is never dull. Visitors always seem to find some resemblance to the home sod somewhere and anywhere around them.

On one occasion I met a young Cornishman direct from the southwest boot-toe of England, outfitted with a keen interest and observation, and, like most foreign visitors, intensely thrilled with what New Mexico offers. The foreign traveler has a sense of the archaic which most forward-looking Americans too sadly lack, and the alien presence among the ancient ruins was a great joy to me. I asked the young man from Penzance if there was any resemblance in the immediate scene to the landscape of Cornwall. None at all, was his reply. But later, driving down from Santa Fe in the vicinity of La Cienega, he admitted that the long grassy sweep of terrain made him a little homesick for his native, treeless peninsula.

On another happy day I escorted a Swiss around the ruins, one who had settled in California. He was on his way to a vacation at Red River in the highest mountains in the northern part of the state.

"For a breath of my homeland," as he expressed it, "without the expense of ocean travel and all the bureaucratic red tape, I have gone to Red River many times. There I find myself again in the Alps of Valais."

The early Spanish settlers found themselves immediately at home in New Mexico. For this northern region bore a keen resemblance to the motherland, particularly to the high, dry plateau of Castile. Right from the start, the chroniclers who accompanied the various expeditions commented on the similarity. Alvarado, when describing to Castañeda an old pueblo in the vicinity of Acoma, told how the wall was "well built of fine cut stone, with gates and gutters like a Castilian city." Andalusia may have been the cradle of American colonization, but the Spaniard of the mountainous north found a familiar atmosphere in the region that in 1598 was chosen for New Mexico's first capital at San Gabriel de Yuque Yunque. And even today, Truchas, Cordova, Trampas, and Peñasco could be taken for villages transplanted from the Pyrenees.

The popular saying, "Africa begins in the Pyrenees," applies to Spain and the Moorish influence brought to that country during the era of Moslem dominance. Truly, those implicit African qualities can be found in New Mexico in the works of the Spaniards who carried all they could of their homeland across the Atlantic to Vera Cruz, to the Valley of Mexico, and northward to the plaza of Santa Fe. So Spanish culture was established, folkways spiced with the flavoring of Morocco and Algiers.

Some time ago, a lady just returned from residence in Spain, was among others at a picnic supper with us at the Monument. From where we sat at a table in the brush-roofed *tipéstle* on the river bank, the museum building stood out in bold relief against the night sky, starlit, blueblack, the moonlight silvery and intense. She remarked on the Santa Fe-Pueblo style architecture, as genuinely adobe as any structure can be.

"How Indian!" she said. "Yet so Spanish and so Moorish! The high *portal,* the corbels, the building itself so harmonious to cobblestoned lanes and a sunny hillside. It may indeed be something out of pre-Columbian America, but give it a red tile roof, a donkey or two, and a rank odor up from the flea market, and I'll say I'm back in Ronda again."

A few years ago, when Carl Raswan operated his Arabian horse ranch near Cedar Crest, it was his custom to come occasionally to the Coronado Monument for, as he put it, "another look at Egypt." Raswan—author of fine books, including *Drinkers of the Wind* and *Black Tents of Arabia*—spent many years in Egypt and Arabia where he studied the Arabic language and poetry and the breeding and bloodlines of Arabian horses. Here at the Coronado Monument he would get great pleasure from sitting on the roof of the pumphouse and looking upstream, meditating on the arid flat-topped mesas, the lofty mountains beyond, and the silt-laden Rio Grande. Absolute serenity.

"I find myself again in Egypt," he would say, "and once more I look upon the upper Nile."

4

The same vista was once likened to the Hudson River at West Point by some touring New Yorkers. Others from the East disagree, saying it has no resemblance at all. Said one: "I haven't seen the Nile, so I'll leave that to Mr. Raswan. But I *have* seen the Hudson. If that's West Point, then where are the cadets?"

In March of 1957 it was my pleasure to guide a group of distinguished Iranians around the ruins at Coronado. Among them was the governor of Nishapur, the province of Iran famed for its turquoise, and others who held high positions at the University of Tehran. I explained the archaeology and lectured on both the ancient and contemporary Indian cultures of the area. Then one of them pointed to the north and made a comment in Persian. The speech was incomprehensible to me, but by their facial expressions I knew they had found something familiar.

"Tell me," I asked the governor, "what is your climate like? And your landscapes? Are they similar to this?"

He continued to point northward, toward the desert under a blazing sun. "Yes," he said, "it is quite the same . . . Look that way and close your eyes; open them, and you will *see* Iran . . . Breathe deep of this air, and you will *breathe* Iran."

When I first came to New Mexico in August of 1923, I found here a favorable comparison to the Scottish Highlands, my boyhood home, and to the Border Hills I had forsaken for America that spring. Here I saw the same vast, rugged stretches of terrain, the bare hills, the shaggy mountains. Over here were the rolling plains, over there the same lonely sweep of the moors. In those days before good highways, Picacho Hill on the road from Roswell to Hondo sported a curve sharp enough to test the sense and skill of any motorist. It reminded me of the Devil's Elbow on the Pitlochry to Braemar road, which I had travelled annually as a boy with my family when we went as clansmen to attend the Highland Gathering.

Over here, a broken plain with a mountain background takes me back to bicycling days at my aunt's house on a hilltop between Loch Lomond and the Gareloch. Again I see the Cobbler that is chiseled out of the Highland Hills, and the far-famed romantic bulk of Ben Lomond.

5

And again, just before descending La Bajada on the highway between Santa Fe and Albuquerque, there is a Scottish scene that lacks only the gorse and the heather and a flock of black-faced mountain sheep to make it truly Highland. It is the view toward the Ortiz and San Pedro Mountains seen over the treeless plain to the south and west. Its counterpart is the great coned mountain Schiehallion lording over the Moor of Rannoch. To the nostalgic eyes a sweep of violet distance becomes the beloved heather, a chamisa clump in golden bloom the shaggy gorse. Here in New Mexico—southwestward seven thousand airline miles—I found the hills of home.

Haniel Long, in his *Piñon Country*, compares the Bonito Valley at Lincoln to certain verdant spots in Pennsylvania and New York. And Canadians will breathe familiar air at such places as Chama, Gavilan, Eagle Nest, and Cloudcroft. And Regina, New Mexico, is not too climatically different on a January day from Regina, Saskatchewan. A winter day at Columbus, on the Mexican border in Luna County, rates on a par with Jacksonville, Florida—without the pea-soup-thick humidity.

Eric James, headmaster of Manchester Grammar School, one of England's famed institutions of learning, visited the Coronado Monument and provided me with the opportunity of doing him the honors. On hearing that I came to New Mexico from Scotland he told me that he was a lover of mountains and therefore spent his summers in a part of the West Highlands I knew very well.

"Apart from the rain and mist," I asked him, "can you see any similarity between here and there?"

"Why of course!" he said most enthusiastically. "Coming down from Santa Fe, this morning. That view one sees to the south. It's the Hills of Morven, exactly. You know, seen across Loch Linnhe from the road to Ballachulish...."

And so it goes, never failing.

Tanganyika, Cornwall, Spain, Algiers, Iran, Morocco, India, China, Egypt, South Africa, Scotland ... Even Texas and the Hudson at West Point.... The frigid prairies of Saskatchewan, the Arctic atmosphere of the Kicking Horse

Pass, and a dozen miles away a climate identical to balmy Catalonia . . .
Switzerland, the Alps of Valais... Darjeeling....

In New Mexico is seen and felt a touch of all the world.

6

Some years ago, a brilliant young traveler from Tel Aviv visited me, and
remarked how closely New Mexico resembled Israel, not only in its arid climate
and sun-drenched land, but in the Indian pueblos and their architecture and
pattern of living. He compared them to rural villages of ancient Galilee. . .

Only recently, at a ceremonial, I watched the walk, the poise, the beauty
of a Pueblo woman as she deposited a heaped basket of bread before a spruce-
covered shrine. Her head and shoulders were draped with a sky-blue shawl; her
face was serene, not of this age.

Was she María, or Guadalupita?

Was she one of the countless Rosas or Luisas we know?

Or was she Rachel at the well?

2

HAWIKUH: CITY OF CIBOLA

Rumors were circulating in the Valley of Mexico that had the Spanish conquerors all astir—a cluster of mystery towns somewhere in the far, bleak north! Tale after tale went the rounds that year of 1528, tantalizing the ambitions of the high-born cavaliers who had followed Cortez to the New World. The Seven Cities of Cibola, so went the talk, possessed wealth beyond a man's wildest imagination.

Nuño de Guzman, Governor of New Spain and President of the Audencia, was inspired, for hadn't he heard an eye-witness report from his own Indian servant, a boy named Tejo, son of a trader in the Valley of Oxitipak? Tejo, it seems, had boasted to the other servants of tagging along on an expedition his father had made to trade parrot feathers in the north. There they had found seven towns, said Tejo, each the size of Mexico City, situated between two seas and reached after a forty-day crossing of a vast, grassy desert. Whole streets were occupied by silversmiths in whose shops the beaten silver was heaped waist-high!

Fired by this vision and confident of the authority of a heaven that governed the fortunes of Spain, Nuño de Guzman organized an army of 400 mounted Spaniards and 20,000 Mexican Indians. The following year, with banners flying and spearheads flashing, they set out in search of the Seven Cities of Cibola.

What Nuño de Guzman expected to find north of Tejo's "grassy desert" was an edifice the size and grandeur of Solomon's Temple, honeycombed with the Halls of Croesus, underlaid with the Cellars of Midas, and stocked ceiling-high with the Coffers of Moctezuma—for of such gilded substance was made a cavalier's dream. The direction Nuño de Guzman took was toward Cibola, but

7

he and his army failed to ride that far. They stopped at a delightful spot on Mexico's west coast to found the garrisons of Culiacan and Tepic. They spent part of the two-year exploration looking for an island inhabited by beautiful women—the island called California—as it was reported to Cortez by some native chiefs. Men from the mainland were said to visit the women only occasionally. The prospect of such a find!

But Nuño de Guzman and his army were to return to Mexico City later that year emptyhanded, without a cargo of silver and gold or the women of California. And when Antonio de Mendoza became first viceroy in 1535, one of his first noble acts was to ship de Guzman back to Spain—shackled and handcuffed, a condition shared with many another gentleman of the day.

Just a year later, four strangers entered Mexico City from the north, bedraggled and footsore, wearied from a long journey. Three were Spaniards of gentle birth, namely Andres Dorantes, Alonso de Castillo Maldonado, and the leader of the group—a name ever to be celebrated in Southwest history—Alvar Nuñez Cabeza de Vaca. The fourth member was a gigantic black, Estevan, who would be remembered through four hundred years by the Zuni Indians as "The Black Spaniard." The four travelers made their way directly to the viceregal palace, there to report to Mendoza all the trials they had suffered in a land vastly different from salubrious Mexico and to relate the wondrous accounts given them by certain Indians of seven towns of such wealth and architectural splendor that they defied all human imagination. Actually, Cabeza de Vaca and the others had not set eyes on the towns themselves, but the descriptions given them were so geographically clear that Estevan could lead any investigating party straight as a dart to the gates of the Seven Golden Cities. Mendoza was thrilled to his avaricious quick.

The four explained that they were survivors of the ill-fated Panfilo de Narvaez sea expedition to Florida, which had set sail from Vera Cruz in 1528, plunder-bent for the glory of Spain. After first getting lost, then almost massacred, and finally being shipwrecked off the Texas coast, this able quartet posed as medicine men and lived among the Indians long enough to gather facts about the southernmost part of the country destined to be the United States. Practicing magic, gaining respect, they edged their way westward across what is now southern Texas and New Mexico, and then along the chain of the Sierra Madre southward to Mexico City.

And just how rich were the Seven Cities?

Cabeza de Vaca elaborated far in excess of any tale related by Tejo. True, he said, the streets *were* lined with silversmiths' shops; but it was not the silver that was stacked waist-high, it was the beaten *gold*!

9

Cíbola had to be true because the Spaniards wanted it to be true. So an investigation had to be made and the sooner the better. But Spanish officialdom being what it was, two years were to elapse before Mendoza had the Franciscan Provincial, Fray Antonio de Ciudad Rodrigo, dispatch two friars to the region north of Nueva Galicia, to convert the Indians and, at the same time, keep their eyes and ears open for anything like the Seven Cities. These two missionaries walked through Nayarit into Sinaloa, beyond Culiacan to the vastness of Sonora. And even farther. The archaeologist Bandelier believes they got as far north as the Colorado River upstream from Yuma; and if so, then Juan de la Asuncion and Pedro Nadal would have been the first white men to step inside the boundaries of California.

The friars returned to Mendoza. Yes, they had heard. From the mouths of the tribal wise men themselves. The Seven Cities of Cíbola were fabulously rich; the people wore cotton and wool; the gems, gold, silver, and coffered treasures surpassed that already wrested from the Moctezuma and the Inca.

Mendoza listened as he had listened before. But now the conquest *must* be made. The hoard of Cíbola, shipload by shipload, would be cargoed to the treasury of Madrid. The King expected it and the King would be satisfied.

Cabeza de Vaca left for Spain, there to regale Charles the Fifth with the glories of Cíbola. Mendoza purchased the slave, Estevan, from Andres Dorantes to make sure *his* property would lead the expedition to victory. And for the "brains necessary" he selected Marcos de Niza, a friar recently come from work in what is today Peru, Haiti, and Guatemala. An Italian of about forty years, he had spent some time at Culiacan, and was therefore acquainted with northern country. And north of Culiacan lay the Seven Cities of Cíbola.

An army of conquest would be sent, of course, but only after De Niza and Estevan, accompanied by twenty Indians, had blazed the way and brought back an eye-witness report. They left Culiacan on March 7, 1539, and on April 12 crossed into what is now Arizona close to the present border station of Locheil, east of Nogales. They followed the San Pedro River down to the Gila and the

Salt; there Fray Marcos carved his name on a rock near the site of modern Phoenix. The trail led northeast, through piney mountains onto high plateaus. Estevan went ahead. Then, on a day in May, word came that he had reached the first Golden City of Cíbola, had entered it in defiance of warnings from the tribal leaders, and had been killed for his daring.

The town was Háwikuh, say the Spanish chronicles, though Zuni legend names the spot where Estevan died as Kiakima. Nevertheless, Fray Marcos continued until, in the copper light of a glorious sundown, from a mesa rim high above the plain, he too looked down on Háwikuh—its walls a glistening gold in the setting sun. He beheld the prize, and "with more fear than food," made fast southward tracks to Mexico City.

Mendoza again listened; this time to a man who had actually *seen* the mighty city of Cíbola. "It is larger than the city of Mexico" was the friar's report. "The doorways of the best houses have many decorations of turquoises, of which there is a great abundance . . . There are many people, streets, and plazas . . . There are some very large houses ten stories high . . . The houses are of stone and lime . . . The portals and fronts of the chief houses are of turquoise."

Fray Marcos confessed that he had not actually seen the riches; but this was a matter of little consequence, for all New Spain was now confident that wealth for the taking was there. When the news fell upon the populace, the details became more and more elaborate. Háwikuh was bigger than two Sevilles! The walls were solid gold! The women wore strings of gold beads and the men girdles of gold!

From such tales was organized one of the greatest land expeditions the world has ever known. The young *conquistador*, Francisco Vasquez Coronado, started north from Compostela in Nayarit, south of Tepic, on February 23, 1540, with Fray Marcos de Niza and a small army of 200 Spaniards and 800 Indians. They reached Cíbola on July 7. They besieged it, captured it, renamed it Grenada, and swallowed bitter disappointment.

All that Háwikuh (or any of the other Cities of Cíbola) could offer the "conquerors" were compact communities of mud and rock, loathing and contempt for the Spaniards, and a complete ignorance of silver and gold. True, some turquoise was found, the only precious stone the Zuni people cherished. But the turquoise "portals and fronts" of the houses turned out to be blue painted doors. And the "gold" that Cíbola possessed was a mere illusion—the coppery hues cast upon the walls by the setting sun.

In the high plateau country southwest of Gallup, there lies today the flattened ruin of a once thriving Indian village, Háwikuh, the most historic of the Cities of Cíbola. The site may be found on the Zuni River, eighteen miles downstream from the great present-day Pueblo of Zuni just east of the Arizona boundary. It was excavated by Dr. F.W. Hodge of the Museum of the American Indian, New York. Unearthed were streets, plazas, corridors among the massive walls—a church with its huge altar, a monastery, even a ceremonial snake pen. But there was found not one trace of beaten silver or gold.

Actually there were but six of the fabled "cities." If there was a seventh, later historic documents fail to mention it and modern scientific research has yet to trace it. The six, all in ruins, are Háwikuh, most westerly of the group, Mátsaki, Kiakima, Kwakina, Kechipáuan, and Hálona. They symbolized the ceremonial six directions: the four cardinal points, plus the zenith and nadir.

Háwikuh lived through 140 years of Spanish colonial history, from that noisy day in 1540 to one equally raucous in 1680. It was visited by Chamuscado in 1580, Espejo in 1583, and Oñate in 1604. The first mission church was built by the Franciscans in 1629, where the pioneer missionary friars were killed by the Indians. Fearing Spanish reprisal, the population fled to nearby Corn Mountain where they remained until 1635. After the return to their homes, the people of Háwikuh suffered little violence until October 1672, when the eternal enemy, the Apaches, attacked with such force that Háwikuh was routed. The missionary priest, Pedro de Avila y Ayala, hugged an image of the Virgin as he rushed across the plaza, only to have his head battered in with the church bell. The wooden cross at the church door was uprooted and thrown on his dead body. Fray Juan Galdo, the priest at Hálona, went to Háwikuh the next day, found the body and buried it in the yard of his own church.

One by one the Cities of Cíbola fell to ruin, Háwikuh and Hálona holding their own in spite of Spanish oppression, only to be abandoned when the Pueblo Indians revolted against the Spaniards in 1680. The Zunis again fled to Corn Mountain, where they remained until 1692, when they returned, building a new town near the site of Hálona—the Zuni Pueblo of today.

12   The bleak winds of the high plateau sweep the ruins of Háwikuh, and each new summer sun continues to parch the out-cropping walls, as tourists walk the town that was, almost four centuries ago, the throbbing hope of the exploiters of Mexico. And while the winds sweep, and the sun blasts, and the tourists gawk, the fathers and mothers of Zuni relate to their children the story of the death of Estevan, here recorded by the ethnologist Cushing:

It is to be believed that a long time ago, when roofs lay over the walls of Kya-ki-me, when smoke hung over the housetops, and the ladder-rounds were still unbroken in Kya-ki-me, then the Black Mexicans came from their abodes in Everlasting Summerland. . . . Then and thus was killed by our ancients, right where the stone stands down by the arroyo of Kya-ki-me, one of the Black Mexicans, a large man with chilli lips. . . . Then the rest ran away, chased by our grandfathers, and went back toward their country in the Land of Everlasting Summer.

3

KUAUA—EVERGREEN

To a Pueblo Indian of the Rio Grande Valley, perhaps to all Indians everywhere, the word "evergreen" is of special significance. It has a deep religious meaning, connoting strength, providence, beauty, eternity. Evergreen is the giver of life, the sustainer of life for all time to come, beyond this world, and everlasting.

Of the several evergreens, spruce is majesty, the tallest of all, dwelling in the upper reaches of the mountains. The ladders that give access to the depths of Pueblo kivas are spruce, their uprights protruding from darkness and pointing to the sky—a marriage of female Earth to male Sun. Legend tells that it was spruce growing from the floor of the underworld ages upon ages ago that provided a way through an opening in the sky, the Emergence that introduced human life to the light of the world.

Today, at Pueblo ceremonials, evergreen bedecks the dancers, fronds of it attached to limbs and held in hands, a prayer for eternal providence. And, as the legend goes, it is the spruce ladder that gives access downward to the spiritual core of life, downward to the blessedness, the source of all Indian life.

In Tiwa, the language of Sandia—a well-known pueblo situated about fourteen miles north of Albuquerque—the word for "evergreen" is *kuaua* (koo-ah-wah). Sandia Pueblo lies in the shadow of Sandia Mountain, the height of devotion for the faith of all Pueblo Indians in the southwest. And in the same shadow, another five miles up river, lie the ruins of another ancient Tiwa pueblo, a huge spread of buff adobe, featuring plazas and kivas and the ground floor remains of a sizeable community. This complex could once have risen several stories with ladders reaching to the upper terraces, the air humming with the

13

activities of a people filled with faith, hope, and industry—a village appropriate-ly named Kuaua.

14   The ruins of Kuaua are an easy twenty-mile Sunday afternoon drive from Albuquerque, three miles out of Bernalillo, along the Rio Grande. They may be reached through Coronado State Park, just west of the river bridge on Highway 44.

In the mid-1930s, this site was excavated jointly by the University of New Mexico, the Museum of New Mexico, and the School of American Research in Santa Fe. It was a five-year project headed by Dr. Edgar L. Hewett to determine the exact location of Coronado's camp. The work failed to uncover any evidence that it was the Tiguex named in the *Castañeda Narrative*, a journal kept by one of the expedition's members, although bits of copper mail and tubing, square-forged iron nails, and majolica sherds were discovered, all of Spanish origin.

Of more importance, however, Indian cultural artifacts were brought to light, all of great scientific value: human burials with mortuary offerings, pottery, ceremonial objects, and a huge mass of foundation house walls laid around three spacious plazas. Finally, the greatest prize of all, the Painted Kiva in the south plaza.

Kuaua must have presented a dramatic picture in Coronado's day, with the tall grasslands of the wide valley sweeping southward to northward and endlessly to the west. And looming to the east, the panorama of the Sandias.

The Rio Grande was wider and deeper then, and the channel a mile or so further east—probably where the Santa Fe railway tracks are today. Between the river and the pueblo was an alluvial plain where crops of corn, squash, cotton, and tobacco were grown, irrigated by primitive dams and ditches. Even in prehistoric times the Pueblo Indians of New Mexico were among the world's most ingenious farmers—they had to be, to withstand the rigors of the terrain and arid climate—a strength inherited by their descendants today.

Excavated at this extraordinary site were some 1,200 ground floor rooms, so very small they are almost like bins in the blocklike community house surrounding the plazas. They served mainly as storage space for crops, out of inclement weather or the reach of raiding enemies, chiefly Apaches. A burned section at the south end reveals granaries that contained charred corn still on the ear. A few of these very definitely were ceremonial rooms given to the complex system of religious fraternities. One fairly large south room contains a ventilator and adobe deflector block, always a part of kiva design.

This southeast corner of the ruins is termed the Lummis Section, excavated at about the turn of the century by the famed archaeologist Charles Lummis. Upon re-excavation in 1934 this section was left just as it lay, without the modern style adobe brick restoration a few feet higher given the rest of the Kuaua ruins.

15

Until about a decade ago the Lummis Section was a fine exhibit showing the prehistoric method of "puddle mud" construction—mud reinforced with ashes, fashioned into balls by the builder and slapped one against the other to give height to a wall rising six or seven feet. Kivas, square or circular, were dug sometimes ten feet below ground and walled with a thickness of puddled mud. The square kivas at Kuaua are unusual for Rio Grande Valley pueblos.

Around A.D. 1,300, a migration of Tiwa-speaking Indians moved into the valley section that is now Albuquerque, Bernalillo, and their environs. As farmers they laid out their irrigated fields; as warriors (though not aggressive) they built their pueblos as huge walled-in fortresses, compact and terraced, with entrance to the plazas from outside by narrow passageways.

Their clothing was of animal skins and cotton. Their food was corn, beans, and squash of the fields, and abundant wild game. Medicinal plants were everywhere to be found, their use and values thoroughly understood by the medicine men. And as these people were born artisans, they developed a distinct class of pottery, molded, fired, and decorated by the women, the designs finished in a glaze that shines even after six hundred years in the earth, the highly acclaimed Rio Grande Glaze.

This little nation extended upriver some thirty-two miles, from Isleta below present-day Albuquerque to northernmost Kuaua. According to Castañeda, there were twelve villages speaking Tiwa, called by the Spaniards Tiguex (Tee-wesh) province. Among these were Puaray, Kuaua, Alameda, Sandia, and Isleta. All have gone to ruin except Sandia and Isleta, with only Kuaua partially restored.

At the time of Coronado's arrival in 1540, Kuaua was no doubt a village of only several hundred. But the Tiwas were at the height of their culture. Castañeda's description was lengthy and thorough, comparing much of what he saw with Spain. He went on to describe the fiercely cold winter when the Rio

Grande was so thick with ice that it would support horsemen and ox carts. It was this frigid weather that brought on conflicts between the Spaniards and the Native Americans, for Coronado's men made demands upon the Indians for materials they could not supply—down to the blankets on their backs. Insurrection was the result. And the Indians, of course, got the worst of the battle.

The Coronado expedition was declared a failure by the viceroy in Mexico City, even though it had spent two years on the high northern frontier, had discovered the Grand Canyon, and from Tiguex explored the plains country northeast into Kansas. This they called Quivira. Mythical, golden Quivira!

When Coronado and his army returned to Mexico in 1542, his two priests elected to stay behind, to become the first missionaries and, as it was bound to be, the first martyrs. Juan de Padilla and Luis de Escalona were clubbed to death. As the years passed and no reports arrived concerning the priests' fate, authorities in the capital became more and more anxious to find out why. But they took their time.

Thirty-nine years later, in June 1581, Fray Agustin Rodrigues arrived in Tiguex with two fellow Franciscans to investigate the whereabouts of Padilla and Escalona. It was Captain Francisco Sanchez Chamuscado, with twelve soldiers, who led the three clerics to their destination, so the venture has gone down in history as the Rodrigues-Chamuscado *entrada*. Theirs was a new route north, a shorter distance up the Rio Grande from the Paso del Norte.

They were told the sad truth. Here, too, the soldiers returned south without priests: Rodrigues and his companions elected to proselytize where Padilla and Escalona had failed. Here, too, the missionaries were lost.

This time the viceroy would not delay: in 1582 he sent Captain Antonio Espejo with Fray Bernardino Beltrán to ascertain the fate of Rodrigues. And with this expedition the name *Nuevo Mejico* is first applied to the region north of El Paso del Norte. After learning of the friars' deaths, the small expedition explored the Pueblo country and returned south by following the Pecos River. Father Beltrán, prudently, departed with the soldiers.

Lesser expeditions, with or without the sanction of the Mexican viceroy, pioneered New Mexico in search of the elusive gold, one gallant exploring as far north as the Platte. But it was up to the greatest of the conquistadors, Juan de

Oñate, "the Colonizer," to begin the flow of Hispanic culture circulating in the Rio Grande Valley.

Did he visit Kuaua? Probably, but he concerned himself mostly with her sister pueblo, Puaray. Back in 1582, Espejo's party had stopped at Puaray and was given a room for the night—possibly a ceremonial room, for it contained wall murals. And what paintings they were! One set of figures depicted the killing of the martyred priests!

Sixteen years later, Oñate's expedition saw this painting, or one similar. The most dramatic recording of the horrifying experience was by Oñate's chronicler, one Gaspar Perez de Villagrá, a poet of extraordinary talent, who described the painting in his *Historia de la Nueva Mexico*, an epic of thirty-four rhymed cantos vivid enough to raise the hair on any seventeenth-century Spaniard.

Three hundred thirty-seven years later. . .

The day's work began in good order on February 14, 1935. The excavators at Kuaua took up their shovels, trowels, and sieves, while workers pushed their wheelbarrows across the dusty site. Little did anyone know that an important find in Southwestern archaeology would come to light that day. The supervising archaeologist, Gordon Vivian, walked across the south plaza until he came upon a parked wheelbarrow heaped with excavation rubble. His expert eye caught a fragment of something blue within the waste: paint on dry adobe—prehistoric paint. Asked where the earth came from, a laborer pointed to the spot where the famous Painted Kiva lay buried.

The excavators dug a test trench across the site, cutting their way deeper and deeper until an uplifted hand and the upper portion of a ceremonial mask came into view. All hands were put to the job of digging around the walls, and in time four sides of a square kiva were exposed. The east wall was badly eroded, but the paintings on the south, north, and west walls were clearly of anthropomorphic and zoomorphic beings, deities in the complex Indian religion. Although the upper walls had eroded away, the figures on the lower sections were intact: they stood about four and a half feet tall, had been drawn full-face without perspective, and had been painted in earth pigments of black, white, red, yellow, brown, and green.

The painted walls were cause for still further excitement upon the discovery that the murals were made up of layer upon layer of painted plaster, adobe laid over adobe throughout the centuries the kiva had been used. So Wesley Bliss of the University of New Mexico, who had done considerable work previously in removing paleontological specimens, was assigned the task of removing the walls from the kiva to the university laboratory where they could be taken apart layer by layer and preserved. The walls were cut into sections and jacketed in burlap, lath, and plaster of Paris. They were raised from the ceremonial chamber by derricks set over the excavation and hauled by truck to the laboratory where the jackets were removed except for the back permanent base. The tedious and extremely delicate work had begun.

Pallet knives and various solutions cleaned away the outer layer of adobe and exposed the murals. Each layer—about the thickness of heavy wrapping paper—was peeled away from the wall with solvents and chemicals and endless patience. As the layers were removed they were applied to a permanent base of commercial pressboard, or masonite. In time the last layer—the first one painted by Indian medicine men on the kiva wall centuries ago—was reached and the mighty task completed. Altogether, the walls had contained eighty-five layers of plaster, seventeen of them painted in fresco, pre-Columbian art at its finest.

However, the Painted Kiva failed to deliver the painting of the martyred priests described in Villagrá's epic poem. One set did show prone figures in Indian ceremonial attire but they were definitely not Franciscans.

But Tiguex was not one village. It was a province of twelve. And Kuaua was just one. There were other sites. . . *Maybe* within their ruins. . . *Perhaps* down in their depths . . . Quite *probably* (to use the three most important words in the vocabulary of anthropology) someday the much-hoped-for painting will come into view: when the site of Coronado's camp is established and Puaray pinpointed, Padilla, Escalona, and Rodrigues will be brought to the light of the sun.

Today the Painted Kiva at Kuaua has been completely restored to exact size, and a true reproduction of the murals put to the walls, the work of Santa Fe artists Zena Kavin and the noted Cheyenne painter Paul Goodbear. Other painted kivas have been found, principally at Pottery Mound near Los Lunas and at Awatovi in the Hopi country, but only Kuaua is maintained in the public interest.

Kuaua—Evergreen

The Coronado State Monument stands as a memorial to those who lived and died there, and as a reminder to those who visit it today for a brief plunge into prehistory, that here came an army of Spaniards, who, though avaricious, were brave and daring, the advance guard of European culture in the Southwest.

The museum at the Monument exhibits artifacts taken from the excavations, including panels of the original murals found in the kiva. Visitors may follow the pathways through the maze of ruins, descend the ladder into the kiva, and, if of a sensitive mind, relive the ancient mode of life that was destroyed by the Spanish sword, taken to the Earth Mother of the Indian, and reclaimed by the archaeologist's spade.

4

THE SHELL BEADS BY THE WATER

A BRIEF FILLER appeared in the *Albuquerque Journal* a few years ago:

> CITY WAS FOUNDED ON VILLAGE SITE
> The city of Santa Fe was founded in 1610 by Spanish explorers on the site of an abandoned Tano Indian village. Even today, Santa Feans digging foundations for their homes come across remnants of the past in the form of pottery, stone implements and human bones.

"Well now!" I said to myself. "That must be Kwapoge. . ." *Kwapoge* (Kwa-poh-gee, hard G) the Tanoan *Place of the Shell Beads by the Water.*

Centuries ago, alive with motion and the sound of ancient, long-forgotten industry, the village, we know, thrived and finally went to ruin atop a low hill overlooking what was to be Santa Fe Plaza. It was no doubt built of puddled adobe, its form similar to a modern apartment house, two or three stories high and terraced, its upper floors reached by ladders from the ground. Taos Pueblo today, four stories high, is an excellent example of this type of pre-Columbian construction. But this is all conjecture. Kwapoge's personal ruin is a mystery. . .

Kwapoge's high position above the plain cut by the narrow Santa Fe River—where corn, beans, and squash are cultivated—gives the sentinels a clear view of the fields and any approach of enemy raiders. Blocklike dwellings surround the open plazas, and in these squares all workaday activities take place: commerce with the gods, ceremonial dances—smoke from kiva hatchways is incense to the ritual. Here at the foot of ladders women prepare the family meals—corn, venison, beans. Here the children play naked, their shouts and cries the treble sound of childhood everywhere.

20

Traffic is heavy up and down the ladders, through the roof-hatchways that give access to the interior rooms. The artisans are at work, the male dressers of buckskin, the weavers of primitive cloth, a fabric of mixed cotton and rabbit fur. The stone-chippers ply their craft, creating arrowheads, knives, spearpoints of flint or obsidian, fetishes essential for ceremonial use tastefully executed to satisfy the gods. A woman grinds corn on a stone *metate* to the rhythm of a man's piping on a bone flute. Fires make flame on the plaza, the female potters molding into shape the *ollas* and utility vessels peculiar to the pueblo, painting the simple designs and firing the products to a permanence that will last through centuries. Out of the ceremonial rooms the warriors prepare to go into battle, painted, feathered and breechclouted.

Kwapoge. . . Where the hunters bring home the game. Where hearts throb to the emotions of joy and sorrow as regularly as the sun gives of its winter or summer solstice, each in its season. Kwapoge on the hill, once a sanctuary of human breath and brainpower, and by grace of the gods "The Place of the Shell Beads by the Water."

There is no trace of Kwapoge to be found today, except for a stray potsherd naked to the sun, a rarity in these days of modernization of everything extant. It is said that a housing development has been constructed near or over the site. And once such squares or rectangles of progress are planted in the earth, even though the earth be ever sacred, they are made to stay. Not so military installations. Well over a century ago Anglo shovels desecrated Kwapoge when troopers of the Republic built a fort on the ancient mound.

Fort Marcy occupied Kwapoge's ground for forty-eight years. Work began three days after General Stephen Watts Kearny and his Army of the West had routed the Mexican forces in Apache Canyon some fifteen miles east of town. On August 18, 1846, Kearny had raised the Stars and Stripes above the Palace of the Governors and with little fanfare had declared all New Mexicans to be no longer subjects of Mexico, but rather, citizens of the United States.

The brand-new Territory of New Mexico, including all of present Arizona plus a sliver of southern Colorado and Utah, was huge in scope and a diversity of altitudes and climates. Mother Mexico was to remain as only an affection in the hearts of New Mexico's people, an emotion that survives today as pride rather than allegiance. Kearny, a true conquistador, moved his army westward to conquer California. Colonel Doniphan was left to supervise the building of a fort on that pleasant elevation with a south view of Santa Fe Plaza and the little river valley.

22

As everywhere else in New Mexico the panorama is magnificent. From atop the hill a scanning eye can move from east to west over the second-oldest town in the United States and the very first seat of government. With the highest altitude of any state capital, 7,000 feet, and the thinnest of air, which could be the most unpolluted were it not for the necessity that has a carburetor for a heart, Santa Fe is blessed.

A glance eastward runs to the bulwark of the Sangre de Cristo Mountains, the Rockies themselves, that begin to rise from the very pulse of town—the Plaza. Canyon Road is the vein that commands all entrance to the forests that reach over the Pecos Wilderness to Hermit Peak (10,260 ft.), the dropoff to the plains, a thirty-mile crowflight trip toward the rising sun, *otra banda*, "the other side," as the idiom has it.

Until recent times, when with one huge measure of concrete and reinforcing iron Santa Fe took a leap at keeping up with the world, Canyon Road was narrow, unpaved, and a lovely thing to walk upon. It was lined on both sides by artists' studios, all flat-roofed and of pure adobe, dried mud alloyed only with straw. The patios were green with weeping willows, chestnut or poplar, and the sweetest Rose of Castile. The people who inhabited Canyon Road then, were they of the world's gracious and most talented artists or humble *paisanos* whose color and lifestyle enlivened palette and easel, all felt the American stereotype far away and alien to their own. And they rejoiced for the distance.

But alas! Canyon Road is now paved, and the old studios have been stuccoed and modernized. Galleries, restaurants, craft shops, and so-called Indian trading posts stand on either side with their shingles of commerce swaying in the sunlight. . . For the world of the 1920s, 30s, and 40s has passed away, gone to make room for ever-changing fashion. Canyon Road is no exception. But some of us can remember it as it was fifty, forty, thirty years ago, when it was warm and alive, when life was simple and inflation was unheard of, when even in the gloom of depression (which didn't affect us much) people were kind to each other, when great paintings were made and fine books written, and sculptures and bronzes were created of love, and poets gloried in the muse. Then, when all was done at the last faint glow of twilight, parties were staged in a dozen studios, and the talk was of art and of words in books and stories. The wine flowed and the cheer was there with the creative instinct and the passion to give.

The view from Fort Marcy Hill—Kwapoge Hill of centuries ago—includes the tricklet called the Rio Santa Fe, which can become a raging torrent when a summer cloudburst pours down the slopes of Santa Fe Baldy and Lake Peak. The river bisects the town and meanders down to mix with the Rio Grande at Santo Domingo, the Indian Pueblo thirty miles west. Not so long ago reservoirs in the Canyon provided sweet and velvety water, but with the increase in population, wells have had to be drilled and the water chlorinated. The velvety sweetness, like anything pure and simple, had to go with the onslaught of progress.

On a clear night you can even see the lights of Los Alamos, a mere twenty-five miles beeline to the northwest. How we wondered, hoped to know, and expressed our opinions as to what it was all about back in the World War II years! The secrecy of it, the eyes of government agents prying into everyone's business, especially at the cocktail hour in the La Fonda Cantina. There slouched the human hawks, watching, screwing the gimlet eye. Some of us thought they were building a giant submarine up there, others were sure it was a sanctuary for pregnant WACs. We knew better in July 1945 when the "thing" was exploded on our own Jornada del Muerto, and doubly sure with later news from Hiroshima and Nagasaki.

As all tourists know, after reading the pamphlets and guidebooks, and as the better informed residents are aware, Santa Fe was founded in 1610 by the noted governor Don Pedro de Peralta. The capital was moved up to the mountain bench from the Rio Grande near Española where Don Juan de Oñate had established the first capital in 1598 at Yuque Yunque, directly across the river from present-day San Juan Pueblo. There are mixed opinions about Oñate's town being a "capital," but undoubtedly it was, because Oñate lived there and he was New Mexico's first governor. But historians will be historians... They opine that the first was a mere settlement, nothing more official than that.

Oñate named his capital San Gabriel de Yuque Yunque in honor of the angel with the trumpet. Peralta, later, called *his* town *Villa Real de la Santa Fe de*

San Francisco de Assisi, or "Royal City of the Holy Faith of Saint Francis of Assisi"—and fair enough, for the friars of New Mexico at that time were Franciscans. Tourists of today have it drummed into them that Santa Fe Plaza is the center of the "oldest" capital city in the United States and that the Palace of the Governors (once called the *Casa Real* or "Royal House"—it housed the governor) at the north side of the square is the nation's "oldest" public building.

How *old* is Santa Fe, in terms of world chronology?

In 1610, as the Plaza was laid out by order of the Spanish governor, while his Palace was in the process of construction and the Franciscans wielded their might by authority of the Inquisition, all the civilized world was either at peace or in turmoil. Elizabeth the First of England had been dead only seven years; and James the First, son of the beheaded Mary of Scotland, celebrated the union of the two kingdoms by having the King James version of the Bible translated from the Greek. Shakespeare was alive and at work. King Henry the Fourth of France was assassinated and succeeded by Louis the Thirteenth, and Marie de Medici began her regency. In Sweden, Gustavus Adolphus the Second was readying for a conflict against the Danes—throughout the globe events all better remembered than is the founding of Peralta's Spanish-American capital of New Mexico.

But on the Atlantic coast, Captain John Smith had founded Jamestown only three years before and just twelve months had gone by since Henry Hudson sailed his *Half Moon* up the Hudson River. Ten years were to pass before the Pilgrims would land on Plymouth Rock. Sometime in the same year Adriaen Block set up his small trading post at the south end of New York's Manhattan Island. All America north of Mexico was a wilderness. And California, of course, was inhabited only by Indians. (However, New Mexico's Governor Juan de Oñate had already glanced at the glamorous landscape when he reached the Pacific Ocean five years before.)

The charm of Santa Fe is immediately felt by newcomers—the clean cold of winter, the bracing sunshine of summer, never sultry. Blizzards are seldom recorded. And New Mexico is *not* tornado country. This is especially so west of the series of mountains that chain down from north to south central of the map. Santa Fe's average annual rainfall is a scant 14.34 inches compared with New York's 41.61 at La Guardia Airport. The average January low is 29.3

degrees, not much higher than New York's 26, but without the chilling humidity.

The July maximum average for Santa Fe is a cool 68, again without humidity. In the same month New York swelters at 84. It will snow sometimes in Santa Fe, a crisp high-altitude mountain fall. The upper peaks of the Sangre de Cristo will hold their white patches into June, while down in the town the hollyhocks and lilacs blaze their colors against buff adobe walls. The lilacs are especially riotous along the Acequia Madre and the Camino del Monte Sol, two quiet lanes favored by people who live by and for the arts that have set Santa Fe above other communities in the state less rich in color, less blessed with an easy pace, both essential for feeding the creative drive.

Santa Fe's population is made up of two separate interest groups: people concerned with politics and commerce, and those with the arts, historical research, and anthropology. If the capital complex is the "heart" of the city, for Santa Fe is first and foremost the seat of state government, it is the merchants and other commercialists who are taxed and fill the coffers who may be termed the "muscle." And the painters, writers, sculptors, historians, poets, ethnologists, composers, and sundry craftsmen who live and work here are the "complexion." For more than a half-century they have proclaimed Santa Fe's fame as an art center to the nation and the world.

Although Santa Fe is without doubt the "oldest" capital city in the United States, the present capitol and surrounding buildings are the shining "newest." The state motto—*Crescit Eundo* (It Grows As It Goes)—throbs in the heartbeat of every soul within those political walls. The design of the capitol itself, called "The Roundhouse," is inspired by the circular Indian Pueblo kivas. This building houses the legislative and executive branches of state government. Loyal to the mighty tourist industry that keeps New Mexico's tri-cultured blood flowing, there are daily guided tours featuring historical, anthropological, and cultural displays, and paintings by selected artists hang in the shadow of the governor's desk.

But the business conducted is precisely that of other state capitals from Oregon to New Jersey, the thoughts and plans and speeches of it all far removed from such gentle creations and fragile activities as practiced along Canyon Road and other arty lanes. . . Except for the *New Mexico Magazine*, the state publication with offices wedged in the hullabaloo. Staffed with editors, art editors, photographers, and designers who produce an attractive package

25

covering all New Mexico for a wide circulation every month of the year, this section of the State Department of Development should be housed in adobe walls amid the lilacs and hollyhocks on the Acequia Madre or Camino del Monte Sol, where the rest of the creatives reside.

26

The capitol building seems to divide "The City Different" (as Santa Fe prides in calling itself) from the conglomeration of housing developments and commercial enterprises along Cerrillos Road and its offshoots.

Take a walk eastward from The Plaza, with the huge wall of the Sangre de Cristo mountains for your skyline, and you are in an environment that is truly *The City Different.*

The landmarks of Santa Fe relate to history, and chronology is recorded in ancient buildings, the venerable Plaza, winding narrow lanes where dwellings were built and are now maintained to fit the scene, homes of people sensitive to the cultural wealth they have inherited, and who will fight like trapped leopards against the aggressors who would seek to modernize and blemish their stronghold.

Santa Fe is a Spanish town in spite of many alien accents and complexions. It is also thoroughly American, its beginning in line with Plymouth and St. Augustine, Jamestown and Quebec. The streets in this residential area bear appropriate Spanish names: Camino San Acacio, Camino Ranchitos, Calle la Paz, Callecita Mera, Plaza Fatima; with, naturally, a sprinkling of Johnson Lane and Miller Street . . . And to harmonize with the Hispanic flavor are homes flat-roofed as Pueblo Indian dwellings, of the same dried mud adobe, ceilinged with *vigas* and *latillas*, floored with flagstone, and with corner fireplaces as whitewashed as the interior walls giving off the perfume of the gods when their fires are fed with New Mexico's own most fragrant piñon.

For well over three centuries and a half the Plaza has been the hub of town. In the beginning it was a square, either dusty or muddy, where the commerce of all New Mexico was concentrated. It was the bartering place for oxcart and pack mule caravans arrived from Chihuahua, from Durango and the Valley of Mexico. The ruling Spaniards, then, forbade all trade with the east and northeast, with the French of Louisiana, and with the Americans who were rapidly pushing their frontier westward and southwestward from the central Mississippi.

But by 1822, following the great revolution when colonial New Spain became the Republic of Mexico, and New Mexico turned to a province of that union of states, the ban was lifted and introduced what Josiah Gregg called "The Commerce of the Prairies." In that year, William Becknell, "Father of the Santa Fe Trail," brought in the first wagon loaded high with Yankee merchandise from Westport Landing (now Kansas City) on the wide Missouri.

He blazed the Trail across Kansas, touched southeastern Colorado, suffered over the Raton Pass, skirted the Rockies at Glorieta, and came to a terminus on that highly unsanitary square of trampled dirt fronting the Palace of the Governors. The church of San Francisco stood at the east side, La Fonda (the inn) on the south. The dismal hovels of the *povres* and the elegant homes of the *ricos* were in company with reeking corrals and noisy gambling houses. The Plaza was the gathering place of gamblers, tradesmen honest or otherwise, trappers, frontiersmen and Indian fighters, *vaqueros*, desperados and swindlers, a cassocked friar or two, and hospitable black-eyed *señoritas*. Becknell had purchased his cargo in Missouri for $150, and sold it in Santa Fe for $700, after dodging hostile Indians along the way and paying out bribes. But it was a profitable venture, blazing the Santa Fe Trail for future merchant barons of St. Louis and St. Joseph and laying out the departure point that was to become modern Kansas City.

The arrival of a wagon train from the "States" was sound reason for holding *fiestas* on the Plaza, and the wagons came in at frequent intervals once the Trail got into operation. There would be music of fiddles and guitars, songs rendered in paisano Spanish or frontier-American, gambling, eating, dancing, laughing. Josiah Gregg, in his *Commerce of the Prairies,* one of the great books of the Southwest, described the joyous event in eye-witness style:

> The arrival of the caravan always was productive of great excitement among the natives. "Los Americanos! Los Carros! La entrada de la caravana!" were to be heard in every direction. Crowds of women and boys flocked around to see the newcomers... Each wagonner must tie a brand new *cracker* to the end of his whip, for on driving through the streets and the *plaza publica* everyone strives to outvie his compadres in the dexterity with which he flourishes this favorite badge of authority.

Trade was brisk, and continued so for fifty-eight years. Drygoods, foodstuffs, hardware all piled high on freight wagons rolled westward to be bartered on Santa Fe Plaza. The trains were long, the hoofed traction plodding over the wide swath of ruts, slowly laboring to the crack of the drivers' whips. Some consignments reached the coveted destination, others fell along the way to hostile Indians or bandits, to tornados and the cruel winter storms that were natural elements of the prairies. The successful traders returned to Missouri over the same route, their carts and wagons heavy with buffalo robes, hides, furs, Indian blankets, and silver bullion and gold.

Throughout the 1850s the Santa Fe Trail was a business of immense proportions. One Missouri-based trading firm alone employed 3,500 wagons, 4,500 men, 40,000 oxen, and 1,000 mules. All on the job of hauling 8 thousand tons of merchandise annually. Prominent among Santa Fe merchants were the Spiegelberg Brothers. Solomon Spielgelberg established his firm in 1846, and his story is a book in itself. Goods handled by the Spiegelbergs found sales in the eastern states, homebound with the Missouri wagons, while they distributed produce from east of the Mississippi throughout Arizona, California, and down the Chihuahua Trail to Mexico. Europe was a market for New Mexican products by grace of the Spiegelbergs, and long awaited items from New York, Ohio, and New England found homes in the remote pueblos and *placitas* at Trail's end.

The volume of the Spiegelbergs' trade is staggering: in the course of one day in Kansas City they loaded a train of eighty-three wagons carrying over two tons each with goods for their Santa Fe store. The merchandise was valued at $125,000. The freight bill paid, $30,000. The calculated profits, $51,000. And the entire cargo was sold out in three weeks.

Wagon trains from the east pulled up before the Spiegelbergs' warehouse to discharge their cargoes almost daily. An item in the newspaper of July 29, 1868, marveled at the speed of commerce over the Santa Fe Trail.

> The Messrs. Spiegelberg Bros. received a train on Monday 27th loaded with goods shipped from New York only forty days ago. This, we understand, is the quickest time ever made.

Then came February 13, 1879, when the first passenger train into New Mexico crossed the Raton Pass, its cowcatcher pointed for Arizona and California. This, the precursor of the new "Commerce of the Prairies," arrived puffing, steaming, and whistling 'round the bends. It heralded speedier progress for the American Southwest and an end to the Santa Fe Trail.

Things have changed around the Plaza since Josiah Gregg's day. The square has been "built-around" to give it less space to call its own, and the rowdy wagon train commerce has been replaced in almost the last hundred years by surrounding shops. Today, patronage of any of these would offer no cause for *fandangos*, murder, or getting drunk on *aguadiente*.

Two original buildings remain, both so modernized that their original style of architecture can be fully appreciated only in books and drawings by artists of the day. These are the Palace of the Governors, now the Museum of New Mexico, and the famous La Fonda, the hotel everyone knows, once the hub of gaiety and commerce in Trail days.

Sometimes called the Exchange Hotel, it was the arrival and departure station for stagecoach traffic over the Santa Fe Trail, as well as for coaches serving El Paso and the south and the Barlow-Sanderson route to the north. Throughout the 1920s, 30s, and 40s La Fonda thrived as one of the finest of the Fred Harvey hostelries. Under Fred Harvey management La Fonda had a flavor of Old Santa Fe in its architecture, in the attire of the employees, a quiet dignity in its very air. It was linked by the Harvey company to the Indian Detours and the Santa Fe Railway, to all that was purely New Mexican, blazing with Southwestern color.

But the years following World War II introduced a nation's overflow to the desert, and people came to realize that the desert was nothing to be dreaded—in fact, it might be a good place to live. . . Which brought on changes: the sunlight became less bright, space shrank, and all the ills of a dense population proliferated. Now the Hilton and all the ultra-modern ambassadors of the mighty motel chains, each almost identical with the other, flourish in the city where La Fonda once stood alone as the finest hotel of its kind in all America. Now even the beautiful old Convent of the Sisters of Loretto has been converted to a luxury hotel. Its chapel containing The Miraculous Staircase, happily, has been spared.

No tourist would want to miss exploring the Palace of the Governors which occupies the entire north side of the Plaza. The construction is of thickwalled adobe, long and narrow, its front doors and windows separated from the street by a wide and shady portal. Its length of four hundred feet from east to west is a type of architecture favored by the early Spanish *hacendados*. On a smaller scale this construction was known to Anglo pioneers as a "shotgun house." Behind the main building—once the offices, residence and private chapel of the Spanish and Mexican governors—is a wide *patio* or walled-in enclosure, its outer boundaries giving space to lesser shotgun structures. There in colorful but unsanitary times were the sheds and corrals housing the livestock, plus quarters for servants and the military. Today the tourist may relive in a brief hour the events of a long chronology by inspecting the exhibits offered by the Museum of New Mexico, which in 1909 this ancient complex became.

Villa Real de la Santa Fe—Royal City of the Holy Faith—.

The French-Romanesque Cathedral of Saint Francis stands at the head of the street east of the once-extensive Plaza. The cornerstone was laid in 1869 by the Jesuit from France, Jean Baptiste Lamy, Bishop and later Archbishop of Santa Fe. A statue to this pioneer greets parishioners at the cathedral entrance, and in literature the man himself is famed throughout the world in Willa Cather's novel, *Death Comes For The Archbishop*.

The cathedral was erected on the site of a church and monastery built in 1622 by Fray Alonso de Benavides, *custodio* of the mission province; it was destroyed by Pueblo Indians in the revolt of 1680. A second church, or *Parroquia*, was built in 1713, and the sacristy at the rear of the present cathedral is an actual part of the older church. The construction is of native sandstone and shows the French influence evident in most church buildings dedicated in the Lamy era. It has been said that the remains of Don Diego de Vargas, the reconqueror of New Mexico following the Pueblo Revolt, lie under the high altar, but recent researches suggest he is in repose elsewhere. The north chapel contains the large *bulto*, or image, of *La Conquistadora*, brought to New Mexico by the earliest Spanish settlers and revered for centuries as the Madonna of the Southwest, saved from desecration by the Indians when Santa Fe was evacuated by the Spaniards in 1680. She was with them during their twelve-year exile at El Paso del Norte: to her guidance De Vargas credited his 1692 victory and resettlement of New Mexico.

Santa Fe is the home of many Spanish Catholic churches. Rosario chapel, for one, is said to be on the site of the hastily built sanctuary De Vargas raised for the image of *La Conquistadora* at his camp before entering Santa Fe for the reconquest. And there is the Santuario de Guadalupe which dates back to the early nineteenth century, its architecture suggesting the California mission style. Over the high altar is an old painting of the Virgin of Guadalupe, Mother of Mexico. The high ceiling is supported by finely carved beams and corbels.

Along upper Canyon Road is the modern Church of Cristo Rey, the largest adobe structure in the United States, built in the true Classic Spanish Mission style, its walls ranging from two to seven feet thick. The altar screen, or *reredos,* was carved of native stone in 1761 and is said to have once graced the old military chapel on the Plaza.

31

The church visited most by tourists in Santa Fe is the Mission San Miguel on the Old Pecos Trail south of the Plaza. For long it has been celebrated as "the oldest church in the United States," which, unfortunately for the celebrators, is not true. It is an eighteenth-century church, but beneath the present floor is the older one built in 1626. If the presence of an earlier floor gives a church the authority to be considered "the most ancient of all," then a wall in the church of San Miguel in Socorro could well qualify *it* for the title of "Oldest—*The First.*" The wall site, said to be that of an Indian house in the Pueblo of Pilabó, was chosen by a priest of the Oñate expedition of 1598 for briefly holding Mass as the caravan trekked northward. The old floor under Santa Fe's San Miguel is that of the mission that served the Analco district south of the river. Once the *barrio* of Tlascalan cart drivers, livestock herders, lackeys, and servants who accompanied the first Spanish settlers up from the interior of what is present day Mexico, it is now the site of fine shops, restaurants, homes, and the complex that is New Mexico's state capitol.

Churches and missions; the Palace of the Governors; La Fonda; the *garita* (the little fortress); the narrow lanes that still retain the charm to match adobe walls and flat roofs and patios and all the loveliness that makes Santa Fe's own style of architecture; plus a distinct human lifestyle, a very special people whose pride is in being different—

It is all there in the air, day or night, anytime of the year.

Santa Fe. . .

Royal City of the Holy Faith of Saint Francis. . .

The City Different.

Different, you say. What difference?

What about Cerrillos Road and the Whataburger stands? And the used car lots and the mobile home sales? What's *different* about those bits of commonplace America?

Who stole the *difference* from The City Different?

Nobody.

Look beyond the condominiums and over the shopping centers, ignore the pavements and the glare of neon, and give never a glance to the look-alike structures that belong to the nationwide hotel and motel chains. Instead, feast your eyes on the mountains—the Sangre de Cristo, named four hundred years ago for the Blood of Christ—too huge and God-sculptured to be changed. As the ancient floor of the oldest San Miguel lies under the veneer of the later, so Old Santa Fe is there in the midst of the town. It is there in the heads and hearts of the few remaining residents who knew the life through the banner years of the 'teens and the 20s, the 30s, and 40s, workers in flagstone, adobe, rawhide, and split cedar—great paintings on their walls and the precious weaving of the Navajo spread on the floors; and patios rampant with the color of lilac and iris and hollyhock, and a *santo* serene in a niche in the wall, and piñon smoke from fireplace-chimneys scenting Cerro Gordo and Atalaya and the Acequia Madre and other narrow lanes. Different because it is the home and hearth of the sort of people who will never let the difference die. The veriest newcomer can spot these people at a glance. It is the difference about *them* that stands to be recognized.

5

HELP FOR THE CONQUERORS

THE HIGHWAY into Socorro is wide and smooth. The tourist accommodations are many. Civic pride is evident everywhere, while the residents sing progress and bounty. Their town is sunbright by day, sparkling by night. In short, Socorro is a compact little community, as typically American as Springfield or Dayton. Nothing seems ancient or especially backward about it, except perhaps for something in the lovely lilt of its Spanish name and the sanctuary within the five-foot-thick walls of San Miguel church—one of the oldest in the nation, if not, in fact, the very oldest north of Mexico.

When the conquistador Don Juan de Oñate arrived to colonize New Mexico in 1598, he found two Piro Indian villages thriving here. At the site of Socorro itself, he found Pilabó, located on the *west* bank of the Rio Grande, and on the *east* bank a few miles upstream, Teypana, its sister pueblo. The Indians prospered as farmers, growing crops in irrigated fields. They were peaceful people.

The Fray Cristobal and Caballo mountains loom south of Socorro. Both ranges slope abruptly on the west down to a rough gorgelike trough that carries the southward flow of the river. At the mountains' east lies a formidable ninety-mile stretch of desert, then completely waterless, and the hunting ground for bands of warrior Apaches dedicated to holding their own, particularly their homeland, against any invader, with fighting methods that were ruthless and cruel. From Spanish-Colonial times this desert waste has been appropriately called the *Jornada del Muerto*—"The Journey of the Deadman."

It is a remote stretch of aridity floored with gravel and shale, dotted with cactus and yucca, a habitat of coyotes and rattlesnakes—one of the most undesirable places in the Southwest for human settlement. So desolate that it is now part of the White Sands Missile Range, the proving ground where in 1945 the first atomic bomb was exploded. No piece of earth anywhere could be more appropriately named.

34

Oñate had forded the Rio Grande at the Paso del Norte (El Paso, Texas) and moved his company of cavaliers, friars, soldier-settlers with their wives and children, Indians and herdsmen, oxcarts, and 7,000 head of livestock northward toward the heart of New Mexico. They followed the river until they met rough terrain. From there they proceeded still north, but east of the mountains and up the dreaded Jornada. On May 28, 1598, after much suffering, the company arrived at Qualicu, the southernmost of the Piro towns. But the people there were most ungracious; they fled for their lives on sight of the Spaniards.

Oñate rested for two weeks near Qualicu, then moved onward toward Teypana. There, to the Spaniards' delight, the Indians met them with gifts of food. Oñate, accordingly gave Teypana its Spanish name, *Socorro*, meaning "succor" or "help."

While at Teypana two friars, Fray Cristobal de Salazar and Fray Alonso Martínez, forded the Rio Grande and walked the few miles south to Pilabó. In the heat of June they found an adobe house with thick walls, erected an altar, and celebrated Mass. They spent a few days in the pueblo, then made haste to rejoin the caravan following the river northward toward Yuque Yunque, the twin pueblos of the Tewas. Within a month, Yuque Yunque would become San Gabriel, the Spanish capital of New Mexico, and last for twelve years until the founding of the new and enduring capital of Santa Fe.

About the time Santa Fe was established, Teypana was attacked by Apaches, the granaries plundered, and the defenders massacred. The survivors made a retreat south across the river, where they were accepted by their kinsmen at Pilabó. Teypana was left to ruin; Socorro had moved to permanent ground.

By January 1626, there were twenty missionaries in New Mexico, all Franciscans. They had built churches, introduced European ways and implements, risked and often surrendered their lives. That month the greatest of them all arrived in Santa Fe from Mexico: Fray Alonso de Benavides, native of San Miguel in the Azores, Father Custodian of the Franciscan Order, first Commissary of the Holy Office of the Inquisition.

With the coming of Benavides, church building and soul harvesting took priority over all endeavors. The custodio himself spent a month in the summer of 1626 among the Piros, but another three years were to pass before the actual foundations of a church would be laid at Pilabó. Friars Antonio de Arteaga and García de San Francisco were assigned the task of construction. Remembering the hospitality of the Indians, the new mission was dedicated to *Nuestra Señora de Perpetuo Socorro,* or "Our Lady of Perpetual Help."

The governor of New Mexico, Don Felipe Sotelo-Ossorio, realized the strategic importance of the southern pueblos. He established a presidio there to protect the mission from the Apaches and to set a line of defense for Santa Fe. Socorro Pueblo flourished for half-a-century; then, in 1680, the Indians, led by the Tewa medicine man, Popé, successfully rebelled against Spanish cruelty and exploitation. At that time Socorro had a population of 600 Indians, one missionary friar, and a handful of soldiers.

The Piro people remained loyal. They took no part in the revolt. Santa Fe was attacked, and the entire Spanish population—including the governor, Antonio de Otermín—retreated southward to the Paso del Norte. The refugees passed through the Piro country on the way and were joined by the Indians of Socorro, and by other pueblos of the blood. It was a prudent move. They were well aware that the Pueblo tribesmen to the north would punish them by slavery or annihilation for not aiding their kinsmen in the Great Revolt of 1680. They left their town to fall to ruin and established themselves down the Rio Grande southeast of El Paso, at a community appropriately named *Socorro del Sur,* or "Succor of the South."

For a hundred years Socorro de Pilabó lay in rubble and weeds, the roof of the church caved in, walls of the houses washed to mudheaps by the rains. But in 1781, Spanish settlers, with names like Montoya, Baca, Abeyta, García, Padilla, Gallegos, Luna, and Vigil, ancestors of Socorro's present-day Spanish-American community, arrived at the deserted town. They built new houses, laid out irrigated fields, and reconstructed the old church. Cattle and sheep grazed the hills and valley. Land grants from the Crown of Spain were awarded the settlers in 1817. Then in 1867, silver ore was discovered and the town became the center of the largest and richest mining district in New Mexico. The silver klondike continued until the 1890s when the price of the metal dropped. But while it lasted, Socorro gained a reputation for being one of the "wildest towns of the Frontier West."

Tradition has it that sometime between 1629 and the Revolt of 1680, a mission supply caravan from the south drew up at the church of *Nuestra Señora de Perpetuo Socorro,* carrying with it a communion rail and companion vessels wrought in solid silver. Its weight was staggering, the workmanship exquisite. Could it have been a gift from the silver-rich Oñate family of Zacatecas in gratitude for the "succor" the Piro Indians had bestowed on their own Don Juan in 1598?

Whatever the source, it was used in the church until both Spaniard and Indian abandoned Socorro and joined the refugees from Santa Fe as they fled south. But before leaving their church, they prudently buried—somewhere at a safe distance from the town—the communion rail and the precious vessels, along with other sacred objects. A map of the location was made and lost. In later times the Mexican Government sent experts to seek the hoard, but to no avail. In the 1880s, someone offered a million dollars to anyone uncovering the treasure. No one did.

Even the change of dedication from the Church of Our Lady of Perpetual Help to that of St. Michael carries a dramatic story. During the first year of the nineteenth century a band of Apaches took to terrorizing the Spanish settlers in the Rio Grande Valley near Socorro. Ranch after ranch was plundered, buildings set afire, and livestock driven off. Many settlers gave their lives, while others retreated to the shrine of the Lady of Perpetual Help. If they ever needed "help," *this* was the time.

The raiders pursued the settlers into town. Women, children, aged and infirm were packed into the church. Greatly outnumbered by the enemy, the men of Socorro took a fighting stand at the church doors. Inside the church, the priest led the women in prayer, beseeching the assistance of the Lady of Perpetual Help.

Outside, the defenders were in trouble. Arrows were finding targets, brave men were falling, Spanish guns were jamming, and the ammunition was playing out. Defeat was inevitable, death for Socorro was sure. *Where was the Lady?*

Then it happened. Suddenly the arrows ceased to fly and the warriors took to their heels. Some fell writhing on the ground, their faces ashen, screaming in fright. A terrible apparition had risen before their eyes. An Apache was caught, tethered, and when he came to his senses told of a warrior in full armor, fourteen feet tall, holding aloft a mighty sword, with eyes blazing curses on the heathen.

And where was Our Lady of Perpetual Help?

In Spain, perhaps. Or in Mexico or Peru. For her help was needed and given all over the earth—everywhere the Spanish tongue is found, everywhere folk hold in high esteem the saint whose mission is "succor" in times of peril or need. So to the faithful she sent her warrior saint, Michael the Archangel, to succor Socorro on the Rio Grande.

6

THE STONE LIONS OF YAPASHI

THE PUEBLO INDIANS of New Mexico recognize their tribal world to be ceremonially bounded by four sacred mountains. These rise at the cardinal points, each a home of the ever-watchful guardian spirits, all a source of prosperity for those who look to them for help. And, by fate or good fortune, four towns of the White Man's Way lie adjacent to the peaks: Taos at the north, Santa Fe at the east, Albuquerque at the south, Los Alamos at the west, all within the limits of the Pueblo Indian World. When the Indian thinks of material goods, he uses the towns for his convenience—for trade opportunities, jobs, and entertainment. He finds the latter especially cheap: watching the white man go about his peculiar ways, offering amusement and evoking comment.

And similarly, the Indian World is employed to advantage by the white man—traders, anthropologists, artists, writers, and those who live by New Mexico's leading industry, "tourism."

The Pueblo Indians of the Rio Grande Valley are the most conservative of all American tribes. They practice to the letter the way of their ancestors who were pure in Indian faith and wisdom, who lived at a time when all America was one vast Indian world. Today, the ancient languages are spoken at the pueblos; although the dress, the construction, and furnishing of the houses, and their transportation and farming methods have been slightly influenced, the Pueblo World in general is blessedly distinct from the overwhelming white society.

The Indian's deeper thoughts, spiritual and temporal, remain unalloyed. Though outwardly Christian, his religion is a substance contained in a hard, unbreakable shell. Valiantly these people hold to what is distinctively theirs despite efforts to convert them to the familiar and somewhat monotonous way of American life.

There are seventeen Pueblo villages on the Rio Grande or its tributaries. Steeped for centuries in the "Indian Way," most lie within the shadow of that special holy of holies, the Pajarito Plateau; all are situated close enough to the Shrine of the Stone Lions for the godly influence to be absorbed.

The sacred peaks at the cardinal points and the vast expanse of the domain within may be viewed from the many high points in Santa Fe. Each mountain is an oracle for its own purpose, eternally solid. But it is the "West World Mountain" that offers the truly magnificent panorama. For against the sunset skyline appears the endless chain of the Jemez Mountains rising to 11,250 feet atop Redondo Peak. Although the massive Redondo is an altar in itself, the lesser Pelado Peak, farther north, is the more sacred shrine—*Tsi'kumupin* (Black Stone Mountain), Guardian of the End of Day, where the Sun God descends to "his sacred place," to rest for the night in *Shi'papu*, the eternal underworld, after showering his blessings on the people of the earth.

Footing these mountains on the east is the long bench of volcanic tufa called the Pajarito Plateau, level upland of "The Little Bird," first step in the rise of terrain west of the Rio Grande. Here are grassy meadows, deep canyons, and timber growing thicker and taller as the elevation increases toward the mountains. This is hallowed earth created by the ancients for the welfare of the people in the valley below.

In ages beyond reckoning, the gods gave humankind great powers, wondrous magic, and sublime happiness in reward for purity of heart, mind, and soul. But in time the people of the earth changed: greed, envy, and weakness corrupted the strife-torn Pueblos. The offended gods forced them to abandon Pajarito Plateau and seek shelter in the valley.

The ruins of their old cities repose today as rockpiles, mounds, and depressions, some desolate, others compact honeycombed patterns that had once been three-storied community houses humming with activity. The finest examples of these remains are to be found within and adjacent to the Bandelier National Monument, forty-five miles northwest of Santa Fe. There is *Tsánkawi* for one, *Ótowi* for another, *Tshirega, Návawi, Puyé, Tyuónyi,* and *Yápashi,* the ruined pueblo at the Shrine of the Stone Lions.

High on the Pajarito Plateau is the watered chasm called the Rito de los Frijoles. Here lies the ruin of Tyuónyi, a town said to have thrived from A.D. 1250 to 1550, whose population numbered somewhere from 1,500 to 2,000. The walls of the canyon rise 300 to 600 feet above a floor of deep, rich soil capable of supporting a substantial population. At Tyuónyi a trail snakes up the southside canyon wall. Leading to an isolated, ancient world, this trail is the starting point for exploration of the ruins and shrines of the plateau's southern section.

40

In a little less than six miles this trail comes to Yápashi and the Stone Lions. Here is a monument so sacred to the descendants of its early consecrators that it may be considered the Stonehenge of America. It is a creation whose age and origin cannot be determined.

Yápashi, Keresan for Place of the Sacred Enclosure, is on high ground between Capulin and Alamos canyons. The Keres division of the Pueblo people also refers to the place as "The Ruined Pueblo to the North Where the Mountain Lions are Resting." In Spanish it is known as *Pueblo Quemado*, or "Burnt Pueblo," for the ruins indicate a razing by fire centuries ago. In its lifetime, Yápashi was a massive pile of terraced houses rising to three stories, laid on rock and made secure from enemy attack. Today, two Pueblo linguistic groups of the valley pay ceremonial homage to the Shrine of the Stone Lions, which lies approximately one-third of a mile northwest of the ruined village. These are the Keres, who live to the south, and the Tewas whose pueblos are to the north. But it is the Keres of Cochití and San Felipe who claim Yápashi to be their ancestral home and the Stone Lions their especial shrine.

Here on the Pajarito Plateau life moved up and down the ladderways and industry was active on the central plaza. Women made pottery, craftsmen dressed skins and chipped the weapon points. Hunters made ready to take the trails—to stalk, kill, and bring home the provision of the gods. But first, before the excursion was made, homage was paid and blessings implored at the Shrine of the Stone Lions.

The sanctuary consists of a stone circle eighteen feet in diameter. It is walled with vertically set rocks up to five feet in height, and approached from the southeast by a passageway of the same construction. And in the exact center of the circle, with their noses toward the rising sun, lie two crouched catlike figures carved in the native rock. In spite of weathering, they are still graceful and easily identified as *múkai*, the mountain lion, one of the animals most revered by the Keres.

A Keres legend tells us that ages ago, before the coming of the first Spaniards, the Cochití and San Felipe Indians occupied the Pajarito Plateau as one nation living in one great pueblo. This could have been Tyuónyi, for it is described as being situated in a deep canyon floored with rich soil, watered by a never-failing stream.

But there were enemies to the north who one day descended upon the Keres and drove them a few miles to the south. There the Keres built *Kuapa'shi* (Yápashi), and another happy phase of their history was initiated. It ended one night when fire swept the town and forced the people to flee their homes and leave behind their war and hunting weapons in the flames. As they moved off the plateau down to the Rio Grande Valley they met a new and formidable enemy. These were the *Pi'nini*, white-haired dwarfs who lived in the Bonito Valley of southeastern New Mexico.

Though small, the Pi'nini were ferocious fighters and greatly outnumbered the Keres. A few Yápashi survivors escaped, but most lost their lives in the battle. The victors then marched southward toward their homes, taking scalps and trophies. Overly confident, they attacked the Pueblo of Kiwa, or Santo Domingo, also a Keres town, whose warriors proved to be a match for the Pi'nini. Half the dwarfs were killed; the remainder made fast tracks south.

Here the Pueblo gods took hand. The Pajarito Plateau, and especially the Stone Lions, was holy ground, the rape of Yápashi was sacrilege. The dwarfs fled, but one by one they fell beside the trail overcome by sickness. Death took them all, their bodies left to be devoured by wolves, coyotes, and buzzards. According to the legend the gods permitted one warrior to be spared, to carry the disastrous report to his chief.

A more academic theory is that after Yápashi's abandonment, for whatever cause, the Keres moved southward into the valley. There they split, one group building a pueblo at the Potrero Viejo, about seven miles north of present-day Cochití, the other band settling yet farther south. The Cochití later abandoned the Potrero Viejo in favor of a new and permanent location on the west bank of the Rio Grande. The second company of survivors shifted about until they settled finally at the foot of Santa Ana Mesa, naming their village *Katíshtya*—the San Felipe Pueblo of today.

While Los Alamos strives with the atomic mystery, a mere eight miles south as the buzzard flies, in the sunrise light at the Shrine of the Stone Lions, the priests and shamans from the valley pueblos are voicing their sacred chants: these are the *Shaiyaik*, the most sacred Order of Hunters, who have come to show their devotion to *Gutsa,* god of deer-hunters. They sprinkle the stone effigies with the sacred meal ground of the colored kernels of the Six Directions, paint the noses a ceremonial red, and place offerings of deer antlers and pointed weapons in the narrow space between the precious symbols. They plead for success along the hunters' trails, and beseech the spirit of the game to forgive the necessity to kill.

42

7

WHERE THE SOUNDING THINGS ARE SUSPENDED

IN 1706, by order of the illustrious governor Francisco Cuervo y Valdez, thirty families from upstream Bernalillo resettled at "a place of good pasturage" where the Rio Bravo del Norte makes a sweeping bend.

We learn from the archives that the governor, in the presence of his secretary and other witnesses, picked up stones and handfuls of grass and threw them to the four cardinal points, shouting, "Long Live the King!" Then Old Town Plaza was measured for the convenience of all, lands portioned out, irrigation ditches dug, and squat adobe houses erected. The new *villa* was named to honor the governor's friend and boss, Don Francisco Fernandez de la Cueva Enriques, Duke of Alburquerque, then in Mexico City as the viceroy of New Spain. By 1800, the "r" had been dropped from the town's name. But the Spanish duke has never been forgotten. Non-Hispanic city fathers and boostering Chamber of Commerce officials have nicknamed Albuquerque "The Duke City," and the local baseball team bats and pitches as "The Dukes." The viceregal bones must rattle in their tomb.

At an altitude of 5,000 feet, Albuquerque—population about 400,000—occupies a terrain as "Southwestern" as any between the Pecos and the Colorado. The Rio Grande, flowing north to south, cuts the town down the middle. Sixteen miles to the east the Sandia Mountains crest at 10,678 feet, while sixty miles west, mighty Cebolleta, Mount Taylor, rises at 11,358 feet above sea level. Five extinct volcanic cones, once well outside the city, are now encroached upon by a subdivision called Volcano Cliffs.

North and south the broad fertile Rio Grande Valley yields its green bounty within a checkerboard of irrigation ditches and fostering canals. Fields of alfalfa and corn, watered pastures, orchards and gardens flourish in the sun—acres of *chiles,* the comestible dearest to Mexican-American hearts. All by grace of the "Bold River of the North."

44

Here is a sun so famed as to lure health seekers from the far reaches of the nation. A dry therapeutic golden light beams an annual seventy-seven percent of possible, a blessing of heaven during the dry winter months. And a scanty annual precipitation of eight inches or so falls mostly in July, August, and September. Cures are attested to by the countless now-healthy men and women who once arrived as "lungers."

The trouble with Albuquerque, when viewed by faraway critics and even New Mexicans residing elsewhere in the state, is that it is a commercial hub, and places given mostly to trade are never lovely to look at. Here interstate highways cross one another at intricate swirls of the cloverleaf, the railroad gives its tracks to all directions, and the International Airport is one of the finest and busiest in the West. Albuquerque is not so much a manufacturing town as it is a warehouse center. With retail outlets spread all over the place, it is here that the New Mexico hinterland comes to shop. It's an honest town, without pretentiousness. Except for its brilliant sunshine it is very much like the town you came from, that one way back yonder. Its real charm is in its horizons, however, the long skyline of mountain or desert or river valley open to view from all sections of town. For this great slab of concrete and towering pylon, of clean streets and green lawns, of trim homes, of everything a complete modern city should contain, was laid by ambitious men over one of the softest, historically romantic, magnificent deserts in the West with a history of swashbuckling conquistadors, mission bells and cassocked friars, Indians once proud of their humble lifestyles, cowboys and herds of longhorned cattle, multitudes of sheep peppering the mountain benchlands, arrogant hacendados, outlaws and hanging-judges—all the ingredients that comprised the rawhide West.

Three words belong to New Mexico as aptly as *chile, tortillas,* and *frijoles.*

Pasó por Aquí
Passed by Here

These are the words that were chiseled on the buff-colored side of El

Morro, Inscription Rock, now a national monument, located a hundred beeline miles west of Albuquerque, words carved by the hand of the great conquistador and first governor of New Mexico some three hundred seventy-five years ago—

Here passed the Adelantado Don Juan de Oñate from the discovery of the Sea of the South on the 16 of April of 1605

The Sea of the South—Gulf of California—
The Pacific, no less!

As greater Albuquerque swells to greater progress in other sections of the city, Old Town Plaza holds its own against frightful odds. *Old town. . .* a quiet oasis of flagstone and adobe, ancient timbers and loving hearts. . . A glad reminder of the Spanish way of life, serene, blazing with color, alive with shops and restaurants and places to rest. . . a monument to Albuquerque's earliest years, to all that has "passed by here."

In Old Town the seed of the city's beginning is healthy and genuine. An array of colors greets the visitor as in no other plaza in New Mexico. Here people have a heart for things genuine and precious, and a will to preserve them in the face of obstacles. Crowded shopping centers, high-rise temples of progress like giant gravestones, and the clamor of streets and blaring of police car and ambulance sirens all seem miles away. Here is a square surrounded by venerable buildings. Shops sell "things of the land," made by hand, wrought or carved. Art galleries are everywhere, up and down the side streets—like the lane called Charlie Vox, or rather Charlevoix. You can find items stitched and embroidered, originating on the plaza or imported from Guatemala or Oaxaca or Tzintzunzan. There are craftsmen producing exquisite handmade furniture and carved doors—and restaurants serving Mexican and New Mexican dishes red or white or green, all *picante*.

A bandstand is center of the plaza, as Spanish as any in Castile or Jalisco. The old spreading trees may have been replaced with younger ones, but the flagstone and grass are there. There are old-style benches for rest or observation. Or for meditation and thoughts of times "passed by here."

Pasó por aquí.

It was in 1930 that Bryce and Nelda Sewell purchased the Casa de Armijo that occupied almost all of the plaza's east side. Now the oldest still-occupied house in Old Town, and therefore the oldest of all Albuquerque, this was the hacienda of the rich and powerful Armijo family whose forebears were early colonists from Zacatecas. Most prominent of these Armijos was Don Manuel, last Governor of New Mexico under Mexican rule (1812–46), in office when the province fell to General Stephen Watts Kearny's "Army of the West," to become a Territory of the United States. It was a bloodless defeat of the Mexican forces. Armijo fled into hoped-for oblivion.

Old Town, as the Sewells first saw it, was an oasis of quiet living in a moderately busy town. It had all the color of the Spanish-Indian Southwest. Several well-to-do families resided around the square, and commerce was confined to a meat market, a general store on the site of today's Basket Shop, the residence of a bootlegger, and an establishment that catered to the natural propensities of gentlemen. At the north side of the plaza was the *convento* and church of San Felipe de Neri quietly attending to the business of God. Tranquil even was the sound of the bells that rang merrily at times, sometimes solemnly, high in the twin towers.

What had the Sewells gained in their purchase? Well, for one, the huge mass of adobe that contained a maze of rooms, stately *salas* (banquet halls), *zahuanes* (breezeways), *portales* (porches), *patios*, especially one where once the culinary affairs of the great household were conducted. Besides all that, they had bought all New Mexico's stages of history—first of Spain, secondly of Mexico, then Territorial New Mexico and briefly the Southern Confederacy— altogether an acre or two of earth that had held true to tradition and charm throughout its eventful life unspoiled, solid in its age. In the rambling Casa de Armijo for untold years past some of the great names in New Mexico history had been born.

It was the Old World set in the midst of brassy America.

Here were shades of people, and animals; and industries no longer in practice, for they were of the completely finished, old-fashioned, no-longer-needed times gone by. The ghosts were colorful in their attire, whether they wore the tatters of poverty or the flamboyant magnificence only the rich could afford. There were urchins and beggars and whores—There were outlaws hiding from the threat of the gallows, gamblers and thugs, professional swindlers called "bunco steerers." Bright-eyed *señoritas* and proud *gran señoras*. *Caballeros*, usually bowlegged and suntanned from their fresh air activities.

Spanish or Mexican *vaqueros*, sly or noisy about their tastes for wine and *muchachas*. Highly respected Jewish traders, such as the Zeckendorfs and the Ilfelds. A sprinkling of *Yanqui* cowboys. Even Tejanos, loud and brazen. And friars from the *convento*, briefly out of the shade and into the sunshine.

Nothing was too sanitary, and the healthy odor of livestock was everywhere. Sounds were plentiful and varied. The noise made of fuss and argument over trade and barter. Oaths—and oaths shouted in *paisano* Spanish are oaths indeed. The clatter of hoofs, the bray of mules and burros, bleating of sheep and goats, barks of a hundred dogs, nickering horses. The grating of oxdrawn *carreta* wheels—huge carts loaded high with products of the valley, or up from Mexico via the Chihuahua Trail. And laughter, for there was much happiness in the lives of these vibrant people.

And sometimes there was noise of battle, when Apaches and Navajos made their periodic raids, letting fly their arrows, hurling their firebrands at windows, teaming up to batter their battering rams. For that reason the church was also a fortress with adobe walls five feet thick, and windows twenty feet above the ground. And there were the *borrachos*, God bless them. For a *borrachon* when he is *muy borracho* may be heard to the four horizons.

Through the Territorial years, after the annexing of 1846, an American flavor was injected to the plaza. It was the frontier sort that didn't sap the Spanish atmosphere a mite. Albuquerque was still a station on the Chihuahua Trail—the Royal Highway, the *Camino Real*—and one of many points along the way vital to commerce, like Socorro and Mesilla, Guadalupe del Paso, Chihuahua and Durango, Zacatecas and the Valley of Mexico.

The Chihuahua Trail terminated at Santa Fe Plaza, where the trade route continued as the Santa Fe Trail northeastward to the land of the *Yanqui* beyond the wide Missouri. Old Town Albuquerque even had a newspaper in those Territorial days, whose owner was both a butcher and the editor. Seek him, and you'd find him either at the copydesk or in the slaughterhouse.

Pueblo Indians from the Rio Grande villages made trips to town with produce of their fields, with laden carts and pack burros, from nearby Sandia and Isleta, Santa Ana and San Felipe, or from the more distant pueblos of Cochití and Santo Domingo. Even Navajos made trading visits to the alien town, hostile tribesmen friendly for the time being. They were horseback people, bright of dress and somber of countenance. And while they made their presence, peaceful or otherwise—while life was lived here harshly or kindly, joyously or mournfully—the bells of San Felipe de Neri sounded their summons to Vespers or to Mass.

48

So the Navajos gave a name to this strange village, a name appropriate and known to the Four Corners, to Monument Valley, to the red earth below the San Francisco Peaks: *Be'eldiilahsinil*, "Where The Sounding Things Are Suspended."

And this designation is applied by them to *all* Albuquerque—even to the day-bustling, night-glistening Heights.

The history of Albuquerque may be portioned into three distinct periods—the Old Town era from 1706 to 1880; the grand and glamorous Railroad Years from 1880 to about 1950; then the three decades of exploding population following World War II, when newcomers seeking sunshine and elbow room combined their efforts to pattern their new home after other great cities of America. Neither health seekers nor retirees, many were sought by the established town fathers to help attract industry and lay out a new city. Today the east and west approaches to Albuquerque drop into the valley from heights that offer a magnificent display of lights by night, and a panorama of high-rise construction and urban planning made possible by the newcomer invasion.

New Mexico in 1930 was one of the little-known states of the West, supposedly a dusty sunblasted desert region that many Americans, then as today, linked with the republic of Mexico. It took the many military bases installed throughout the state during World War II, the Los Alamos project, and finally the atom bomb test on the Jornada del Muerto to educate the rest of America that this sovereign state had a star of its own on the national banner.

But the great event that introduced New Mexico to the world took place with fanfare on April 22, 1880. That's when the first train of the Atchison, Topeka and Santa Fe Railroad—later officially called "railway"—pulled into the crudely built Albuquerque depot to be greeted with cheers from the populace and a musical blast rendered by the Ninth Cavalry band. The train rolled to a halt at noon that day, bringing excursionists and Territorial celebrities from Santa Fe, all primed to let Albuquerque know that although the great trunk line that would connect east coast with west had taken the name of the capital city, this little community by the Rio Grande would benefit as a station along the route.

Little did the speechmaking Santa Feans realize, in spite of the petty compliment, that Albuquerque would in the years to follow become a most important division point along the main line of the far-reaching network of track—1,338 miles from the Santa Fe's start at Dearborn Station in Chicago, and 885 miles to Los Angeles. Since December of 1879, tracklaying had moved mile by mile westward into the Territory, from Raton Pass at the Colorado line, through Las Vegas and around the Rockies at Glorieta Pass, down to the Rio Grande Valley and Albuquerque. At Isleta Pueblo, twelve miles down river, the first line took the name of the Atlantic & Pacific and continued as such to Needles, first station in California, on the Colorado River. All right of way was later absorbed by the Santa Fe.

No point along the line was better known than Albuquerque. The Santa Fe was, in the days of the great streamliners, the "Highway to the Southwest"— and all through the Southwest the company stressed the color of the region, its passing landscapes and peoples: east of Albuquerque the plains and mountain Southwest, westward the deserts and red rock country of the Navajo past the old Pueblo villages of Laguna and Acomita. And last, before slipping over into Arizona, came the frontierlike town of Gallup. So Albuquerque, then, was where the curtain was raised to stage the grandeur that could be feasted upon from Pullman windows and observation car platforms as the train moved west.

After the Chicago Railroad Fair of 1948–49 introduced the Santa Fe and all the glamour it possessed to hundreds of thousands, all unaware but eager to learn about the country it served, Conrad from Zuni in his colorful Pueblo attire boarded *The Super Chief* at Albuquerque to walk the corridors and explain passing landmarks of history to the passengers—the Indian country and the lore of its people. The Santo Domingo Indians affectionately nicknamed *The Super Chief* "Chili Mouth" because of the locomotive's red front that harmonized with the long silvery train. Even the Pullman cars of all the streamliners bore Southwestern Indian names such as *Tsankawi, Shonto, Toroweep,* and *Betatakin.*

But, in those memorable years, Albuquerque's pride was the hotel at the railway station, Fred Harvey's finest, *The Alvarado.* Built in Spanish Mission style, it spread from the street to occupy almost the entire length of the tracks

49

where trains arrived and departed. It featured portals and shaded galleries, patios green and flowering, fountains and flagstone walks. The upper floor windows, facing east, offered views over the tracks to the city beyond, and the dramatic mountain skyline of the Sandias and Manzanos.

50

At the turn of the century efforts were made to build Harvey hotels in harmony with the Southwestern environment. All were to be given names out of New Mexico and Arizona history, or in appropriate Spanish. There would be *El Tovar* at the Grand Canyon, the *Fray Marcos* in Williams, and *La Posada* at Winslow, all in Arizona. For New Mexico came *La Fonda* in Santa Fe, the *Ortiz* in Lamy, the *Castañeda* in Las Vegas, *El Navajo* in Gallup—and the finest of them all, the *Alvarado* in Albuquerque. And the Alvarado was the first to be built to suit the cultured demands of Fred Harvey himself. For Albuquerque, nothing but the best in dignity and service would do.

Accordingly, Mary E.J. Colter, renowned architect and interior decorator, was given the project of designing the entire structure, exterior and interior. Even the furnishings were to harmonize with the Spanish-Mission atmosphere of the hotel. In preparation for the exacting task, Mary Colter spent considerable time in the Southwest studying towns, villages, and Indian Pueblos, obtaining authenticity to match the quiet decor.

There were 120 guest rooms in all. A Santa Fe timetable of 1950 listed rates per night for all the Harvey Houses up and down the line including the Alvarado. For one person (European plan) a room was priced at $2.50 without bath, and one with bath would cost $4.00 and up. Table d'hote service offered breakfast for $1.00, luncheon for $1.25, and dinner, which could be a sumptuous one, for $1.50. A la carte orders were available at very reasonable prices. And along with the delectable fare served in the dining and lunchrooms went the courtesies and graciousness of the strictly trained, world-famed Harvey Girls— waitresses extraordinary.

Or, as S.E. Kiser, "The Sweet Singer of the Prairies" put it to harmony in 1906:

Oh, the pretty Harvey Girl beside my chair,
A fairer maiden I shall never see,
She was winsome, she was neat,
She was gloriously sweet,
And she certainly was very good to me.

Whenever a train from the east pulled into the Albuquerque railway station the passengers were given their introduction to the Indian Country, actual contact and conversation with its residents rather than merely passing pueblos and villages along the way. When their train was stopped for exterior cleaning and general servicing, they had ample time for crowding into the Fred Harvey Indian Museum at the Alvarado adjacent to the track. They could talk with the Indian crafts venders seated beside their pottery, textiles, beadwork, and silver and turquoise jewelry in the shaded walkway at the doors. And while some passengers inspected the museum, or purchased the handicrafts, others preferred to exercise by strolling beside the long silvery train while California-Missionlike melodies, such as *Ramona* or *My Rosary*, chimed from one of the Alvarado's towers.

Ever since the Los Angeles suburb of Hollywood had become the hub of the nation's motion picture industry, the Albuquerque townfolk, then in the great years of railroading, adopted the quiet diversion of going to the station and meeting the trains, hoping to get a glimpse of some movie idol on a stroll, while the train was being serviced. In the early *California Limited* days, Pola Negri or Norma Talmadge or Lili Pons could be seen smiling down on her adorers from the open observation platform. Later *The Chief* might discharge to the brick walkway Gary Cooper, Betty Grable, Dorothy Lamour, or Henry Fonda. And finally *The Super Chief* with Jimmy Stewart or Joan Fontaine or Liberace. All glittering stars of Hollywood in their turn, who favored the Santa Fe for the glamourous service it provided, and for its route through the sunbright, pastel-painted Southwest.

In 1971 the beautiful Alvarado was razed and its site converted to a parking lot, the station complex whittled down to suit the needs of matter-of-fact Amtrak. If the ghost of the *Super Chief* haunts the rails where it once stopped, it must be borne in mind that Robert Taylor and Norma Talmadge have also passed on, but with hardly a chance of being forgotten.

A mile-and-a-half separates the railroad depot from Old Town Plaza. The wagon road blazed to connect the two historic points was first known as Railroad Avenue, and now as Central Avenue, a parent concourse for all the streets and thoroughfares in the city. From the first tent-saloon hastily erected to greet the first train and to bolster the cheers of the celebrants, to the architectural masterpiece that is the Civic Plaza of today, Central Avenue was the course to empire. On East Central Avenue the University of New Mexico was opened in 1892, to become a city within a city, a source of learning for all New Mexico, the West, and the world. Progress and development used it to climb out of the valley and spread to the mountains, building a metropolis for the tastes of newcomers, the current pioneers who have more than tripled the population of Albuquerque since 1950.

By 1930, when the Sewells found themselves with the Casa de Armijo in their possession, every nook and cranny of the huge house in Old Town Plaza was loaded with history, bright or tragic. From under the long front door portal, which occupied the entire east side of the town square, could be viewed the quiet Spanish charm established 224 years before. Fearful that in time an increase of population and commerce for Albuquerque would mark this monument of the past as a lamb for slaughter, the Sewells got busy and mapped a course for preservation. From their ideas sprang Old Town Albuquerque as it is today, a haven of color with an aura of the past, the residence and marketplace of people with discretion. Nelda Sewell, now Mrs. Jack Moorhead, is hailed as the founder of it all, the pioneer. And she is still owner of the Casa de Armijo.

Through her efforts the plaza is now almost wholly shops and restaurants. In the Casa de Armijo is the Patio Market, shops built around a space that was given to artists' studios when the Sewells took over, bright little emporiums whose names speak of the things they sell: *The Wood and Iron Shop, Craftwear, La Piñata, The Glass House,* and other specialty shops as well as an art gallery, the *Galeria del Sol.* From the start, the Sewells tried to get a restaurant going in the Casa, with a few attempts made, strangely enough, by anthropologists from the University. But *tacos* are not artifacts, nor is *chile con queso* a culture to be explored. All attempts were dismal failures. Then, about 1940, Cyrus and Marie Brown took over a large section of the building and *La Placita* became a reality and a success. Along with the neighboring *La Hacienda,* it is the largest and finest restaurant in Old Town, with color and menu extraordinary.

Within a short time, residences around the plaza gave way to shops and galleries and smaller restaurants serving Mexican fare. And when the plaza was filled, the side streets, especially San Felipe Street, made room for more galleries and *tiendas.*

To retain the flavor of New Mexico's past the area is now protected by Historic Ordinance No. 1493, "to promote the continuation of the traditional characteristics of the Old Town Plaza." Buildings here date from the three periods of Albuquerque history—Spanish-Colonial, Territorial, and Western Victorian. Historic buildings are gradually being restored. New buildings in this zone must be built in these styles. The new and attractively-designed Albuquerque Museum—a treasure house of art, history, and anthropology—is just off the Plaza, as is the Sheraton Old Town Hotel.

53

At the start of World War II, one of the most genial and lovable of America's writers chose Albuquerque for a home. He selected a spot at the city's edge, close to the Sandia Mountain foothills, then alone in the sun, now swallowed by urban development. Ernie Pyle was among the greatest of war correspondents; and because he was great, and brave, and the most ardent of the loyal, he was killed in action, the victim of a sniper's bullet. His Albuquerque home was planned for his return from battle, after the havoc, for the victory and the reward of settling down to quiet writing on ground he loved.

Before leaving on his last mission he wrote an article for the *New Mexico Magazine* about why he chose Albuquerque for his home:

> We like Albuquerque because, in spite of the great comfortable sense of isolation you feel here, still you do not suffer from over-isolation. For people here, too, live lives that are complete and full. We want for little, even in the nebulous realm of the mind. There is no famine of the mind. There is no famine of thought in our surroundings. In the Southwest character there is sufficiency which, though not complacent, has in it something of the desert's charm.
>
> We like it because the sky is so bright and you can see so much of it. And because out here you actually see the clouds and the stars and the storms, instead of just reading about them in the newspapers. They become a genuine part of your daily life, and half the entire horizon is yours in one glance just for the looking, and the distance sort of gets into your soul and makes you feel that you too are big inside.

8

THE GREEN CORN DANCE

THE INDIAN PUEBLO of Santo Domingo lies sprawled on caramel earth where the lesser Rio Galisteo meets the Rio Grande. It is reached by a four-mile access road that takes off Highway 85 at a point twenty-seven miles southwest of Santa Fe and thirty-four miles northeast of Albuquerque.

This is ancient Kiwa, the "Hub," the place of the Great Council. This is the metropolis of the Keres, one of the linguistic divisions that make up the Pueblo nation. It shares the Keresan language with six other related nearby towns, namely San Felipe and Cochiti, Santa Ana and Zia, Acoma and Laguna. And with about 1,500 residents it is the most populous.

Here the earth is cut by the muddy brown river; ditches provide irrigation for the fields that are laid out green and well tended—alfalfa, beans, barley, wheat, and the precious ears that cling to the tasseled corn.

And to Santo Domingo every August, on the feast day of its patron Saint Dominic, come the spectators from everywhere in the world to witness one of the most elaborate religious ceremonies to survive prehistory. They come as they have year after year, the alien majority, to stand, to watch, to absorb, and to be assured that religion in its ancient form is alive in this village of low, mud-plastered houses built along earthen lanes and around dusty plazas. It is estimated that in recent years an average crowd of 8,000 annually witnesses the "spectacle." But to the Indian it is more; it is the beginning, the continuation, and the strength of all existence.

As the crowds gather on the dance plaza, the wait seems endless. But this is Indian business, never hurried. In time the drums will throb. In just a little while the double line of brightly dressed dancers will give themselves to ecstasy and the chanting chorus will be heard. And at last the prayer received by Iatik, the Corn Mother, who said at the dawn of creation, "You are my children, I am your mother. I will nurse you and sustain you. I give to you my corn, the very milk of my breasts."

Among the strangers, the tourists, artists, business people visiting for the day, mingle with the close friends and acquaintances of Santo Domingo: Spanish-American and Anglo neighbors from Peña Blanca, Algodones, and Bernalillo; teachers, school administrators, Bureau of Indian Affairs officials; concho-belted folk from other pueblos—Tewas, Tiwas, and Towas; Hopis and Zunis; and Indians of the nomad tribes, Apaches, Navajos, Utes—garbed in their best, loaded with silver and turquoise jewelry, the men stoic under high, wide-brimmed hats, the shy women with shawls held over their faces.

Since the first seed was planted in the spring, since the initial flow of irrigation water was cut from canals into the ditches, since the cornfields first sprouted their tender seedlings, preparations have been made for this day. Since April, *T'shrai'katsi*—the *cacique,* the village chief, the living presence of Iatik herself—has fasted and prayed and communed with his divine mistress. He has commanded the prelude ceremonies to be performed: the rain dances which successfully brought showers from heaven—gala events, open to public view—and the age-old secret rituals held in the firelit dark of the ceremonial houses, too sacred for any but the initiated.

The Great River responded with the spring runoff, with thick, brown water tumbling down from the snowfields high in the Colorado Rockies. July sent its contribution—torrential thunderstorms full of power and lightning. Plant life flourished. And now has come the finale, the year's benediction, the Day of Saint Dominic, be he Christian symbol or Indian kachina. Truly the difference is slight.

The houses sparkle inside and out, smooth with fresh coats of plaster or whitewash. Every lane has been raked and swept. And for days and nights the food has cooked on the kitchen ranges and outside in beehive ovens. Now the tables are set, ready for the guests: stacks of fry bread, tortillas, all manner of store-bought bakery creations; meats—beef, mutton, goat—roasted, stewed, fried, and boiled, with or without the most popular of all New Mexican ingredients, chile; coffee brewed to suit powerful Indian tastes; soft drinks of various pastel shades. The village air is saturated with aromas and every dwelling bustles with culinary enterprise.

The massive adobe mission church shines as well with its annual plaster-ing of mud, with the festive sprucing up. But today something is missing inside. Now, at midmorning, the image of Saint Dominic is not on the altar, his residence throughout the year. This day he occupies a temporary altar in a brush shelter erected at the far end of the dance plaza. The fiesta Mass has been celebrated, the congregation off to prepare the festivities, and the little *bulto* (carved image in wood) of Saint Dominic has been carried without fanfare to his place of honor.

This is the last day of a four-day ceremony; it is the noon and sundown of *iyan'yi*—the earned "blessing of the gods"—when maturity of the field crops, and especially the corn, will be assured the people. The Green Corn Dance is *not*, as is popularly supposed, a ritual pleading for rain. It asks for an abundant harvest, survival for Santo Domingo, and a blessing on every beating heart in the world.

For three days and nights smoke has curled from the open ladder-hatchways cut in the roofs of the two kivas. Smoke symbolizes life, the vapor of breath. In this Indian faith, every object is a symbol—every sound, color, move-ment and action; every material piece of apparent insignificance—a pebble, a button on a coat, a nail, a coin—anything under the sun, has, like flesh and blood, the gift of a living spirit. And corn is symbolic of every good thing possible in this life. And the most sacred elements of Pueblo Indian life are "female."

The depths of a kiva symbolize Shipapu, the dark underworld from whence came all living things—the womb of *Naya Ha'ah'tsi*, the Earth Mother. The spruce ladder down the kiva hatchway reminds us all that we climbed the tree itself on the day of creation up to the surface, to find our peculiar methods of living on this tricky earth, until death transports us again to the depths of the underworld, and to bliss eternal—to the loving arms of Iatik.

The clans are matrilineal, each Indian child inheriting his "descent" from his mother. Grandmothers are held in greater esteem in the Pueblo community than grandfathers. The Rio Grande is a gently flowing river, therefore "female," in contrast to the turbulent San Juan, which is "male." The cacique, although male in body, is considered female in spirit. He represents the Corn Mother on earth.

Related to the clans are the two tribal subdivisions, the Squash, or "Sum-mer People," and the Turquoise, "Winter People." Every child is born into one of the two groups. The Squash kiva is located at the south side of the village; the Turquoise kiva, at the north. Turquoise people are the masters of ceremony for the winter dances; Squash, for all summer events.

Now, *Oshatsh*, the Sun God, is high overhead but not yet at his zenith. Since dawn he has lifted himself above Sandia, the sacred East World Mountain, place of shrines and home of the warrior gods. Now the pueblo "officers" take their places against a house wall facing the sacred precinct on the plaza, where the dance will be performed. They are the governor and his lieutenant; the two war chiefs, *biscales* and *sacristano; nawais*, or headmen of the many secret societies—purely Indian, unrelated to Christianity. And in the center of them all sits the cacique, white-haired, wrinkled with age, blissfully composed by the almost ceaseless occupation of meditation and prayer. They wait.

Little Saint Dominic in his spruce ramada waits.

The thousands of spectators wait—the *simpatico* knowing that they will see and hear the fervent prayer of one of the most devout peoples on earth.

Thunderheads are building over the mesas; some white as shells, others dark as the matrix in turquoise.

Look to the kivas, north and south. The smoke still spirals from the roof hatches, the great spruce ladders slope their highest uprights to the sun. And now out of the kivas, to herald the human emergence, may be seen the 12-foot long standards that will be carried beside the dancers throughout the day. Attached to these poles are embroidered kilts, identical with those worn by the men who comprise the male *Shi'wanna*, or corn dancers. The kilts are somewhat narrow and hang vertically from the head of the pole. At the very peak is a knob, containing shells and seeds, from which sprout eagle feathers, eagle down, parrot, woodpecker, macaw, and Swenson hawk plumes. And bound to the peak is a fully furred pelt of *Mast'ya*, the gray fox, whose purpose is to dangle over the dancers, chorus, and drummer and shower upon them the most potent iyan'yi in Indian religion.

Now the dance plaza provides a show of drama. The Green Corn Dance of Santo Domingo has begun with a historic prelude, a demonstration to the Sun God by the society of sacred "clowns"—who are not clowns at all, but solemn masters of ceremony for every Corn Dance. These are the renowned *Kosh'airi*, or "Delight Makers." Their bodies are painted an ashen gray crossed with black stripes—physically hideous as the dead beings they represent. Their loins sport breechcloths; their hair is done up with cornhusks. To be effective, the entire ritual must be performed without a flaw. The Kosh'airi's duties are to watch and to ward; to spot offenses that would instantly render the day sterile; to aid the dancers, adjust bits of their costumes should they come loose; to dance, to circle about, and to pantomime fertility.

58

The Summer Kosh'airi have emerged from the Squash kiva. Once out of the depths, they trot single file to the south half of the village, circling and sanctifying it for the presence of the dancing Shi'wanna. They enter the plaza and excitedly run for the sacred precinct in the center. They seem to ignore Saint Dominic standing in his brush shelter. Meanwhile, the Winter Kosh'airi have performed the same ritual of circling their north section of the pueblo. They join the Summer group in the plaza and show, by acts and gestures, that there is a threat to the village and to the people's welfare. They dramatize a raid on the pueblo and cornfields by the *Mo'shomi*—the nomad enemies, Apaches, Navajos, or Comanches. In short, by a heated discussion, gestures of excitement, and deep concern, they indicate doom for Santo Domingo if the matter is not speedily attended to. A suggestion is made; agreement seems unanimous. Runners are sent to the four cardinal points, soon to return to the waiting Kosh'airi. True enough, the enemy threatens. The performance goes on to show the purification of the warriors, the warpath, the battle, and at last the victory— the raiders vanquished. Now the historic prelude is completed; the crops remain healthy and unmolested. Now the great prayer must be offered to the Power— Himself. The Kosh'airi disband, to hurry off to their respective kivas, and disappear down the ladder hatchways.

But not for long. A drum sounds at the Squash kiva, and the spectators' attention is turned to the south. The plumed banner with the dangling fox skin is lifted high by its bearer. Now the Kosh'airi are dancing on the kiva roof. The chorus—a hundred voices building up to religious ecstasy—begins the day-long chant to which the dancers respond with symbolic movement of their bodies. The volume is tremendous; it vibrates the surroundings.

The banner is held over the hatchway, to shower its iyan'yi—the same blessings the gods gave generously to the people as they emerged from the depths of Shi'papu climbing the spruce ladder on the day of creation. Out of the kiva come the corn dancers in full ceremonial dress.

Men and women appear singly and alternately in the sunlight. They descend the steps from the kiva to the ground, where they form a procession—following drummer, chorus, and standard bearer—and move toward the church. They stop in a double line, male facing female, in front of the gate to the walled yard at the church entrance, where they give their brief token of respect to Christian participation in the events of the day. Then the dancing Kosh'airi lead the way to the plaza, which is entered at the west side where little Saint Dominic waits to receive the power of the ritual and to give his own power in return.

Two lines are formed at the sacred precinct in the plaza, directly in front of Saint Dominic's spruce-covered shrine. The lines of fifty or more couples face each other, one line male, the other female, and the standard bearer moves up and down around them showering them with blessing. This, the most sacred fetish, is at first carried by an elderly Rain Priest who later turns it over to a younger man once the dance gets under way.

Now the drumbeats become more forceful, and the chant from a hundred voices resounds through the crowd. A man at the center of the dance line motions with his feet, others follow in step, and the Green Corn Dance begins, the Kosh'airi dancing up and down and between the lines.

A woman dancer's costume consists of a short black skirt of native weave, the waist rising to the right shoulder leaving the left bare. All the jewelry in her possession is draped about her neck and wrists; around her middle is a belt of woven red yarn. Her feet are bare, for her flesh must touch that of Naya Ha'ah'tsi, the Earth Mother, throughout the ceremony. And the dancer's long black hair flows free; atop her head she wears a *tablita,* a thin board shaped and painted with sacred symbols—sun, moon, and clouds. The tablita is worn erect, the tips potent with wisps of eagle down, token of the *t'stats winoshka,* or "breath-heart," the breath of life. In each hand she carries a sprig of unblemished spruce. Her cheeks are painted red. Her eyes are downcast while she dances.

A male dancer wears a knee-length kilt embroidered with potent symbols and a white "rain belt," its long fringe streaming down his right leg. A fox skin, attached to the belt, is suspended behind him. His hair also falls loose down his back, but is held tight at the crown with tufts of woodpecker and parrot feathers. A girdle of seashells is slung over his left shoulder and down to his right hip. Painted rawhide bands, inserted into sprigs of evergreen, decorate his arms.

A rattle made of dry land turtle shell is attached to a garter at his left knee, and around each ankle a band of skunk skin. In his right hand he holds a *ki'ah'weh*—a gourd filled with seeds, which sounds like falling rain when vigorously shaken. If the male dancer belongs to the Squash kiva, his body is painted a pinkish tan. Should he be of the Turquoise people, the paint is a turquoise blue. Otherwise the male costumes are identical.

And so the Green Corn Dance is presented to the gods. Squash and Turquoise, each in turn, dance to the prayer-chant, to the hand-and-arm gestures of the chorus, to the thundering drums. The gestures, in time with the rise and fall of the voices, are symbolic of the blessings for which supplication is given. The falling rain, the crack of lightning, the roll of thunder, clouds forming in the heavens, water from the river trickling down the corn rows, a breeze rustling the leaves, the abundance of ears clinging to the stalks, joy expressed by the people for the gift of the Great Benevolence.

The men pound the ground with moccasined feet, rattle their gourds, and turn, while the women, in a gentler performance, sway their sprigs of evergreen and never for a second's time allow a bare foot to leave the Earth Mother.

Just before noon, at intermission, visitors may help themselves to refreshments from bowls of food, baskets of bread, and coffee and Kool-Aid that have been placed before Saint Dominic's place of honor. Then both the Squash and Turquoise peoples, who perform four dances in turn throughout the day, join together for the "Push Dance," two hundred dancers, two hundred chorus voices, two drummers, two groups of Kosh'airi. And when the drama is completed, everyone takes time out to feast.

When the Squash kiva leads off with the afternoon ceremony, Oshatsh the Sun is moving westward to descend to his "Sacred Place." Minute by minute a spiritual zest is building. The standard bearer waves his wand, and every Indian present, whether of the village or visiting from elsewhere, manages to pass under it and receive a blessing. The Turquoise group presents the last dance of the day, filled with all the ecstasy and thanksgiving the day's "work" has provided.

And with sundown it is finished. The spectators begin the return to their world, some having experienced the true purpose of the day, others with little understanding of what they have witnessed. But at the village the rejoicing is extreme, for the sweat of the brow has triumphed: the corn will mature, the earth and the field will provide a bountiful harvest. And there will be not only a bounty of the field, but of the heart in the continuing faith that Santo Domingo will survive and increase.

9

LOS MATACHINES:
DANCE OF THE MOROS

THEY ROASTED San Lorenzo (St. Lawrence) on a gridiron, and the event is remembered throughout the Spanish-speaking world every August 10th with a solemn Mass followed by feasting, music, and dancing. True, his martyrdom calls for a certain expression of solemnity, but the associated merry-making is appropriate, too. For San Lorenzo, a Spaniard, is said to have been a man of extreme good humor, devoted to the happy things of life, such as choice wines and heavily laden tables, laughter, and good fellowship.

Pope Sixtus the Second employed him as his deacon in Rome. He was especially valued for his wise administration of church funds. But the Emperor Valerian, persecutor of the Christians in A.D. 258, condemned Lorenzo to death. Legend has it that even during his ordeal, the saint's good nature prevailed and he entertained his executioners with humorous quips about the basting process . . .

San Lorenzo has been worshiped throughout the world for centuries. In 1563, King Philip of Spain built the Escorial, the somber palace-monastery near Madrid, and dedicated it to the saint's honor because, it is claimed, the Battle of St. Quentin had been won from the French six years before on August 10. But nowhere else in the world do Hispanos prepare with such zeal the exalting of the ancient Spaniard as do the people of Bernalillo, New Mexico every August.

Bernalillo, twenty miles up the Rio Grande Valley from Albuquerque, is one of New Mexico's first-settled areas. Francisco Vasquez Coronado, the conquistador, occupied a nearby Indian Pueblo from 1540 to 1542. Haciendas on Spanish land grants were laid out in the vicinity before 1620, fields were

62

cultivated in the valley, and flocks and herds ranged the grassy flatlands. Before the Pueblo Indian Revolt of 1680, Sandia Pueblo, three miles south of Bernalillo, had become an important Spanish government post. Twelve years later, Diego de Vargas who regained New Mexico for the Spanish crown in 1692, died in a ranch house in Bernalillo. However, the actual laying out of the townsite was probably not begun until the early nineteenth century, when the town became an important stopover and trade point on the wagon train route between Santa Fe and Mexico City.

63

The ruins of adobe buildings that made up the old town, locally called *Las Cocinitas*, "The Little Kitchens," may be seen just off the main business block. In 1856 the church of *Nuestra Señora de los Dolores* was constructed by direction of the famed Archbishop Jean Baptiste Lamy, hero of Willa Cather's *Death Comes for the Archbishop.*

No one seems to know when in the course of Bernalillo's history the bulto of San Lorenzo was put in the chapel to become the patron saint and recipient of long-standing reverence. But it happened a long time ago. A Franciscan friar astride his donkey could have been the bearer of the object that now shows considerable age.

Although Lorenzo died in Rome four-and-a-half centuries before the Moorish invasion of Spain, it is the *Matachines* dance—of African origin—that is performed today in his honor on Camino del Pueblo, Bernalillo's main street. Like the Spanish horse (the Barb and the Andalusian), it was brought to Spain by the Moors in A.D. 711. Related forms of the dance spread to other parts of Europe to become *Les Mattachins* in France, the *Matacinio* in Italy, and the Morris (Moorish) Dance in England. The Moorish-Spanish version arrived in Mexico following the conquest of Cortez in 1519, was eagerly adopted by the Indians and given Aztec characters and symbolism, in place of, or in addition to, the original Afro-European form.

The word *matachin* comes from the Arabic *mudawajjihin*, meaning "those who face each other." Whatever its remote origin in the regions south of the Mediterranean, the Pueblo Indians of New Mexico have adopted the dance and look upon it as an ancient Mexican ceremony honoring Montezuma. And Montezuma in their belief, was not so much a sovereign of the Aztec Empire, as a deity who once lived among them.

August comes to New Mexico at midpoint of the summer "rainy season."

Thunderheads are apt to pall the summit of nearby Sandia Mountain while the Bernalillo *gente* make preparations for their fiesta. The alfalfa fields are moist with irrigation and fruit is ripening in the orchards; now chile peppers come to the kitchens, freshly plucked and green.

64

Housewives perspire about the stoves, well ahead of the festive week. Good food calls for slow, steady cooking; all the ingredients are on hand for *chile colorado, enchiladas, albondigas* and *posole, tacos, tamales* and *chile con queso,* and breadstuffs such as *tortillas, empanadas, biscochitos,* and an assortment of homemade *dulces.*

Gay apparel is made ready, and buying is heavy in Albuquerque stores that cater to Spanish-American needs in drygoods and foodstuffs. For weeks the Matachines group has practiced its steps, chant, and the precise fingering of guitar and violin. The carnival has been set up on a vacant lot, handy for all the *niños* in town, the *padre* knows his fiesta homily by heart, and the numerous saloon keepers wait in anticipation.

Then, on the seventh day of the auspicious month, the glorification of San Lorenzo begins.

Although he is the object of the five-day gala, it is during the final three days that his wooden image takes an actual part. August 7 and 8 are given to worldly cheer—dancing, feasting in the homes, the sparkle of wine, much laughter, jesting by local wits, and riotous pleasure for the niños on the Ferris wheel and merry-go-round. A parade is sponsored by the sheriff's posse. If the object of veneration is at all present, his spirit is in the food and wines, the laughter and cheer. But come the evening of August 9, church bells summon all faithful to the Novena. Then the Matachines appear, and, with song and string music, dance the beloved bulto of their patron up the Camino del Pueblo from the home where it has resided for the past year to a special place of honor in the church.

Again, no one knows just how long the statue has gone through this aspect of the ritual of veneration, but for an entire year it resides with a local household outstanding for some extra show of devotion or active in parish affairs. Except for the two fiesta nights of August 9 and 10 when an altar in the church gives it shelter, the bulto is a guest of the honored family who earn a special blessing for their great responsibility. For almost a year San Lorenzo lives among the people, the center of a home altar as elaborate as an Italian wedding cake, amid imitation blooms and shrubbery, glowing candles, and pristine lace.

Of the nineteen performers in the Matachines, twelve are dancers, called *dansantes*, who carry a *palma*, three sticks pronged into fanshape and painted with ceremonial designs. Over their shoulders and back is draped a fiesta-bright and floral printed shawl.

65

Because it is a *Morisca* dance, the faces of the Bernalillo dansantes are blackened to impersonate *Los Moros*, the Moors, even as the Morris Dancers of England blackened theirs. Wherever the practice is found it symbolizes the victory of good over evil, Christianity over paganism, Spain over Africa.

Between the dansantes is *El Monarco*, representing Montezuma, the power of good over evil, and *El Toro*, the Bull, the counter-symbol, a truly hellish personality.

La Malinche is there as well, Doña Marina of the conquest of Mexico, Cortez's Mayan mistress and interpreter. Here she is revered as the first Indian convert to Christianity, portrayed by a ten-year-old girl in virginal white and a conspicuous look of innocence on her darker contrasting face. She plays her part daintily. Here in Bernalillo, where the residents consider themselves more Spanish than Mexican, she symbolizes Christian victory over paganism, in contrast to Mexico where the Spaniard is not so exalted and Malinche is remembered as a traitress who helped the invaders topple the Aztec empire and bring an end to the Montezumas.

Then there is the comic touch, two clowns called *Los Abuelos*, the Grand-fathers, who prance between and around the lines of dancers. They seek to amuse as they have done year after year for centuries. And, of course, the musicians, uncostumed, playing the violin and the guitar, accompanied by a man with an ancient shotgun, whose duty it is to blast away at any intrusion of the devil. He fires into the air, with care not to hit El Toro, the very personification of Satan.

. . . Look! The Matachines are approaching the house where the saint is snug on his altar, awaiting the moment of departure. But before he leaves, his convoy must eat—and with the same heartiness that the pleasure-loving Lorenzo enjoyed when he was flesh and blood and not a graven image. For on this feast day hospitality is extended everywhere in the spirit of San Lorenzo, especially so at the house where the saint has spent the past year, and then again at the home where he will live next year after he has "gone to church." The aromas are rich and penetrating, chili and Mexican *comida, sabrosa y muy picante.*

Spectators line the Camino del Pueblo for a full mile as the Matachines dance the patron saint to the church, while the musicians play their ancient folk tunes. . . The late Prospero Baca, who came to Bernalillo many years ago from the Penitente country in the Sangre de Cristo Mountains, was responsible for the strong interest shown by the townspeople for the ceremony and for the preservation of the accompanying music. Ninety-year-old Luciano Nieto was violinist for many years and handed the songs down to his grandson, Charles Aguilar.

The important event of San Lorenzo Day is the Fiesta Mass, celebrated in the morning of August 10, the one day in which the bulto of San Lorenzo spends a full twenty-four hours in the church. The Matachines appear on the street at intervals throughout the day, the steps and music ever the same. The fiddle's whine, the strumming guitar, the shotgun blasts at Satan who hovers above in the blue New Mexican sky, the laughter of onlookers at the comical Los Abuelos.

And on the morning of August 11, the Matachines call at the church again, take the saint from his perch of honor, and dance with him to the house that will be his home for another year, and where, of course, now there is feasting once more.

By midnight it is over, the festive spirit has fled, and the sounds of the town are the cries of late celebrants leaving the bars at 2 A.M.

Bernalillo shares the Matachines pageant with a few other Hispano villages in New Mexico, with seven Indian Pueblos, with the Yaquis of Tucson, and with many Indian communities in Mexico such as the Tarahumara, the Huichol, the Otomi, the Mayo, and the Tarascos on the shore of Patzcuaro in Michoacan.

In Mexico City, every year on August 21, ten days after Bernalillo has danced its dance, a little group in authentic Aztec costume walks up the Paseo de la Reforma, probably the loveliest concourse in the world. They move to the music of violin and guitar, and their destination is the second *glorieta*. Their mission is to dance, to chant, to recall the greatness of the ancient Aztec empire in the purest Nahuatl at the base of a huge figure in bronze. In all the republic there is not *one* statue to exalt Cortez, Coronado, Alvarado, or any of the so-called conquistadors. But there amid the floral splendor of the exquisite glorieta, the first cousins of the Bernalillo Matachines pledge continued loyalty before the sculptured memorial to Cuauhtemotzin, last prince of the Aztecs.

10

THE SUN SYMBOL PUEBLO

THIRTY-FOUR MILES out of Albuquerque on State Road 44, Zia—the Sun Symbol Pueblo—can be seen spread atop a high black mound beyond the creek, a sort of footstool for the gods of benevolence that dwell upon the mighty lava rock precipice to the north.

The impression one gets on entering Zia is strongly tempered with awe—awe for the surrounding desolation, coupled with admiration for a people who can adapt themselves and survive now as their ancestors lived and survived for centuries past. Jemez Creek here is silty and sluggish, often a mere trickle, sometimes no stream at all. The meager cultivated fields are sandy and parched. But the men of Zia are Pueblo Indians—therefore farmers and herdsmen, skilled at cultivating earth that the white man would shun. They can bring to harvest their crops of corn and beans, wheat and alfalfa, their chile and melons, and graze the hillsides with fat ewes and lambs. Being Pueblo Indians, the people of Zia are equipped with courage and faith unmatched by almost any others.

The great symbol that has been made official in New Mexico shines with warm affection on Zia.

Because of its basalt foundation, the village is reached by hard pulls up calloused lanes. At the top are the homes, plazas, church and kivas—a masterpiece in Pueblo architecture. Walls are of masoned rock and substantial adobe.

On the height of the bluff stands the mission church of Nuestra Señora de la Asuncion (Our Lady of the Assumption), built in 1692 at the time of the De Vargas reconquest. It is a massive structure with heavy buttresses on the front facade; the adobe walls are several feet thick, forming a simple architectural pattern except for the stepped adobe gable where the bell is hung above a railed outside gallery. Willa Cather, in *Death Comes for the Archbishop*, makes reference to an original *El Greco* among the old Spanish paintings in the church. If one ever existed, it isn't there today. This church was built on the ruins of the first that was consecrated after the Oñate *entrada* of 1598 and destroyed in the revolt of 1680. On the Feast of the Assumption, held every August 15, the Green Corn Dance staged on the plaza as a religious ritual is one of the finest Indian pageants to be seen in New Mexico.

Zia is the birthplace of some of the finest Pueblo artists—painters, weavers, and potters, including Velino Shije *(Ma-Pe-Wi)*, Ignacio Moquino *(Waka-Yeni-De-Wa)*, Rafael Medina, and Lorenzo Medina. Almost every woman is a gifted potter. Delicate hands mold the famous ollas, trays, and mixing bowls that are distinctive of Zia. Trinidad Medina and Vicentita Pino have year after year taken prizes at fairs and exhibitions throughout the nation, their creations very, very beautiful in design and symmetry.

Colors are red and black applied to a white slip; the designs may be floral, or represent the rainbow or cloud. Characteristic of Zia is the Chaparral Cock pattern, known to the people themselves as the "Zia Chicken." It is given frequent use. But the symbol that put Zia on the map—or, better still, to blaze in deep scarlet in the center of New Mexico's official flag—is "The Sun."

Antonio de Espejo, after visiting Zia in 1583, made mention in his report of figures painted on a wall in one of the Keres pueblos showing moon, stars, and one that obviously could be taken to symbolize the sun, though its disklike center with surrounding leaves gave it more the look of a sunflower. Centuries later, a woman of Zia carefully painted this motif on a water jar she had made, which ultimately found its way to the collection of the Museum of New Mexico in Santa Fe.

A design by the late Dr. Harry Mera, a Santa Fe physician, was chosen by the Daughters of the American Revolution for a state flag that would incorporate in colors and pattern the Indian and Spanish traditions that make this "Land of the Sun" unique among American states. The Sun Symbol on the water jar—then in the Laboratory of Anthropology—was selected for a center design in deep scarlet on a plain field of rich yellow, the colors that accompanied the Spanish conquistadors to New Mexico more than 400 years ago. In March 1925, Governor A.T. Hannett signed House Bill 64, creating the official flag, with the Zia symbol alone against its sunbright background. The governor's action repealed a law of 1915 which had adopted another state flag.

Some years ago, Charles E. Minton, of Santa Fe, executive director of the New Mexico Commission of Indian Affairs, presented the state flag with the Sun Symbol to the Zia Indians as a gift from Governor Simms. Upon arrival he discovered to his delight that a dance was in progress on the plaza. He had wrapped the state flag, carefully tying it with scarlet and gold ribbons. He presented it to the Pueblo Governor, who graciously received it and carried it to the kiva. After a few minutes a procession emerged, at the head of which was one of the Zia officials with the state flag tied to a stick in lieu of a flagpole. The procession moved solemnly to the center of the plaza where the flag was secured upright and remained throughout the day. When the Buffalo Dancers came on, the scarlet and gold streamers that had wrapped the presentation flag were seen to be flying from the horns of one of the buffalo! No greater honor has ever been bestowed on New Mexico's official colors.

The Zia Indians are proud of the state's use of their sacred symbol—on the flag as well as to decorate official state letterheads and publications. Even automobile license plates. But they are showing displeasure in the sad fact that commercial concerns too numerous to mention have adopted it for their own insignias.

Age-old Zia, in the flood of New Mexico's golden light, sits today on its basalt mound as tranquil as it has for centuries past, content with Indian ways, with Indian things—and with the Divine promise only Indian faith can bring about. The cold products of Pittsburgh, Oshkosh, and Grand Rapids have invaded their homes, the various channels of television flash their signals on the screens, and Venetian blinds work to perfection on a few windows. It is rumored that there is even an electric can opener in the village. But in spite of gadgets, "household thoughts" carry the ancient substance—for the wise "old people of Zia" were wiser than the inventive moguls of white America today. They spoke words of caution, blazed spiritual trails, and manufactured Wisdom for the good of their people, never to become obsolete, never to fall out of style. While the gadgets perform their mechanical duties, those who employ them give exercise to the mind with thoughts of the *real* things, the *good* things, the *genuine* and *truly benevolent*. The life-giving Sun, the life-giving earth; the life-giving rain, the life-giving corn . . . of fertility, the Indian's wealth-abounding . . . of the field, and of the loin.

11

THE CHRISTMAS PUEBLO

THE CHANCE is favorable that silver-blue-black will be the colors to bedeck New Mexico's Indian Country this coming midnight of Christmas Eve; blue-black of the star-speckled firmament, clearest of clear, over a landscape silvered by a moon fast riding toward its full. San Felipe—"The Christmas Pueblo"—serene by the night-sparkling Rio Grande, will wear the colors for the occasion of performing with humble devotion one of the finest pageants on the Indian's ceremonial calendar.

The lovely dance-tribute to the Christ Child follows Midnight Mass on Christmas Eve at San Felipe Pueblo.

The stage setting is within the walls and before the altar of the massive old mission church, itself one of the purest examples of early Franciscan architecture.

The atmosphere in San Felipe at midnight of Christmas Eve is certainly not of the modern world, but of some place far away and long ago. A sense of peace can be felt in the starlit silence; a victory in the escape, be it ever so brief, from the materialistic sound and fury generated by the white man in his own peculiar fashion—the mad race for status, for culture, such as it is, from the Christmas of Santa Claus to this, here in San Felipe, the *real*, the *true*, the unalloyed reason for commemoration of the Nativity.

Midnight—the house doors open and close; in pairs and in groups the shawled and blanketed figures move down the lanes from the far limits of the village, they cross the plaza to the waiting church. All is still; voices that must be heard are given in hushed tones. For this is the gentle night—*La Noche Buena*, the night of the *Santo Niño*, the Man Child among men known to the Pueblo people ages before the coming of the first Franciscans.

The Christmas Pueblo

The church doors are opened wide, the interior a blaze of candlelight. The floor is earthen, hardpacked after two centuries of devout attendance; there are no pews, for this is an Indian shrine. Anglo and Spanish-American visitors who are seasoned to Indian ways bring folded blankets to kneel or sit upon, though much of the ceremony demands standing. The throng pours in from the dark, to find a place and await the Mass. One by one the congregation makes its way to the Manger, to view the Christ Child, and to note that the crib is filled with gifts of an appropriately humble nature. There is a bite in the air, made of so much interior space under so high a ceiling, mixed with the smell of burning candlewax and the forest tang of the Christmas trees.

The Mass, of course, is sung in the conventional manner, as the midnight Nativity is celebrated in churches to the earth's far reaches; but here in San Felipe the priest's assistants are of the Keres Indian world, and the Keresan world is unique, the champion of the "Indian Way."

Now the priest and his assistants move from the altar and disappear into the sacristy. The ritual of the white man is complete—the Nativity is now actual, the Christ Child is born. The congregation—Indian, Spanish American, Anglo—clears the center floor and packs itself against the walls. A broad aisle reaches from the entrance door to the altar rail. It is an arena kindly to the foot, of good Indian earth made firm by the tread of centuries. More pilgrims from the outer world enter the church, mostly Anglo, now that the Mass is finished. They, too, mingle with the throng standing at the walls.

Now the "Christmas Way of the Indian" begins: out in the dark night can be heard the faraway sound of beating drums. And within the church another sound is evident; high in the choir loft a chorus of Indian-made bird warblers operated by as many little boys as the loft can support, each enthusiastic with the spirit of the occasion, sends trills and ripples to the high vigas, as though a thousand birds had arrived to take part in the ceremonies. It is an expression of the delightful legend that tells how all the birds of the earth burst into song at the birth of Christ; an expression doubly sincere with these people who are so closely harnessed to Nature in thought and action.

The drumthrob is now at the entrance, a stern bass that seems to command the treble birdsong to cease. Now the drummer is inside, moving to the open space between the two long rows of spectators; his chanting chorus is behind him—makers of sound, full of power, but still not strong enough to cause the small boys with the bird-warblers to desist. The altar is a blaze of candlelight, a receptive glow that welcomes this contribution of the Holy Night—that receives the substance and carries it to the Destination for which it is intended. A male dancer moves in through the open door; he is bedecked in the costume that befits the ceremony—deerskin and shell, turquoise and coral, feather-down as light as the breath of life, his own brown skin. His movements are graceful, each step exact to the rhythm of the chorus, touching the precious earth with the respect it deserves; arms rising and descending in action to the tempo of the chant, without flaw as befits the occasion.

Behind him comes a line of women, each in her *manta* of ceremonial black, but glistening with all the silver and turquoise her body can support—of paint correctly applied, of the symbolic squash blossom; and, each holding in her hand, a sprig of *hakak*—spruce, the sacred tree that grew to help create mankind, the evergreen, the emblem of eternal life.

The dance is performed to its dramatic end. The male leads the way, the female line follows; their destination is the wide door that gives exit to the starry night. The drum continues to throb, the chorus drones as its members shuffle to the outside, leaving within the church the happy, grateful trill of the bird-warblers.

But San Felipe has more to offer. A second drum is heard at the door, and this time the impersonators of the deer enter to act their part of the pageant. The drumbeats become rapid, the chorus carries a lively sound. The dancers—each correctly garbed for the ritual, with antlered heads and faces masked, with bodies fitted in buckskin complete with tail—dart here and there, performing their antics. There is a clown-deer among them whose purpose is to make people laugh. And each is an actual quadruped, for a cane is held in every hand to represent the forefeet of the animal, given by the same Spirit that fathered the Christ Child—sustenance, food for the body, strength and nourishment—to the Indian of today, tomorrow, even those of old times who lived by the deer—by its venison, buckskin and sinew—folk of the Great Age when all America belonged to the Indian alone.

Then the deer prance out to the open dark and the first group of dancers returns to the candlelight. Each in turn they give their prayer, the male and female of mankind and the essential provision of the animal kingdom. One is too absorbed to count the acts, but probably four are given by each group. For the number "four" has a symbolic purpose in all Indian ritual, just as "seven" had within the walls of Solomon's Temple. Then, at about the time when the hands on the white man's clock turn to 4 A.M., when almost three hours yet remain before Christmas dawn, the drums, chorus, and dancers move off to the ceremonial houses and the birdsong is stilled. Christmas Eve at San Felipe has come to an end.

The outside air is crisp, clean, the sky darker but the starlight brighter than at any previous hour of the night. The drumbeats continue to throb in Anglo ears as those destined for a different kind of Christmas walk to their cars. To the light of Albuquerque and Santa Fe, blazing their multicolors for the joyousness of the occasion. And each carrying a Christmas gift from little San Felipe— appropriate for times such as they are—a token of peace for heart, mind, and soul.

12

DON FERNANDO PLAZA

TAOS IN THE YEARS OF ITS PURITY, which was not so long ago, was a little town of adobe walls and piñon smoke spiraling from mud-plastered chimneys—of the Spanish tongue and the easy pace. It thrived in its own way in fresh mountain air under blue skies—a community of humble paisanos and immensely proud damas y caballeros, painters and writers and poets, sculptors and patrons of the arts, dilettantes, bohemians, and hangers-on, all feeding on the creative atmosphere—and leading them were great names among the artists of the world, like Blumenschein, Sharp, and Phillips. All were gifted to labor by the then unspoiled Spanish-Indian lifestyle convenient to their doorsteps.

Among them was D.H. Lawrence, who lived in Taos no more than a couple of years but left behind a cult of doters not equaled anywhere on earth except, perhaps, in Hollywood or Mecca. In all the American nation there was, and to a great extent still is, not another environment like Taos.

The color of the town, the simplicity of the paisanos. The deep humility of the Indians. Architecture as nowhere else except in North Africa or, perhaps, the Holy Land. The biting cold of winter, the cool, high-altitude air of summer. Away, far away from commercial, stereotyped America, from the mediocre and the trash of popular taste.

The painters, the sculptors, the woodcarvers, the novelists, the poets, the composers, the host of lovers of things kind and lovely, all in their castles of sun-dried mud, saw the simple daily lives lived by neighbors, and were fired with creativity. Taos at the time of the creatives was a side-prop in the drama of what had been one of the wildest, wide-open, hell-for-leather, wicked, and most brutal settlements west of the Washita. It was a town with a past—and what a past!

Taos is not one town but three—and all three are the loveliest in the West. There is Don Fernando de Taos, the town proper, population three thousand, and the seat of Taos County. It has been here since the Spanish colonization of New Mexico in the seventeenth century. The altitude is a healthy 7,000 feet. Here's the Plaza, supermarkets, filling stations, and other conspicuous bits of commerce. But until recently there was only one traffic light in town. And not so long ago the streets were unpaved and the houses single story, with thick walls made of the earth itself—of hand-hewn timbers axed and adzed of pine and juniper, felled in the provident mountains.

The wood venders, then, plied the streets with their strings of pack burros, crying,

"*Leña, leña!*" into the clean mountain air.

And the housewives opened their doors to greet them, to buy a burro-load for perhaps *dos reales*—that is to say, for twenty-five cents. And the perfume made of the purchase drifted through the town, clean smoke from a hundred chimneys—piñon always for the fireplaces, juniper for the cookstoves and ranges. Each gave off its sweet incense, matched nowhere in the nation. There were sounds of mission bells and hoofbeats, burro brays and rooster songs. The speech everywhere was Spanish, and the scant English was gentle and *simpatico*. All that aglow in a blaze of color . . . not too long ago.

Then there is the *second* Taos—the oldest in centuries and the best-known throughout the world. This is San Geronimo de Taos, the Indian village two miles to the northeast. Here are the ruins of the old mission erected in 1704; and here the two huge four- and five-story communal houses of the people, homes built in tiers and terraces of solid adobe, stand to face each other across Pueblo Creek.

The Taos Indians, a Pueblo division, are so conservative of the Native American way, so adamant, and so repulsed by the white man's rape of the environment, so possessive of the beauty of their own, that they ask nothing of available electrical conveniences, or running water, or the presence of propane tanks or gas meters. Sufficient to their eyes is sunlight through mica-glazed windows, kerosene lamplight, and water dipped from the cool clean mountain stream that flows swiftly by their homes.

The *third* of the Taos villages is Los Ranchos, three miles south on the road to Santa Fe. This, in turn, is surrounded by villages of the same rustic loveliness, all with lilting Spanish names—Talpa, Córdova, Prado, Cordillera. And as in Don Fernando itself, the Old World feeling is alive in all. Many nationally renowned artists and writers have made their homes in Ranchos. The church here—a massive but delicate sculpture in adobe—is among the most photographed and painted in America.

And the horizons of Taos!

The skylines surrounding the three Taos communities are built of mountains. East are the highest peaks in the state, Wheeler and Truchas, both over 13,000 feet. To the north the snowy ranges of Colorado glisten in the winter sun as west Canjilon and San Antonio peaks rise majestic over the hogback of the Brazos—beyond the wild gorge of Rio Grande. And south the valley of the river descends to bless the desert Southwest, downward past Albuquerque and El Paso, to nourish "The Valley" dividing Texas and Mexico, and at last mingle with the green waters of the Gulf.

And what of the people, the salt of this magnificent earth?. . . Not the artists with the understanding hearts. Not the writers who give solitary labor to exalting the beauty of their chosen home. But, rather, the humble villagers whose forebears left them this legacy of clear light, a language that is their own, and abounding peace away from highways and crowds.

If ghosts walk these haunts as a goodly number of people suppose, the streets of Taos are jammed with restless friars and armored conquistadors, with mountain men in fur and buckskin, with gamblers and harlots, frontier judges, cowboys and sheep-barons—with poor wretches doomed from the beginning of their murderous or horse-stealing lives, whose spirits yet retain the feel of the hang rope. . . . And "Taos Lightning," the most dreadful of all decoctions that have desecrated the honest name of Whiskey—the imaginative odor of it lurking about where *cantinas* and *fandango* halls and *monte* banks and cribs of the *putas* used to be.

And sounds—the laughs and shouts of the revelers, hoofbeats on the earthen lanes, pistol and rifle fire, the crash of the gallows-trap, a scream in the night, fiesta music and the creaking of oxcarts, the rattle of a stagecoach at the portal of La Fonda. Sounds wrapped in the death of history but alive in the ears of folk who can dream.

"It was the greatest experience of the outside world I ever had, it certainly changed me forever," wrote D.H. Lawrence of his brief two-year stay in the early 1920s. He found a ranch near Arroyo Hondo, which he left in favor of a home in France, there to die after declaring New Mexico a refuge from the hostile world. He returned only as ashes in a suitcase, for burial in the earth that transformed his life. Today the Lawrence Ranch is a shrine maintained by the University of New Mexico, where thousands of readers of *Lady Chatterley's Lover* pay homage at the site.

Don Fernando Plaza, the heart of it all, has been remodeled to suit modern taste, as has happened to the major plazas in the old Spanish towns— Santa Fe, for example, La Mesilla, Albuquerque, Socorro. Taos plaza is now paved with brick and flagstone. . . Yet the flavor still hangs on. The old hotel, La Fonda, occupies most of the south side, once long ago the Bent and St. Vrain store established in 1832. The former Taos County jail and courthouse takes up the north side. Once in tune with the famous art colony, it exhibited paintings of the greatest—Lockwood, Bisttram, Phillips and Higgins. The new courthouse located at the south end of town seems like a block of masonry without doors or windows. But all around the plaza square are tasteful crafts shops and art galleries.

The bandstand with the copper roof is too big for the environment, more in harmony with a prop for a Billy Graham crusade than with established Spanish dignity. . . . But the flagpole on Taos plaza is something special. . . . for the American flag may be flown day and night, without being raised or lowered, an honor decreed by authority of Congress. And for a reason.

When the Civil War broke out in 1861, sympathy for the Confederate cause was strong in Taos. One day a group from this faction tore the flag from the pole in the plaza and left it trampled in the mud. Union backers cleaned it, and again it was raised to dignity, only to have it desecrated for a second time. Capt. Smith Simpson, a prominent resident, retrieved the flag and held it until a new pole could replace the old, one cut and trimmed by his own hand and axe. He nailed the flag to the pole and raised it on the plaza. Two stalwart defenders were recruited, men of Taos and famed in frontier history—the trader Ceran St. Vrain, and the scout and trapper Kit Carson. The three took turns at guarding the flag, and armed to the teeth, vowed to shoot the first person who attempted to remove the standard. Not a soul challenged them.

The Confederate forces were defeated at Glorieta Pass in March 1862, after holding Santa Fe for a brief period, ending the war in New Mexico. The American flag flew over Don Fernando Plaza without benefit of a rope that could lower or raise it. Firmly nailed to the timber, its colors had never been folded since the three defenders planted it. The military command recognized the loyal action taken by Simpson, St. Vrain, and Carson, and the nailed flag was sanctioned by Washington to fly twenty-four hours a day.

Like Santa Fe Plaza and Albuquerque Old Town, Don Fernando de Taos is a tourist attraction to stagger the imagination. Taking the flagpole as the axle in the hub, the spokes point out to all directions, enclosing in a three-mile rim more than sixty art galleries, a half-dozen museums, and some of the state's finest restaurants. Points of historic interest may be found along Ojitos Lane, Santa Fe Road, Kit Carson Street, Dragoon Lane, Bent Street, and Martyrs Lane. Of special visitor interest are the graves of Kit Carson and the spectacular Padre Martínez. The latter without doubt was the most fascinating character in Willa Cather's novel, *Death Comes For The Archbishop.*

There is the Stables Gallery, housed in the old Arthur Manby house where that eccentric Englishman was found murdered in March 1929, his head severed from his body, a mystery that seemingly never will be solved—and God forbid! For as long as it remains it will forever fuel the lucrative tourist industry. There is the Governor Bent home, where New Mexico's chief executive was scalped by Indians in 1847 while his family escaped by digging an exit through the three-foot thick adobe wall.

At the outer rim, three miles from the hub, there is the classic mission church of San Francisco de Assisi de Ranchos de Taos.... Then, of course, two miles toward the mountains, there is Taos Pueblo.

Any day of any season is right to visit the Indian town. In the dry brightness of spring, the cottonwood gold of autumn, the high-altitude cool of summer, or the bitter whiteness of winter. Here the two communal houses, the north and the south, stand, brown and sculptured against the mountain backdrop, overlooking the clear stream that supplies the households as well as the moisture-craving fields.

Taos Indians are taller than other Pueblo Indians as a result of their relationship with the Plains tribes who ranged east across the mountains, with the Comanches and Kiowas especially. And the dignity of it all shows on their strong, proud, terribly stoic faces. They can be seen at the stream, on the plaza, or on the terraces, the men draped with blankets about their shoulders, their hair long and braided. In winter the blanketing is heavier. The women are bright with shawls of sundry colors and white moccasins with high and flapping tops—as photogenic as the beehive-shaped ovens, or the ladders to the upper tiers of the houses. . . . But beware, there is a standard monetary price for picture taking, and a hundred eyes are on the lookout for tourists who can't seem to adhere to the rules.

Northern New Mexico is Fiesta Land. These fiestas honor saints whose names were attached long ago by mission clerics to succor towns and villages of the godly. In Albuquerque it is San Felipe de Neri, at Santo Domingo the gala goes to Saint Dominic, in Bernalillo it's San Lorenzo. The widely publicized and heavily attended Santa Fe Fiesta not only commemorates the Franciscan saint but also a victory of the conquistadors in 1692. Likewise Taos Pueblo has its patron saint, San Geronimo, or Saint Jerome. His fiesta is held every September 29 and 30. It is not only noisy in exalting his beatitude, but it keeps an ancient custom alive—trading with other Indians.

In line with all fiestas throughout the Spanish-Indian world there is much feasting, drinking, dancing, and meeting friends from near and far. But the over-indulgers are mostly from other communities, for San Geronimo's day in Taos is one of devout commemoration. More important, the native Indian religion is observed. As with all pueblos when honoring saints the event is not strictly Catholic.

Throughout the 1700s and early 1800s, it was custom for the nomad Plains tribes, particularly the Comanches, to cross the mountains from the east and converge on Taos Pueblo for a trading "party" which lasted several days. In spite of the trouble that never failed to mar the event, the Comanches were welcomed by both the Indians of the Pueblo and the Spaniards of Don Fernando Plaza—even by the settlers of the outer vicinity who would suffer most. The nomads pitched their tipis outside the pueblo wall, and some thousand head of cattle and ponies were grazed nearby.

The trade goods were Comanche trophies of the hunt—buffalo meat and robes, stolen cattle and horses, and human captives offered as slaves. The Pueblo people exchanged produce of the fields, especially cornmeal, tobacco, and Spanish ponies. Don Fernando townsmen brought to the market commodities dear to Comanche hearts—like guns and cloth, hatchets and axes, knives, and, no doubt, kegs of the villainous whiskey called "Taos Lightning."

The festival often turned into a mighty drunk, with casualties on both sides, and with the Comanches getting the worst end of the barter. To make up for their loss, on their way home they raided and plundered Spanish farms and ranches in several Taos valleys, thereby garnering bounty without the courtesy of exchange. Today, the San Geronimo fiesta is a reminder of such lively times, and perhaps Kiowas and Comanches still attend—in from Oklahoma—but the trade goods no longer consist of buffalo meat and robes, or slaves or guns or ammunition, but rather a supply of necessary United States currency. For sale are stacks of red and green chile, sacked pinto beans, corn both shelled and on the ear, livestock fodder, and maybe a few head of cattle. Even a horse. But more likely a Ford or Chevrolet pickup truck that someone yearns to get rid of. Booths set up in the plaza offer Indian handwork, buckskin, and beaded moccasins, fruits and vegetables, hot dogs and hamburgers. And a brisk business in tamales and soft drinks.

The chief attraction on September 29 is the Sundown Dance, performed in the plaza when daylight dims into twilight. Chosen men of the village, wrapped in bright blankets, shuffle in line carrying branches of yellow aspen and chanting the song of the occasion. They perform the same at sunrise the next morning, this time a prayer to the reappearance of the deity. There's a footrace then, the young men of the north and south communal houses competing with each other. Dances are featured through the day around the event of events—the pole climbing—when clowns with cornhusks in their hair, carrying bows and arrows made of straw, show their acrobatic skill by climbing a high slippery pole planted in the center of the plaza. Tied atop the pole is a prize to test any athlete's strength—bundles of *horno*-baked bread, pastries, assorted native foods, and home-butchered sheep.

In all, the fiesta of San Geronimo is one of the most colorful in the Pueblo round of celebrations, a worthwhile adventure into a living tradition in the clear light of an aspen fall.

Taos history has also been rank with the harshness of the frontier. There have been hard living mountain men, fur traders, and trappers, as well as outlaws and murders committed for retribution or thrill.

Once, when Taos was wilder and woolier, Judge Lynch kept hard at work with his vigilantes, hanging hard cases on cottonwood trees, in the jail, and courtroom.

Don Fernando Plaza

Today the frontier spirit lingers in the air. In 1976 the law enforcement element was so corrupt, there were reports that prisoners on felony charges ranging from burglary to murder were permitted to leave and return to the jail as they pleased. No wonder television's fictional Sam McCloud, a trigger-pulling go-getter for order and decency, served New York City after leaving the rigors of Taos, often and pridefully expressing his point of origin.

Taos' nineteenth-century violence matched Dodge City's, Tombstone's, and Socorro's. The ruthless but thorough methods of enforcing law and order by sheriffs, U.S. marshals, and judges of the early day West provided juicy meat for chroniclers of that period. Famed "characters" of the bench in the drama of Wild West history were Judge Roy Bean of Texas and Isaac Parker, the Hanging Judge of Fort Smith, Arkansas. But New Mexico had its Judge Kirby Benedict, administrator of justice in the northern counties, including Rio Arriba and Taos. He served from 1858 to 1871, winning fame throughout the Territory for conducting his office with a certain flavor of black-robed justice and pounding gavel. Second to law, his interests were historical research and literary pursuits—the latter perhaps injecting into him a feeling for drama in the courtroom.

Born in Connecticut in 1811, he came to Santa Fe in 1853, having been appointed to the Supreme Court of New Mexico by Franklin Pierce. For a time he served with distinction on the Illinois bar, winning a warm friendship with Abraham Lincoln and Stephen A. Douglas. For that reason, in New Mexico, he was one of the "Lincoln County Men"—those who in 1869 drafted the bill creating the famed, and at times violent, domain named for the martyred president, the largest county in the United States.

He was one of the most brilliant of frontier judges, and erratic to his downfall. Every session of court was tempered with emotion and flamboyant oratory that kept all concerned glued to their seats. When it came to sentencing hard cases, either to the hang tree or to the chain gang or to durance vile. . . Well!

He was suspended from practice in 1871 through difficulties with the Supreme Court. He had reached sixty years, and although robust while active, the suspension wounded his pride and he began failing in health. He petitioned to be restored to practice on January 16, 1874, but died the following February 27—the petition not yet acted upon. He was buried in Santa Fe on March 2 with honors. The funeral service was read by W.W. Griffin of Montezuma Lodge;

and, as the *New Mexican* reported, with "the band of the Eighth Cavalry in new and flashy uniforms, leading the procession, playing funeral dirges to the grave."

It was either in 1861 or 1867, when holding court in Taos, that Judge Benedict delivered the classic death sentence on José María Martín, a murderer of the most dastardly sort, at a time when killers were as plentiful as rattlesnakes in the sagebrush. His crime was horrible and unprovoked, his status and reputation that of a weasel among men, uncomely to look upon and heartily disliked. José María Martín was someone society could do without. The jury had given its verdict, and now it was time for Judge Kirby Benedict to deliver the sentence:

Judge Benedict [to the condemned]: "José María Martín, stand up!

"José María Martín, you have been indicted, tried, and convicted by a jury of your countrymen of the crime of murder, and the court is now about to pass upon you the dread sentence of the law. As a usual thing, José María Martín, it is a painful duty of the judge of a court of justice to pronounce upon a human being the sentence of death. There is something horrible about it, and the mind of the court naturally revolts from the performance of such a duty. Happily, however, your case is relieved of all such unpleasant features, and the court takes positive delight in sentencing you to death!

"You are a young man, José María Martín; apparently of good physical condition and robust health. Ordinarily you might have looked forward to many years of life, and the court has no doubt you have, and have expected to die at a ripe old age; but you are about to be cut off in consequence of your own act.

"José María Martín, it is now the springtime; in a little while the grass will be springing up green in these beautiful valleys; and, on these broad mesas and mountainsides, flowers will be blooming, birds will be singing their sweet carols and nature will be putting on her most gorgeous and attractive robes, and life will be pleasant, and men will want to stay.

"But none of this for you, José María Martín!

"The flowers will not bloom for you, José María Martín!

"The birds will not carol for you, José María Martín!

"When these things come to gladden the senses of men, you will be occupying a space about six by two beneath the sod, and the green grass and those beautiful flowers will be growing above your lowly head.

"The sentence of the court is that you be taken from this place to the county jail; and that you be there kept safely and securely confined in the custody of the sheriff until the day appointed for your execution.

[To sheriff]: "Be very careful, Mr. Sheriff, that he have no opportunity to escape and that you have him at the appointed place at the proper time.

[To the condemned]: "That you be so kept, José María Martín, until—

[To court clerk]: "Mr. Clerk, on what day of the month does Friday, about two weeks from this time, come?"

Clerk: "March 22nd, your honor."

Judge Benedict [to the condemned]: "Very well, until Friday, the twenty-second of March, when you will be taken by the sheriff from your place of confinement to some safe and convenient spot within the county—

[To sheriff]: "That is in your discretion, Mr. Sheriff, you are only confined to the limits of the county.

[To the condemned]: "And that you be hanged by the neck until you are dead; and the court was about to add, José María Martín, 'may God have mercy on your soul,' but the court will not assume the responsibility of asking an All-wise Providence to do that which a jury of your peers has refused to do. The Lord *could not* have mercy on your soul. However, if you affect any religious belief or are connected with any religious organization, it might be well for you to send for your priest or your minister, and get from him— well—get such consolation as you can. But the court advises you to place no reliance upon anything of that kind!

[To sheriff]: "Mr. Sheriff, remove the prisoner."

A few days before the appointed time for his execution José María Martín escaped from the Taos jail, and as far as the courts of justice were concerned was not heard of nor seen again.

13

THE EARTH—THE FAITH—
THE BLESSING

THE BROAD HIGHWAY north out of Santa Fe is hard, smooth, paved, and runs straight through the rugged terrain. But a turnoff to the right, at mile twenty-four on the official map, leads the traveler into one of the softest, most mellowed landscapes in the Southwest—the Valley of Chimayó, home of generations of weavers and the site of a shrine revered by thousands upon thousands for a century and a half, trusted for its help in the battle against physical ills.

The Rio Santa Cruz falls from its source in the high Sangre de Cristos, down from the Truchas Peaks, and forms the Valley of Chimayó, a narrow swath of fertility, lush and provident, blazing with manmade and natural color. It is an oasis bordered by rock-metal hills, where grass is sparse and juniper, scrub. There, by the fast moving stream, the irrigated fields provide for all the traditional wants of a proud, contented people. The apples and peaches are succulent, sweet. The chile grown at Chimayó, it is said, ranks as the world's most torrid. The houses are thick-walled, squat, adobe. The people are of Andalusian descent, their language Spanish.

But like many American place names, Chimayó is of Indian origin, for long ago, before the time of the conquistadors, an Indian Pueblo thrived on the site of Chimayó and it was called *Tsimajo*, Tiwa for "a flaking stone of superior quality." The men of the village were said to be fine weavers, using such prehistoric yarns as sheared rabbit fur and clipped turkey feathers fluffed into wool. . . .

This district of squat sunbright adobe villages is in the heart of New Mexico's Pueblo Indian country where the mixing of conquered and conqueror's blood has for 350 years bred an insatiable love for color into the people of the Chimayó Valley, who have woven honest beauty on simple looms into the fibers of the blankets for which these communities are world-renowned.

Contrary to popular belief, Chimayó is not one village but many. Ten or more Spanish-American villages situated on or adjacent to the Rio Santa Cruz make up the Chimayó Valley. Each village has a name with a piquant flavor to match the color-spiced landscape. There is *La Puebla* (the town), *Potrero* (fenced-in pasture), and *Cuarteles* (quarters), so named because a company of Mexican soldiers were once quartered there. There is also *Plaza Abajo* (lower plaza) and *Los Ranchos* (the ranches), each a contrast of sunswept earth and the cool verdure of cottonwood shade and irrigated alfalfa. *La Cuchilla* (the knife) is properly named for its location on a hill with a knifelike edge. *Rincón* (corner) and *Los Ojuelos* (the little springs) are gems sculptured in adobe and carved in cedar, as are *El Llano* (the plain) and *Rio Chiquito* (the little river). But the uppermost settlement toward the mountains, *Plaza del Cerro* (village on the hill), is known popularly—and officially, since it contains the district post office—as Chimayó.

The finest of textiles the world over are created by people in remote places who give devotion to the simplest of looms and much use of the hand. Kinsmen in spirit to the Chimayó craftsmen are the Scottish weavers of Hebridean tweeds and the Aran Islanders off Ireland's west coast. Brothers in art are the Turcoman makers of Bokhara rugs, and they who offer the priceless Persian *Kashan*. The love of the loom is strong in Spanish blood, for it was the Moors who first introduced into Western Europe the true art of textile weaving. But closest of all to the Chimayó blanket are those woven by the weavers on the vast Navajo Indian Reservation in New Mexico and Arizona and the Saltillo *serapes* woven in Saltillo, Coahuila, Mexico. In fact, it is said that the Chimayó blanket is a cross between the two.

Chimayó village today is sheltered among pleasant hills. Water flows abundantly in the ditches, its influence strong in the cool, tidy alfalfa fields, among the neat rows of flourishing corn and indispensable chile peppers, in the orchards of apple, pear, peach, and plum.

This is a place happily free of the straight line and demanding clock. The houses of adobe, naturally, are neat, squat, flat-roofed for the most part, tastefully dressed with patios and portals. There is quiet here, and a delicious atmosphere, appropriate for these high, crisp altitudes. The fragrance of burning piñon and smoke from the chimneys mingles with the acid cottonwood tang. Flowers are everywhere, a luxury in color and scent that the humblest paisano can afford. There are hedgerows of lilac, patios brilliant with the yellow Rose of Castile.

86

When the Spanish colonists introduced sheep in 1598, the settlers in the vicinity of Tsimajo were inspired by the Indian weavers they found at the Pueblo. Looms were constructed, shears applied to the sheep. The district abounded in vegetation for making the natural dyes. The colonists were in need of blankets, and to think of textiles was to consider Chimayó.

But a brisk demand tends to incite the inferior product, then in rustic New Mexico just as today. Competing weavers set up looms in Santa Fe; and, drowned by production, Chimayó was forced to take second spot. Slipshod creations by the hundred were sold in the Santa Fe market. The capital weavers were not only avaricious—they just didn't know how to weave. In 1805 the few gifted craftsmen of Santa Fe appealed to the Governor for aid. Don Fernando Chacón decided that the best method for improvement would be to instruct the inexperienced and instill in them a sense of pride. This would require a stern tutor. He, in turn, appealed to the viceroy in Mexico City. Consequently there arrived, in 1807, the Master Weaver Don Ignacio Ricardo Bazán, and his brother Don Juan, on a six-year contract. Santa Fe gave them a hearty welcome. With such a captain as Don Ignacio at the helm Santa Fe would become the most important weaving center north of Saltillo.

But destiny is a tricky mistress: the Bazán brothers disliked Santa Fe, its people and their ambitions, and after a short stay moved to Chimayó. The best of the Santa Fe weavers accompanied them, and Chimayó was back in her old stride. Don Ignacio insisted on Spanish techniques, but compromised with native soaps and dyes. The older blankets were made on narrow looms, in two identical parts each about two feet wide and eight long. Then the "twins" were sewn together. In later years, wide looms came into use and the blankets were woven in a solid design.

Wool, of course, was locally grown, cleaned, carded, and spun by primitive hand methods. Natural fleece colors were white, black and gray. Dyes were as honest as the weavers—the bark of the tag alder, mountain mahogany, and red ocher providing the popular crimson. Cochineal, indigo pellets, and brazil sticks were imported from Mexico. Blankets of indigo blue in harmony with natural white and black wools have become collectors' items, lovely to behold. Brazil offered a soft light coffee color. Mixed indigo and brazil resulted in a rich mahogany. Yellow came from the local *chamisa*, or rabbit brush. Green, orange, violet, and rose were made of combinations of the natural and imported dyes.

In the 1880s commercial dyes came into some popular use. But the century was to turn before the weavers' interests were directed toward machine-spun yarns. Traders, then, took heed of the tourist industry and dealing with Chimayó became a lucrative enterprise. The situation could have been akin to that of a hundred years before, when Don Ignacio Bázan came to the rescue. But in the head, heart, and hand of every weaver from father to son was pride of craftsmanship two centuries old.

Chimayó, situated as it is between the renowned art centers of Santa Fe and Taos, is blessed with the sympathy of people who understand true crafts-manship. The late Mary Austin was a special friend. As are those responsible for reviving fine old methods and patterns in recent years.

The true test of an old Chimayó blanket is by touch alone. Close your eyes, press its mellowed texture against your cheek. You feel the softness, the honesty of weave, the human art that put the beauty there.

Chimayó lies within a fifteen-mile radius of San Gabriel de Yuque Yunque, now in ruins beside the Rio Grande, the old capital of New Mexico established by the conquistador Juan De Oñate in 1598. Chimayó, therefore, is among the earliest colonial agricultural communities in the Southwest. It was a bastion of New Spain on the far northern frontier.

The descendants of these settlers are unique in this material age: they are rustic, of a sweet, kindly nature, and above all religiously devout. And they claim that the Christ Child—*El Santo Niño Perdido*—The Lost Holy Child—walks the fields by night and gives His spirit to heal and comfort the sick and bereaved. You don't believe it? Then go to El Santuario some midnight, and, perhaps, you will find the Child gone. Or by daylight examine His baby shoes, and you will find them soiled and worn by much travel.

The village of El Potrero is one of several Chimayó communities; it is the last to be met before the road leaves the valley and ascends toward Cordova,

Truchas, and Las Trampas, those alpine settlements closer to the loftiest of all New Mexico's peaks. And there in El Potrero is the low, flat-roofed adobe church, which you'll recognize by the two tapering belfry towers in front.

88

An ancient gateway leads to a courtyard through a thick adobe wall, one shaded by an immense cottonwood tree; and here about are wooden crosses, none too vertical, and inscribed stones that are old and hoary, graves of the privileged dead.

Richly carved double doors lead to the interior narthex. Another of similar craftsmanship gives way to the nave, which is long and characteristic of Spanish-New Mexican Pueblo mission architecture. The roof is supported by closely spaced vigas (heavy pine log rafter beams) and walls crudely plastered with mud under a century and a half of frequent gypsum whitewashings. The nave is alive with every imaginable sort of religious painting, image and homespun decoration, mostly the work of native New Mexican artisans.

Dimly lit, musty with age, there is a feeling of sanctuary here, of an especially blessed quiet and peace. Ahead stands the candlelit altar behind a rail of home-hewn workmanship; the floor is carpeted with rugs of the famous Chimayó weave. The reredos are naively painted with a definite Indian motif, somewhat like the design on a Navajo blanket. And at the center of it all hangs a crucifix—over six feet in height, painted a dark green and (contrary to simple New Mexican practice) decorated in gold leaf. This cross, built by a local craftsman a century and a half ago, is the very reason for El Santuario de Chimayó, the preciously guarded symbol of a cult that has its roots, not in New Mexico alone, but in ancient Central America. It is sacred to people who have faith in the healing power of earth and the benevolence of the color black. This, El Santuario, is the shrine of Our Lord of Esquípulas—*El Cristo Negro*—"The Black Christ."

Any day of the week, but especially on weekends and holidays, folk seeking renewed health arrive at El Santuario. They arrive in all kinds of automobiles, most of the models showing age and wear, many of them pickup trucks, the farmer's favorite. And always there are tourists on the premises, for the fame of Chimayó has carried far.

The pilgrims stand about in the courtyard before moving inside to show their faithfulness at the altar rail before the large cross of Esquípulas. That done, they rise and go beyond the rail, turn to the left and enter the sacristy through a

very low door. This room is also a chapel of the *Santo Niño de Atocha*, whose
image stands in a shrine of its own. Behind the image, at the ends and the wall
opposite, hang crutches, braces, and every variety of medical and surgical pros-
thetic. And to each of them is attached a token of gratitude by the "healed,"
religious medals, rosary beads, cards bearing names, even driver's licenses; but
most conspicuous are pairs of baby or doll shoes, soiled and worn. Lift the hem
of the Santo Niño, and you'll find Him to be wearing doll shoes—also soiled and
worn. (Unless, of course, you catch Him at a time when He has just been given a
brand-new pair, which is said to happen every six months.) Legend has it that His
nightly visits of mercy in the Valley of Chimayó are rough on the footwear.

    Following a prayer, plus an offering, the pilgrim goes farther toward the
main purpose of his journey—to pass through another small door at the north
wall, which leads to the Chapel of the Blessed Earth, *El Posito*. This is the hole in
the floor containing the sandy, yellow, miracle-substance. Above El Posito is a
small altar, draped and supporting many images. But center of the altar, in a
homemade niche of its own, stands a small and very primitive crucifix, again
depicting the Lord of Esquípulas. The pilgrim kneels beside the Blessed Earth,
to rub his hands in the sandiness; apply some to his afflicted part and offer prayer
while in the process. Then from his pocket he draws a small receptacle—a
tobacco can, an empty Band-Aid box, anything convenient—and he scoops up a
sample to take home for continued application. When the healing is
accomplished (and quite often it is), he returns to El Santuario with his token of
gratitude. From near and far they come—from all over New Mexico, Texas,
Arizona, Colorado, California, and northern Mexico.

    The story of the Lord of Esquípulas is rooted deeply in prehistoric and
early historic times: not in the Old World, not in the Holy Land, not here in New
Mexico, nor in Mexico itself, but in southeastern Guatemala, where the air is
humid and vegetation lush, where greenish waters of the Gulf of Honduras lap
the land of the ancient Mayas.

    It seems that at the time when Cortez successfully overthrew the Aztec
Empire in Mexico, there lived in southeastern Guatemala a tribe of Chorti-
speaking Maya Indians, governed by a chief named Eskipurha. The Mayas were
intelligent, highly civilized, seldom belligerent, and deeply religious. This was
especially true of Eskipurha and his Chortis, for their tribal domain was

traversed by the trunk road used by pilgrims from all regions of the Maya—from Chiapas and Yucatán, from all parts of Guatemala—on their journeys to and from the great religious center called Copán, located farther south in Honduras.

90   Also, to give Eskipurha's people added spiritual significance, there was in their country a spring of mud known to have healing properties—so potent with power bestowed by the black gods of the Maya that thousands of the faithful had been cured of various infirmities on their way to or from Copán.

With the conquest complete, with Aztec Mexico reasonably secure for Spanish dominion, Pedro de Alvarado and a military force were dispatched southward to overthrow the Mayas. His was a small but ruthless army that punished any resistance with cruelties becoming the times. And the Mayas resisted, at the expense of great sacrifice among their warriors.... All but the Chortis of the "sacred earth" who were ruled by the wise and peace-loving Eskipurha.

"Why sacrifice ourselves?" cried the chief to his council. "Why give our blood to people and gods we know nothing of? ... They are stronger than we, as they show by the great slaughter. Let us not resist them; then, perhaps, we will benefit by what they have to offer."

When Alvarado's army swooped on the Chortis it was met with peace offerings rather than weapons, with samples of Maya wealth and fruits of the land. Alvarado, the armored conquistador, was astounded. And hand for hand Eskipurha and the Spaniard became fast friends. So great was Alvarado's admiration for the Chortis that he named them for special award. They would retain Eskipurha for their chief and a new town be established as the Chorti capital. The townsite location would be the choice of Eskipurha and his council, and the Chortis selected the most significant ground in the Maya empire—the Place of the Sacred Earth. The Spaniards called the town Esquípulas to honor the chief whose wisdom made it possible.

The Chortis became willing converts to Christianity. The friars gave orders and a church was built, with Eskipurha—now Equípulas—in charge of the construction. It was a new sanctuary, a shell to protect an ancient and holier shrine. The shrine was El Posito, the "Spring of the Sacred Mud."

Nevertheless, there was discontent with the Spaniard's God. The crucifix that was given them to grace the main altar was Christ with a white skin—the same colorless complexion as the soldiers who had slaughtered the Mayas of

Yucatán, Guatemala, and Honduras, who punished with torture any who resisted them. Besides, the idols revered for centuries by the Mayas were black, and the stone god Turkah on the hilltop overlooking Chichicastenango was the blackest of them all. There was power in the color black. A white Christ was alien to Mayan faith.

Would they settle for a brown-skinned Christ—of their own color—a Man God identical with themselves? . . . If so, the friars would provide.

The Chortis agreed, and the famed Portugese woodcarver, Quirio Cataño, for fifty ounces of silver, was commissioned to carve a crucified Christ out of orangewood and balsam. The sculpture was exquisite—an image in brown, five feet tall, on a dark green cross. It was placed above the high altar—to be revered by the Indian congregation.

But the reverence went so far and no further. Brown was a handsome color, fit for a Christ. The Maya idols were black—and there was power and benevolence in the color black. In groups and in secret, the Chortis went to the hills to worship Turkah and his ebony-hued associates.

Yet candles burned beneath the large crucifix in the small Indian-built sanctuary. And being sixteenth-century candles, they did smoke. The Mayan pilgrims continued to arrive there daily, year after passing year, to lave themselves with the healing substance in the shrine of the sacred earth. And as the years passed the ceiling beams above the altar became blackened, the silver ornaments took on a sooty, burnished look . . . And, most of all, the balsam and orangewood *Cristo*—the brown Christ of the Mayas—took on for itself the color black. A miracle!

A cult was born, and here in Esquípulas was a black God to preside over the healing earth. Now the shrine became the "Mecca" of Middle America, to proclaim to the Maya nation that here was another Copán with the same spiritual significance. Thousands attended the shrine yearly to give homage to the small pool of mud. They were the maimed, the crippled, the incurable.

By 1695 the cult was so thoroughly established that Rome endowed it with its blessing. Consideration required sixty-three years; then in 1758 was built *El Santuario de Esquípulas*, a massive baroque temple to house the miraculous Black Christ. Other shrines and sanctuaries were consecrated at springs of healing earth—not only in Guatemala but in Costa Rica, Mexico, El Salvador, Nicaragua, Honduras, and, lastly, in New Mexico, where faith in the color black and in the therapeutic power of earth is as strong today as it was a century and a half ago when the "Miracle of Chimayó" is said to have happened.

Pueblo Indian legend has it that the Chimayó Valley was once a place where springs of boiling water, together with small craters that discharged fire and smoke, was the domain of a giant with a ferocious temperament and a passion for devouring people. This monster was such a menace that the Hero Brothers, *Ma'syuwi* and *Oy-yoy'-yuwi*, journeyed from their South World Mountain of *Oku'piñ* (Sandia) to stop the horrendous traffic for good. They slew the giant with magic arrows, whereupon the fiery craters and boiling springs ceased to flow, leaving only a single pool of clear warm water. This was known far and wide by its Tiwa name, *Tsimahopokwi,* meaning just that—"pool of warm water."

In time this pool dwindled down to a small pit containing yellowish mud, but one so potent with miraculous curing properties that its fame spread to the far reaches of the Pueblo Indian world. Daily, through prehistory into historic times, thousands of Indian pilgrims sought the "sacred earth" for the treatment of their infirmities.

With the Oñate conquest of 1598 the valleys adjacent to the new Spanish capital of San Gabriel were the first to be settled. Chief of these was that of the Rio Santa Cruz, where fields were cultivated, villages established, houses built, and babies born. There were, and are, several settlements up and down the clear stream, and that which was laid out around the pit of sacred Indian earth was named El Potrero—"fenced pasture."

The Pueblo Indians rose in revolt in 1680 to drive off their Spanish masters and hold New Mexico for their own until 1692. Then came the reconquest by De Vargas, which put Spanish ranchers and farmers back in the far settlements and a new population in Santa Fe. Up from Mexico came the caravans of settlers, and among the 1701 arrivals was a certain Diego de Veitia. He made his home near Santa Fe, but a member of the family, Antonio de Beytia, moved to Santa Cruz in 1720 and married there. The family name was changed through the years and finally became Abeyta. By 1806 there was a Don Bernardo Abeyta living in El Potrero, a devout man, fairly prosperous but suffering miserably from arthritis. Day after day, from his adobe ranch house, he watched the Indians arrive to pay homage to the healing earth.

There are, of course, many versions of the story concerning the "miracle" itself. Some are of Spanish origin; others are popular among the Indians. One tells of a day when Don Bernardo Abeyta was watching his grazing sheep on the hillside overlooking the Indians' *tierra bendita*, or "blessed earth." He sat with his crutch beside him, his serape drawn about him because of the cold. And while he rested, his eyes strayed across the Chimayó Valley to the fields and houses of folk far less endowed by heaven with material wealth, though few suffered as he did with painful joints. Their wealth was in things spiritual, Don Bernardo's, temporal—in land and field crops, cattle, sheep, horses, burros—and sacks of money buried under the floor of his house. Alms for the poor was his to give. And as he rested, watching his sheep, he thought of all the blessings the less fortunate could receive—if *only*, only he could have the health to move about and perform the tasks on healthy limbs.

It was twilight. Soon the herders would gather the sheep and drive them to the safety of the nighttime corrals. As the sky darkened Don Bernardo felt himself very much alone with his pious ambitions. Suddenly a brilliant light surrounded the Spring of the Sacred Earth and flashed before his eyes; rising from it stood a crucified Christ, almost six feet tall, one as black as ebony nailed to a dark green cross. A voice cried, "Don Bernardo, come here."

It is told that Don Bernardo Abeyta threw the serape from his shoulders, stood erect, and left the crutch on the ground. Now the pain in his joints was unbearable, but at the divine command he made his way down the slope to where the vision shone of the utmost brilliance above the muddy hole. But before he could reach the spot the Black Christ had vanished; now only the yellow earth remained, yet earth with such a sublime texture that, as Don Bernardo scooped the handfuls and bathed his ailing extremities, the pain departed, and he felt a comfort such as he had never experienced before. He walked to his home a healthy man, with new strength and renewed faith—faith not only in the ancient, dried up pool called Tsimahopokwi but also in Our Lord of Esquípulas, the New World Deity that heals with earth among the Mayas of Guatemala.

Again, this is but a single version of the many stories told of the reason for El Santuario de Potrero at Chimayó. It could have been that Don Bernardo was well read in spite of his isolation and compared the Pueblo Indian shrine of Tsimahopokwi with the similar pit of earth in Guatemala. Much traveling was done in those days between Santa Fe and Mexico City, down the Camino Real.

Travelers then, as today, had much to talk about. And there was traffic, too, on the highway south from the Mexican capital into Middle America. Besides, shrines in reverence of the Black Christ were springing up throughout Mexico, in Campeche, Vera Cruz, Chiapas, Oaxaca, Tabasco and Jalisco . . . Why not New Mexico, the most northerly province of New Spain?

In 1814, Don Bernardo Abeyta applied to the Bishop of Durango for permission to build an *hermita* (small chapel) in honor of Our Lord of Esquípulas at the site of the sacred earth. The request was granted in 1815, and the building of El Santuario was undertaken that year with communal labor. The structure was completed in 1816. Then, it is told, another "miracle" manifested itself in Chimayó.

A local *santero*—a woodcarver whose specialty was chiseling, smoothing, and painting images of the myriad saints—was commissioned to make the large crucifix for the main altar. This man, it is said, had never journeyed out of New Mexico and therefore knew nothing of cristos other than the familiar and very primitive creations common to the Sangre de Cristo Mountains, traditional home of the santeros. Nevertheless, the masterpiece he produced was not only unbecoming of the homespun work of the New Mexicans, more in tune with European techniques and exceptionally beautiful, *but an exact replica of the Black Christ of Esquípulas in Guatemala.* Except that the Chimayó figure has a dark *green* body—not black . . . Then again, the skeptical may say, the santero could have worked under the direction of the more sophisticated Don Bernardo, as did the builders of the shrine.

Don Bernardo died in 1856 and was buried in the Chapel of Our Lord of Esquípulas of Potrero—within the santuario—by permission of the famous Bishop Jean Baptiste Lamy, who became the first Archbishop of Santa Fe. Don Bernardo left a widow and eight children. His daughter Carmen inherited his devotion for the santuario and continued to supervise its upkeep. But from then on there was a dwindling interest in the Christ of Esquípulas, and today there is a complete ignorance of Him among most of the pilgrims. The reason is that the "miracle" of the Santo Niño de Atocha, or the Lost Child, long ago assumed that popularity.

Today it is told, and thoroughly believed, that instead of the crucified Christ appearing at the spring of the healing earth, a voice was heard by someone (not necessarily Don Bernardo), and that upon digging into the yellow sand an image of the Christ Child was found and given a place in the santuario that was built in His honor. All credit for healing now goes to the Infant Deity. For many years the image of the Child looked down on El Posito containing the earth in the special chapel to the left of the nave; but now a small crucifix has taken His place—a Black Christ on a black cross. The Cristo Negro of Guatemala.

El Santuario was in the possession of the Abeyta family until 1929. Then it was that the famous Southwestern author, Mary Austin, received $6,000 from a donor who asked to be unnamed, and El Santuario was bought from private ownership. It was then given to the Society for the Preservation and Restoration of New Mexico Churches and then transferred to the Catholic Church.

Today there is peace and quiet loveliness in the Valley of Chimayó. Though cultivated for more than 300 years, the soil is extremely fertile. There's the stream, tumbling or trickling according to season, made in lofty peaks on the eastern skyline, peaks whose summits reach two-and-a-half miles above sea level. There's a pungent freshness in the air, of irrigated fields and the ripeness of fruit. And, above all, there's a certain quality in the people—a friendliness that reaches out and grips you, and a humility that belongs only to those who are close to the earth.

It is told, in this valley, that in the darkness of night, every night of the year, the little figure of the Santo Niño Perdido leaves His daytime niche in El Santuario de Potrero and walks the fields, lanes and orchards in quest of someone sick or bereaved, someone in need of comfort. If there's doubt in this belief, go to His *nicho*, lift the hem of His robe and see the tattered shoes for yourself . . . Or ask the people, the special kind of people, and they'll tell you it is so. For theirs is the privilege to believe, and to stand firm against all the sophistication alive in the world. They can still look to the horizon and there find the union of heaven and earth.

14

CHILI AND BEANS

IN SPITE OF the deep red richness of its physical appearance, a bowl of "chili" holds insignificant rank in the mighty legion of American comestibles. Its closest kin are the "hamburger," the "hot dog," and the "sloppy Joe." More often that not, it is vulgarly referred to as a "bowl of red," and you'll frequently find it chalked on bill-of-fare boards in the cheaper, short-order lunch counters. Often it is given lowest spot on the menus of restaurants specializing in Mexican food, always a safe distance below the tacos, rellenos, and enchiladas. Another indignity is that a bowl of chili is usually dished with crackers-on-the-side, and its sharp potency gentled to suit Anglo-American tastes.

A sorry state, indeed, for so noble a dish. It wasn't always that way. Look to the history of the Southwest and you'll find that the stamina of our Spanish-American founding fathers was built on a steady diet of "chili and beans."

Chili and Beans, as everyone knows, is an old Spanish dish. . . . But how old and how Spanish? The *bean* is definitely Spanish. The first seeds were brought to the New World from Spain by colonists shortly after the 1521 conquest of Mexico; in 1598 they found their way to New Mexico in the ox-drawn carretas of the Juan de Oñate expedition, and by 1610 they were flourishing along irrigated rows in the then newly settled Santa Cruz Valley near the site of present-day Española.

The Pueblo Indians had for centuries been growing their own sort of beans, cultivated in the same fields with corn, squash, cotton, and tobacco. But the Indian species lacked majesty and was soon eclipsed by the European import. Today in the Mexican border states it's the pinto bean that counts, and there is no substitute.

Cream of body with dark speckles, it's the product of crisp, high-altitude fields. Some buyers prefer that they be grown to dry farming methods, although irrigation seems now to be universally employed. The Estancia Valley of central New Mexico was, until only a few years ago, the "Pinto Bean Capital of the World," its soil and climate unexcelled for producing beans of quality and abundance. But the seat of honor seems to have shifted now into the high, chill valleys of Colorado.

Regardless of environment, whether it be the original Estancia stronghold, or the Animas Valley adjacent to Mexico, or Colorado's Dove Creek, or Cahone in the shadow of the snowy San Juans, the pinto bean is the favored mate for the healthy red goodness called *chili*. For southwesterners *who know*, nothing else will suffice.

So the pinto bean is a Spanish import. . . . but the chile pod is something else again. Here we have the fruit of a native American plant—as American as the "Irish" potato and the so familiar, red-ripe tomato. And like its cousins, chile goes far back in age—countless centuries back—to the slopes of the South American Andes, to the Incas.

Deep in the pre-Incan past, some Indian genius discovered that edible fruits could, with clever propagating, be obtained from one of the best known of the truly poisonous plants—the nightshade family, which includes the deadly belladonna. After centuries of cultivation the plant developed little berries; some were sour and became the tomato, others were hot and pungent and became the capsicum peppers, which includes the "Chile Colorado" of Mexico and the southwestern United States.

Centuries before the European was aware that America existed, the spiciest of the capsicum peppers found their way out of the Andes (where they were unknown by the Quechua Indian word *aji*) and northward into Aztec Mexico—where they were eagerly sought and extensively cultivated, and given the Nahuatl name of *chili*. Which is odd, because the Quechua word for "cool" is *chile* and it referred to what we now call the sweet, or bell pepper . . . . And in New Mexico, today, the correct name is *chile*, never called chili by sticklers for accuracy.

What ingredients combine to make a good mess of "Chili and Beans"?

The Texans, as might be supposed, claim the dish for their very own, admitting no outside interference. Which is nonsense, for who ever heard of a pre-Incan Texan? They pride themselves on the fallacy that "Chili and Beans" is *their* invention, a product of *their* hands and minds and, furthermore, a product of the pot unsurpassed anywhere else in the world. Except for the "invention" claim, they are pretty darn right.

98   Here's a Texas recipe for "chili," one popular at the Great Annual Chili Cookout—a gustatorial event that has helped spread the fame of Texas far and wide:

> Brown one pound of ground beef in a skillet and set aside. In an ample-sized pot put a quarter-cup of chopped onions, along with one minced garlic clove. Sprinkle on a teaspoon of salt, quarter- to half-teaspoon of marjoram, half-teaspoon cumin seed, a pinch of oregano and the same of sage. Add meat, and one or two cups of water; mix in two tablespoons of flour, stir and let simmer. Throw in the chili powder, six tablespoons either level or heaping, gauged as to whether you like your chili with or without authority. Simmer slowly for two hours; or, better still, *all night*, if you can keep it from scorching. *Never, never* adulterate it with tomatoes, fresh or canned, sauce or paste.

And for a mightier "mess," five pounds of meat calls for five times as much of everything else.

The native New Mexican cook spurns ground beef in favor of cubed round steak. And many is the *paisana* who has never heard of marjoram. But she knows all about *cilantro* (coriander) and *chimajá* (wild parsley) and has learned that the wild varieties of onion and garlic are far superior to anything civilized. She also knows that a little beef suet, chopped and browned, with the liquid fat thereof, gives richness to the dish—a little too much richness for some people.

Although the pinto bean is as Spanish as the name Gonzáles, it is the Smiths and Robinsons of the Anglo-Saxon cattle ranges throughout New Mexico who have developed the best formulas for cooking the speckled beauties, called *frijóles* in Spanish. Cowboys and sheepherders have coined "special" names none fit to grace a menu, because of the legume's tendency to produce flatulence. But without the daily mess of boiled pintos the cowpokes and woolie-skinners would never have survived.

> Oh, It's bacon and beans
> Most every day.
> I'd sooner be eatin'
> Prairie hay.

So goes the cowboy ballad. But don't be fooled by it. If the chuck wagon cook hadn't a load of bacon skillet-sizzling under the pot rack, and a bucket of beans hanging from the bar, there would have been grumblings among the dainty diners and sooner or later outright rebellion on the old Diamond K. On every table in every ranch house west of the hundredth meridian was featured the traditional pair—and the first words spoken after a cowboy "set down" was "pass the beans."

A good cow camp bean recipe goes thisaway. It's one that I learned from Tom Weldy, wagon cook for the Block Ranch, about forty years ago. Here was a man famed for culinary skill tastefully blended with a cantankerous nature:

> Heap four cupfuls of pinto beans near the edge of the table, for better wrangling out of stray bits of Estancia Valley earth and herbage. Wash beans, place in heavy lidded pot. Cover with *boiling* water (I got this tip from a Pueblo Indian woman) and let stand overnight. Next morning, start boiling. Do not drain off soak water, but see that beans are well covered. Cook slowly, steadily, and add boiling water as the potful thickens. Add salt and pepper to taste, one chopped onion and the right amount of cubed salt pork, or ham hocks, or sliced bacon, or bacon rind. Above all, several tablespoons of bacon fat. Throw in a couple of dried, red chile pods for a special southwestern bouquet. Boil and boil, until beans and pork are tender—until the liquid is a rich brown. Four or five hours, maybe more, depending at what altitude stands the chuck wagon. Add more bacon fat for the final twenty minutes of cooking; then serve on tin plates after hollering your ill-natured, typically camp-cook invite of "Come and get it!"

Old-time New Mexican sheepherders seldom flaunted their knack for preparing the finest production of cooked pinto beans known to man. But they were never a boastful lot, anyway. Their method was to dig a hole close to the campfire—deep and wide enough to sink an eight-pound lidded lard bucket. Beans, water and all the standard ingredients were placed in the lard bucket, and the lid pushed on tight. They put several inches of red-hot *hardwood* coals (oak does fine) down in the hole and nested the bean bucket in them. Then, they shoveled in some earth and packed it around the sides. Next they heaped another thick layer of coals on top of the pail—covering it with earth and patting the little mound with a shovel.

Walk off and forget about it, is their advice. After eight hours or so, dig out your bucket of beans. You'll have a supper luscious enough to satisfy the most finicky sheepherder. Every particle of flavor is caught, sealed in.

100 This method worked on the ranges of the early West; it can do equally as well for a present-day suburban cook-out, even if the chef doesn't know a Rambouillet from a Delaine Merino.

The pinto bean is to the Indian, and to the rural Spanish American, what rice is to the Oriental. Served with chile—or any of the myriad native dishes made with chile—it is what oatmeal and broth are to the Scots, beef to the English and that godsend to the folk of Ireland—the American potato.

The experts claim that beans are an excellent meat substitute, that a cupful contains 15 grams of protein, while a three-ounce serving of roast beef can boast of 17. In the same cup you have a copious amount of the B vitamins—thiamine, riboflavin, niacin—plus iron and calcium.

Nutrition research at New Mexico State University, near Las Cruces, where campus and fields are in the heart of the "Chili Country," has proven chile to be a rich source of vitamins A and C. This has significance in northern New Mexico, where the fiery pod is grown in abundance and eaten in large quantities by all ages (from infancy to senility).

For more than 350 years the *curanderas* and *médicas* (herb women) of New Mexico have found healing magic in "chili and beans." Decoctions thereof have helped village midwives ply their homespun professions. For the pungency of chile and the power in the bean can (or so they say) not only cure the sick, but abate the sufferings of the lovelorn—and even combat the hellish effects of witchcraft. While matters of *amor*, or of *brujeria* are no concern of the médicas, happily the services of the benign *echacéra* (Spanish for "she who casts out," or an *anti*witch) are available in many mountain communities.

The Aztecs used chile compresses, as well as potent decoctions, for the relief of kidney inflammation. For lung, brain and heart pains. For a purge and to check diarrhea. To clear the blood, ease sore throat and to overcome difficulties in childbirth. And the Spanish Americans of New Mexico have carried on the ancient practices, discovering for themselves other remedies made from the precious chile. It is a sure cure for rheumatism, to name one; and if you will only pound the extra-hot seeds and veins together, and burn them as a fumigant, you will frustrate any invasion of *chinches* (bedbugs) that may afflict your house.

Not to forget the pinto bean, which also provides much relief for the ailing—*if*, of course, one has the know-how. Green leaves from the plant, soaked in vinegar and water, and applied to the forehead, can banish *muy pronto* the ache inside. Three raw beans swallowed by the mother-to-be can speed up a stubborn childbirth.

But first and foremost, chili and beans remains a most tasty food. A most nutritious dish; balm for the body, the mind and the soul. It is the poor man's sustenance and a culinary way of life in the American Southwest. Occupying such an exalted station, then, it is no wonder that the dish has been the subject of some controversy.

Life magazine, in the issue of February 28, 1969, featured "A Chili to Cry Over," one of its "Great Dinners" series. The recipe was superb, with the chile to be served along with chicken tacos, tortillas, guacamole salad, rice, beer, cream pudding with iced oranges, coffee; in short, a feast to satisfy every gourmet. *Magnifico!* That is the word for *Life's* "A Chili to Cry Over."

Yet it has its fault. A single fault, maybe, but a monstrous one: it pays too much homage to Texas.

Repeated is the eternal fallacy; that Texans may have been the inventors of chili con carne.

It does truthfully report that Will Rogers judged a town by the quality of the chili it served. It tells how Jesse James wouldn't rob the McKinney, Texas, bank because the town was the site of his favorite chili parlor. It does publicize the International Chili Appreciation Society (of Texas)—a cookout outfit whose slogan is *"The aroma of good chili should generate rapture akin to a lover's kiss."* An excellent slogan indeed.

But nowhere does *Life* mention New Mexico—the "Red Heart of the Chili Kingdom"! Or the historical certainty that the chile fields of Santa Cruz de la Cañada flourished at a time when about the only animation to be found in Texas was among bison and cyclones and warring tribes, red ants and rattlesnakes and wolves.

Such a slight sparked the ire of Arch Napier, of Albuquerque, a journalist, researcher, gifted writer on southwestern themes, a man of taste and discretion, loyal New Mexican—and self-appointed president of the Gourmet Chili Society of America. Mr. Napier's organization is perhaps alive only in his soul, but he has many fellow members. The estimated population of New Mexico stands at 1.1 million. Perhaps one million of that figure are chili gourmets, and two-thirds of the remaining 100,000 could be if the cooks would only ease a little on the tear-jerking authority of their product. So Arch Napier spoke for most of us in New Mexico when he wrote the following letter to *Life* (printed March 21, 1969):

> Sirs: You are giving this exciting food a bad name by linking it to the crude stuff served in Texas. Texas chili is a test of endurance, primarily useful for terrorizing tourists and fracturing oil wells. Last year, the Texans had a kind of chili cooking contest—conducted like a shoot-out—and it was publicized on the front pages along with crimes and disasters. When New Mexico chili cuisine is discussed in our newspapers, it is usually carried on the Art and Music pages.

15

SHALAKO:
TIME OF THE WALKING GODS

IF YOU LIKE KACHINAS you'll like the Shalako. If you don't like kachinas, or know what they really are, you'll curse the folly that bade you forsake the cozy fireside of Gallup's El Rancho Hotel and drive forty miles southward to Zuni Pueblo, for the purpose of witnessing what is hailed as the most elaborate Indian pageant of the wintertime Southwest. Wait around, and you'll get to like kachinas. Shiver some more in the biting cold, and you'll actually see the gods walk.

Not being an Indian yourself, and especially not a Zuni, you arrived at the pueblo early—ten in the moring—so as not to miss a thing. Now it is four in the afternoon with the sun declining to the Zuni Buttes, and nothing has happened. When will the gods perform? When will New Mexico give up being the *Land of Mañana*?

And what are kachinas?

To learn of the kachina influence upon this spiritually created world you have to come to Zuni. You have suffered a friendless six hours in the numbing cold, waded slush and choked in the dust, visited trading posts for nothing better to do, ached with boredom while young Zunis recounted to you the exploits of their G.I. days. Now, at last, the crowds are moving toward the trickling stream called a river. Your curiosity is about to be satisfied, for the Council of the Gods is planting prayer sticks in the village, preparing the way for the six giant Shalako.

Without kachinas the Pueblo Indian World could not exist. Without the aid of this army of weirdly masked, brightly garbed anthropomorphic beings the lives of the most spiritually rich people in North America would fall to empty, materialistic decay. For every kachina—and there are scores of them, each identified by mask and costume—is an actual messenger, a bringer of good, from the sublime world of the gods to devoted people on this tricky earth. Once upon a time, before the Spanish conquest when America was pure, the spirits came to earth unaided and returned from whence they came after showering blessings on the people. But now the best they can do is to allow their spirits to enter the body of a thoroughly cleansed mortal who dons mask and costume, and make of him a supernatural being, a god who walks among his people dispensing the blessing of the Supreme Power. And the greatest of kachinas are the Shalako, who come to earth regularly every late fall. They never fail.

When the Shalako cease to come to Zuni, then Zuni will be no more. It may remain as a town—of houses, stores, churches, a drive-in movie (God forbid), even a bank, and a solid population. But as an Indian town it will be dead, forsaken of soul as the kachinas will have forsaken it. But today Zuni, happily, rests on its height above the river, still favored by the gods: Hálona, "Place of the Ants," one of the Cities of Cíbola.

Because the Shalako are the greatest of kachinas, and never fail to appear, a special and costly reception must be prepared for them. They come gliding in, six ghostly forms almost ten feet tall—which explains why all rooms within Zuni Pueblo are at least twelve feet from floor to ceiling. The six Shalako houses are either newly built or freshly renovated, the interiors gleaming with a wash of pristine whiteness. For as the gods are immaculate so must be their appointed shrines. Each householder has taken the vow to be host, assuming the labor and expense which enriches him with esteem of his people and blessing of the gods, but which can throw him into long-lasting debt. Besides the money involved in the building or renovation, his women just grind corn day and night prior to the feast, tend the roasting ovens and boiling pots. He himself will butcher some fifteen head of cattle and perhaps fifty sheep. Many of his guests will be Navajos, who are said to have hearty appetites. The whole pueblo will take on a festive air.

Accurate to detail, this event requires a full year of preparation. Just prior to the "first moon," in early January, the company of mortals who will impersonate the kachinas is selected and installed. They are thirteen in number, the six Shalako giants and the seven-member Council of the Gods. The little Fire God, *Shulawitsi*, is all important in the Council, a completely black figure speckled with bright spots to denote sparks, always impersonated by a small boy about ten years old. The most sacred Six Directions are represented, first with *Saya-tasha*, Rain God of the North—a figure in white buckskin, popularly called the "Longhorn" because of the mighty prong that protrudes from the right side of his mask. And there is *Hututu*, Rain God of the South, so named for the call he gives as he goes about his sacred duties. The east and west are honored by two brightly masked kachinas, the *Yamuhahkto*, Warrior Gods of the sunrise and sunset points, while two *Salimobia*, also warriors, bring blessings of the Zenith and Nadir.

From the first moon to the ninth, the chosen Council of the Gods, un-masked and quite workaday, go about sacred duties that are all part of the year-long ritual. They help the six volunteer "hosts," hauling rock and log beams for building or renovating the Shalako houses, cultivating and harvesting the crops, and bringing in wagonloads of firewood in addition to spending long nighttime hours in the ceremonial house practicing and memorizing the difficult chants and prayers. Every morning they offer prayer meal to the rising sun; each evening with long meditation they give a portion of food to the river. Through the winter, spring, and summer the rise of each full moon sends them off with prayer sticks to be planted at shrines outside the pueblo.

Then comes autumn and the morning of the October full moon. The Council of the Gods is given two strings of ceremonial cotton, each tied with forty-nine knots. Here the preliminaries become complicated, preparations heated, anticipation intense. For when the forty-ninth knot is ultimately untied from one of the two strings, the Shalako will have completed their blessing of Zuni with continued life and prosperity, and will be on the way home to their sacred world.

Each morning Sayatasha, the Rain God of the North, greets the rising sun with prayer and sacred meal, and unties one of the forty-nine knots. Now purification rites are rigid, work for the kachinas endless. Building or renovating of the six Shalako houses is almost completed, though none will be lived in until the gods have spent the night. The Council of the Gods builds a new bridge or causeway across the river, one to be used only by the Shalako and their attendants when they cross from the south side to the pueblo on the forty-eighth day and back again on the forty-ninth. Altars are set up and consecrated in each of the six houses. And on the day of the untying of the fortieth knot the first assembly of kachinas appears in the village—masked and in regalia.

These are the *Koyemshi,* commonly called the Mudheads, painted a sickly pink with idiot faces. They symbolize monsters born of incestuous marriages and warn against violations of the sexual code. They act the clown and perform all manner of exercises for the welfare of the pueblo. And with the untying of the forty-fourth knot, now with the coming of the Shalako but four days ahead, the Council of the Gods—masked, garbed, and laden with sacred essentials—arrives to sanctify the ground that annually has been sanctified for centuries. Then comes the forty-eighth day: the day of days, that of the great Shalako.

The sun hangs low, coaxing darkness out of the east. It thins the cold while the gods are signaled to come gliding into the village that waits for the supreme blessing, for the six envoys of the Mighty Invisible Being. Frost and smoke combine to incense the air as the few hundred fires roast, boil, and fry the gala feast. The visiting crowd—composed of Indians and assorted whites, the latter wrapped to battle the frigid night—moves to where the masked Council of the Gods is employed at planting prayer sticks with the long-horned Sayatasha supervising the process and the little Fire God showing his weariness. The Yamuhahkto and the Salimobia, warriors itching for a skirmish, eye the crowd through their mask slits for some act of irreverence or disrespect, or for the presence of a Mexican or Spanish American, who alone have been barred since Coronado found and took the Cities of Cíbola. Hututu, wrapped in white buckskin, moves about with potent fetishes as he gives his odd little call. With planting done, attention moves to the causeway at the river. The six figures come—gliding with poise and dignity out of the south—clacking their beaks while ancient Hálona smokes her welcome and the six Shalako houses are opened for their sacred attendance.

The crowd watches at a respectful distance. Now the waning glint of a winter day provides too meager a light for the ritual to be seen. But the sight is secondary, it is the *presence* that matters. They reach the causeway—six sacred towers of plumage, the very life of Zuni and the welfare of the world bundled within them. They cross the bridge, gliding; they clack their beaks while tiny feet shuffle under the massive superstructures, moving toward their altars as nothing earthly is supposed to move. The crowd of spectators follows.

Should a Shalako stumble, the force of evil will fall on Zuni and all the blessings will vanish. The whippers, the Salimobia, will flog the aliens from the village, while the people who really matter are left to mourn and grieve. The way is tricky, thoroughly Indian, and seemingly endless.

The Council of the Gods is in a Shalako house, seated with masks removed. The host asks them how they came to this world, and they reply with a litany—a chant monotonous and repetitive as it is long. Then they move on, after planting the necessary prayer sticks in the ceiling, after sanctifying the shrine for the greater presence. The altar is laid for the Shalako pleasure, all the essentials for Zuni's breath of life—each piece exact and without flaw. The rooms are draped with extravagance, the color contrast of Navajo, Hopi, and Chimayó blankets, the richness of Sears Roebuck's best. Here is grandeur equal to the taste of an Arab sheik, but without the fragrance. Soon the stench will nauseate as the crowds pack in. But now the Navajo are feasting in the town kitchens, as are the Anglos, fueling up for the great night.

Shortly before midnight, when the room is filled with the reverent and curious, the Shalako rises from its seat beside the altar to perform its blessing on the little world of Zuni, to dance for its people, a giant indeed, one draped in godly apparel. The spectators are awed. They look to the mask, with its tiara of white eagle plumes, rich with down that symbolizes life's very breath. Birdlike, the wooden beak clacks; animallike the twin buffalo horns have their rightful place in the sacred rite. The tips of the plumes almost touch the twelve-foot-high ceiling. The mask is of turquoise, strings of assorted stones and shells drape the neck. Knoblike eyes protrude and long tresses of black hair reach from the peak to midway down the back. The armless figure lacks human proportion, its height beyond reason, neither bird, beast nor reptile, yet all one together. With a gliding motion not of this earth, it is an oracle, a walking holy of holies, the very end of the world if it is not given its due respect. It dances, clacks, bows. Its beating heart is contained in a man whose worldly occupation is that of a farmer, perhaps an expert mechanic or wheelbarrow man for a Gallup construction firm—but one who, for this solemn night behaves like a god and, indeed, *is a god*.

Hours pass, dark and cold in the village, bright and overheated in each of the six houses where a Shalako struts and blesses. Troops of kachina go from house to house, joining the tall ones in the dance—the Koyemshi, for one, clowning in their foolish, idiotic way. But the dance is a religious rite in every step and movement and the breechclouted pink company is aided by masked gods of assorted shapes and colors. They dance until dawn. Then the kachina parties leave for their own ceremonial houses and the Shalako shrines are cleared of spectators. It is time for the wearied gods to rest—until the finale at noon.

As the sun peeps over the horizon, Sayatasha, the Longhorn, climbs to a rooftop and faces the rising glory. All Zuni rests, even the visitors take a nap in their cars and a little repast from their baskets and thermos bottles. From a pouch, Sayatasha takes a pinch of cornmeal, which he throws to the cardinal points and up and down, as he intones a solemn prayer:

> Now this day, my Sun Father,
> Now that you have come out standing to your sacred place,
> That from which we draw the Water of Life—
> Prayer meal—
> Here I give to you.

[Ruth Bunzel translation]

For his people he asks old age, long life, waters, seeds, riches, power, strong spirit; and with the prayer completed he unties the forty-ninth knot, the last, the signal that the Shalako is complete.

At about noon the six gods emerge from their respective houses. With their attendants and the crowd following they cross the causeway to the plain south of the river. There they dance and compete in a race—and glide away for another year.

16

THE WHITE OAKS OF
HEART'S DESIRE

WHITE OAKS, as the old timers say, has "gone ghost." The little mining town that was once alive with frontier occupation, with the dreams and losses of those who ventured, with the labor and gains of sturdier pioneers, lies quietly today in the midst of one of New Mexico's most dramatic settings. Mountain ranges, one seeming to pile against the other with wide sweeps of desert flatlands between, each square mile with a story to tell. And appropriately enough, for out of little White Oaks in the latter nineteenth and the early twentieth centuries emerged some of the Southwest's finest literary talent—writers, story tellers, who unlike the town will never "go ghost."

The gold has played out, they say. The deserted streets are weed-grown and eroded, fallen brick and adobe buildings crumbling further in the sun and wind. Some were homes built with love; others were stores and banks, assay and newspaper offices, wagon yards and livery barns, gambling casinos and brothels —all put together with fortune in mind. Some remain standing—the red brick schoolhouse and a "castle" built by a lover whose chaste lady never arrived to grace the towers. A few homes still house the living, but very few.

But the inspiration is still there in the loneliness: beyond the remnants of the town, off to the stony north slope of Capitan Gap, south to the Carrizo and Patos mountains, the yellowed flats cut by Padilla Arroyo and the Cienega del Macho, north to the long though not too-lofty Jicarilla range—barren cones loaded with lore and legend from Baxter Gulch to Jack's Peak. Lore and legend that fired the minds of Emerson Hough, Harvey and Erna Fergusson, Eugene Manlove Rhodes, Jack Thorpe, to fill the libraries of the nation with the golden bonanza of their combined talents.

Gold and related ores were known to be there in New Mexico's famous Lincoln County prior to 1879. But that year, in the height of the Lincoln County War, in which Billy the Kid was the star performer, two quiet prospectors along with a "helper" were placering in the gulch. They were Jack Winters and George Baxter, and a certain George Wilson. The placers were showing only a sparse return, and the miners were thinking of packing their burros and gear and whacking off further west—say maybe to the Black Range.

Winters and Baxter were hard-rock men, true "jackass prospectors." But Wilson offered only a partial interest in the quest for "color." He was a Texan, a plainsman, who possessed neither burro or gear. He was a freeloader with absolutely nothing. And a surly one at that. But my! Was he about to pay for his keep!

The noon hour came and the three quit work for a taste of lunch. Wilson finished first and rose to say that he "aim[ed] to go for a walk, maybe find some gold." But Wilson had no intention of finding gold. Truth is, he was wanted in Texas for a series of felonies, and, if he didn't get to Arizona fast, the sheriff's posse might catch up with him. He climbed the canyonside, his goal the highest ridge, the best point to survey for mounted posses. Then by command of Queen Luck, whose realm is Bonanza, he sat down to rest on a blowout boulder. He bit a chew off his tobacco plug, one he'd likely bummed from Winters or Baxter, spat some juice on the ground, hit a rock, and

Eureka! The great White Oaks klondike was born!

The rock looked something like dirty concrete, which he took down to show Winters and Baxter. They whooped at the sight of it, thanked the Lord for the feel of it, and danced like crazy. Wilson led them to the lucky spot where traces of gold showed round about. Float, real honest native gold!

Winters and Baxter made plans. Three claims would be staked out, each man to have an equal share of the bonanza. But Wilson wanted nothing of it. He told his partners he'd gladly sell them his rights. After all, what good is a gold mine to a wretch strung up on the gallows? He wanted nobody's wealth, just a healthy distance from Texas.

"How much will you take, Wilson?"

"Anything I can git, but make it quick."

Wilson sold his share for forty dollars, a six-shooter, and an aged pony with saddle. He couldn't have asked for a better deal. He pocketed the forty dollars, drank the whiskey, buckled on the six-shooter, mounted the pony, and rode off to oblivion. He did, however, release his claim to one John E. Wilson. Here Baxter goes out of the picture and Winters remains.

Baxter developed a successful mining company, had a gulch and mountain named for him. Winters and John E. Wilson divided the claim—Winters taking the north half, Wilson the south. Together the North Homestake and South Homestake mines went into operation. As predicted, both mines "struck it rich." Soon an army of prospectors and their burros began to trail up the White Oaks Draw.

To celebrate, "Uncle Jack" Winters brought in a wagonload of whiskey, provided tin cups, and invited every crusty miner to help himself. All men were too drunk to stake claims that day, but they did so upon sobering up. By the turn of the century the South Homestake had produced over $350,000 in gold, and by 1904 the North Homestake reaped $500,000 since its first working day. But Wilson and Winters were not around for the reckoning. Both had sold out to a St. Louis company in 1880 for $30,000 each. Besides, Winters didn't live long to spend his share. He died that same year in White Oaks and became one of the earliest residents of the community's Cedarvale Cemetery.

Trouble started when the Winters relatives in West Virginia, claiming to be heirs, filed litigation against the Homestake Mining Company. "Uncle Jack" hadn't been treated right. At the same time a suit was entered by Henry Patterson, a townsman, charging the Baxter Gold Mining Company. Both cases were argued in 1884. There was so much litigation going on in White Oaks at that time that newly arrived lawyers filled the street. Miners were riled; they threatened to form lynch mobs; they'd hang the lawyers if they "didn't git out of town."

Those that didn't "git" was the firm of Beall, Chandler, Hough and Thornton—representing Baxter. And Harvey Butler Fergusson, a West Virginia attorney, on behalf of the Winters heirs. New Mexico owes much to White Oaks and its year of litigation for introducing one great legislator and three famed writers to the Territory. The Hough in the Baxter case was Emerson Hough, outstanding American author, creator of *The Covered Wagon, North of 36,* and other novels of the West, who was inspired by the town's wild activity to write the novel *Heart's Desire,* the setting laid in White Oaks. Emerson Hough, and later Eugene Manlove Rhodes, referred to White Oaks as the "Little Town of Heart's Desire."

Harvey Butler Fergusson settled to conduct a law firm in Albuquerque, to excel in oratory, and later be elected for New Mexico in the 55th, 62nd, and 65th Congresses. He was the father of literary critic Francis Fergusson (*The Idea of a Theatre, Dante, Shakespeare: The Pattern in His Carpet*); novelist Harvey Fergusson (*Conquest of Don Pedro, Grant of Kingdom, Rio Grande*); and Erna Fergusson (*Dancing Gods, Our Southwest*), nonfiction author celebrated as "New Mexico's First Lady of Letters."

White Oaks, in 1884, was laid out along one street, a half-mile long and a hundred feet wide. Operating mines were everywhere, up the hillsides and along the arroyos. These were given names with affection: The Lady Godiva, The Boston Boy, The Comstock, The Little Mack—and the richest of them all, the Old Abe, which in twenty-five years earned three million dollars. Gold at the time was worth $20 an ounce. From the Old Abe's fourteen hundred-foot shaft ore was brought out assaying $100 a ton. The price of town lots was staggering, and hastily built shacks gave way to buildings of substance. "The Little Town of Heart's Desire" quivered with activity, bellowed its prosperity to the skies.

It was in White Oaks that the law firm of Beall, Chandler, Hough and Thornton lost its Hough. Emerson Hough, while on the Baxter case, began to lose heart with briefs and oratory and dim-lit courtrooms. New Mexico's sun shone along the Jicarilla slopes, autumn frosts changed scrub oak and white-barked aspen to a riot of color in the higher Patos. The town, the noise of it, the bawdy nights of it, the whiskey presence so readily detected along the street.

Baxter Gulch and its people—the miners, the prospectors, the burro bray, the attending loafers, leeches to feast on hard-earned prosperity. The gamblers and bunco-steerers, casino dealers, the Can Can Girls, the harlots in the parlors. Swaggering cowboys off the Block Ranch and Carrizozo Cattle Company, Mexican vaqueros from the Rabenton Draw. Sheepherders, assayers, freighters, stage drivers, itinerant "opera" groups, outlaws and peace officers. Sheriffs, such as the great Pat Garrett himself.

Drummers, cure-all-pill venders in their wagonettes. The glory of the skies, the deep amethyst of the Malpais under the sunset blaze, the liquid sunrise off the Llano Estacado. All the ingredients little White Oaks had to offer, to fire the gift of talent in a novelist to be—

The case of *Patterson vs. Baxter?*

The hell with it!

Emerson Hough was born in Newton, Iowa, 1857. That was two years before Billy the Kid, famous outlaw of Lincoln County, first saw daylight in New York City. Billy the Kid would be killed by Pat Garrett near Fort Sumner in 1881, three years before the young attorney arrived in White Oaks. Hough had earned his degree in law at the University of Iowa, a career the bright drama of the American West would hastily put to a finish.

113

While in White Oaks Emerson Hough made his "hang out" in the office of the *Golden Era,* one of the town's newspapers; and at the *New Mexico Interpreter* his ambition "to write" was further fueled by Ash Upson, the frontier journalist. He published twenty-two books, most of them written in Chicago. Besides *Heart's Desire,* the best known were *The Story of the Cowboy, The Mississippi Bubble, The Passing of the Frontier;* and *The Young Alaskans,* a boys' book. From *The Covered Wagon* the great motion picture was made. He returned to New Mexico in 1904, traveling over Lincoln County with Sheriff Pat Garrett, an adventure that gave material for *The Story of the Outlaw.* An ardent conservationist, he toured Yellowstone Park on skis. It was Emerson Hough who influenced the government to protect the buffalo and all wildlife on the preserve. He died in Evanston, Illinois, in 1923.

Two other noted Southwestern writers followed Hough's trail to the White Oaks country. Eugene Manlove Rhodes, also referred to White Oaks as "Heart's Desire" in his fiction—his great novels being *Once In The Saddle* and *Pasó Por Aquí,* the latter one of the finest Western stories ever written. And the Princeton-educated cowboy, N. Howard "Jack" Thorp, who rode the ranges of the Block Ranch east of White Oaks, and the Bar W to the west. Thorp is best known for *Tales of the Chuck Wagon* and *Songs of the Cowboy*—especially for the cowboy ballad, "Little Joe the Wrangler." The literary fame of Harvey and Erna Fergusson, foremost of New Mexico writers, although neither were born in White Oaks, is deeply indebted to old "Uncle Jack" Winters of the North Homestake Mine.

Fortune's promise brought in the hopeful. The population peaked to over 4,000. Miners staked their claims, sank the shafts. The stamp mills ground out the ores, the assayers assayed, and all commerce flourished. It was calculated at century's end that White Oaks would become the metropolis of New Mexico if. . . .

If the town could be blessed with a way out, *if* faster contact could be made with the great wide world, *if* an outlet for the golden product—

A railroad, for example.

Col. D.M.A. Jewett arrived in 1880 and found all men to be "millionaires but nobody had any money." Adna Lampson was the first postmaster, with an office in the Pioneer Saloon. Mail was brought in by stagecoach from San Antonio, a Santa Fe Railway station on the Rio Grande south of Socorro. The same coach took mail, express and passengers on to Fort Stanton, to Nogal and Lincoln Town. A notice in the White Oaks post office advised patrons that their mail could be picked up or deposited any time they should "find the postmaster sober."

The Pioneer was the saloon of saloons, always filled with good humor, such as it was. Men had been shot and knifed there. From its doors, sometimes, the shackled and doomed were led to the hang tree. (For their convenience was the sanctified Cedarvale Cemetery.) Whiskey cost one dollar for two shots. The Pioneer had three grades—all from the same barrel. As everyone paid for the lowest grade there were no arguments. The brand was Dowlin and Delaney's *Tanglefoot*. Fine Havana cigars were sold—made in Arkansas and imported "in the same box with the late Charley Ross."

Further along the street was Madam Varnish's Little Casino, a place of wide renown. The lady herself was the dealer, who won her name by the slick way she manipulated the cards. She, too, sold whiskey—without bar or bartender. Customers served themselves from a monster barrel. They paid with silver coin. A notice gave simple instructions: CASH ON THE BARREL. And from the Little Casino in White Oaks, handwrit by Madam Varnish, a maxim was created to be used throughout the nation, its modern interpretation "cash, no credit."

There was Starr's Opera House which featured a famed dramatic troupe on its opening night. To celebrate, all mines closed down for the day. After the show, the cast played roulette in one of the several casinos, lost all they had and barely managed to leave town, the cost of horse-and-wagon hire being excessive. Every commodity was priced out of reason. All but the boomtown monopolies raged against them. Everything was freighted down by wagon from the railhead at Las Vegas. Drinking water was bought by the barrel, forty cents each, bring your own barrel. Nonetheless, the going rate of merchandise was just about half that of 1975.

Three churches and a $10,000 schoolhouse were built. There were two false-front hotels, a brick kiln, and a planing mill. Homes of red brick began to form a residential section. A man named Hoyle built a "castle" for himself, complete with turrets, balconies, and the gingerbread decor of a Mississippi showboat. He filled it with priceless furniture and ornaments—all for a prospective bride who was never to set foot in White Oaks.

115

Merchants such as C.L. Pearson dealt in "Agate and Flemishware and Black Blasting Powder." J.T. Butler & Co. carried "the Finest in Photograph Albums, and the Choicest Wines and Liquors." Goodman, Ziegler & Co. advertised in the *Interpreter* "Immense Reductions in desirable dress fabrics and plushes." There was a healthy market for Tutt's Pills, Bile Beans, Dr. Pearce's Pellets, and "Sir Astley Cooper's Great English Vital Restorative For Seminal Weakness Due To The Follies of Youth"—an absolute *must* for the miners. The medical profession was thoroughly represented. And, after the 1884 lynching threat gave way to other pastimes, lawyers arrived to hang up their shingles.

White Oaks was equipped with a set of ambitious town fathers, a machine that led to its downfall. All citizens were certain that soon, very soon, the population would swell with the golden commodity. In this gulch, on this red earth, would rise "The Metropolis of New Mexico," the hub of all territorial commerce. In 1900, a man named Hilton had a 13 year-year-old son named Conrad. They lived in San Antonio where Conrad was born, the village on the Rio Grande, west terminal of the White Oaks stage line. Often the Hiltons, father and son, made trips to White Oaks. The senior Hilton saw a bright future for the town, but not so glowing as in the eyes of the dreamers and schemers. He saw the rise of banks and mercantile establishments, ramrodded by territorial magnates. Here could be strength enough to sway the economy of all New Mexico. The false-front architecture would surrender to impressive buildings— *If* the "way out" to the big wide world could be realized—

The railroad, God bless it!

And who knows, if the "Gem of the Jicarilla Lode" had grown with commercial majesty as dreamed by pioneers, today it might actually sport a White Oaks Hilton.

The railroad prospect was no pipe dream, but very real. As White Oaks thrived on gold, so did Phelps Dodge, the mighty corporation, as it dug copper from its pit at Bisbee, Arizona. In fact, Phelps Dodge *owned* Bisbee. It also operated the Copper Queen smelter in nearby Douglas. For smelting, the Douglas operation was convenient to fifty percent of Arizona's copper as well as the output of the pits at Pilares and Nacozari, Mexico. Hence, an abundance of coking coal was necessary to keep the Douglas stacks belching sulphurous pollution.

So Phelps Dodge built a railroad, eastward to El Paso—the El Paso & Southwestern. Its purpose was to bring New Mexico coal to Douglas. Soon it was to meet the Southern Pacific at Tucson. In 1905, as White Oaks rocked with hope, the plan was to extend the rails north from El Paso to the Dawson coal fields northwest of Springer, New Mexico, and at the same time connect with the Rock Island at Tucumcari. This was later to become the "Golden State Route" of the joint Rock Island and Southern Pacific between Chicago and Los Angeles, way of the luxurious *Golden State Limited*. From Tucumcari a line branched off to Dawson, which brought southward trainloads of coking fuel for Douglas. And praises be! The proposed right of way between Tucumcari and El Paso would hit White Oaks smack in its Baxter Gulch.

So exuberant were the mayor and his council that the project was referred to as the El Paso & White Oaks Railroad. Day after day the tracklaying went on, night after night the work was celebrated by White Oaks men who could drink copious quantities of *Tanglefoot*. Then came the time for land to be purchased by the railroad—for depot, sidings, yards, and even a possible roundhouse.

"Why, of course!" resounded the beaming town fathers.

A price was given, and one quite resonable in view of the fact that White Oaks would be God's gift to Phelps Dodge. Or so the local gents thought. The money asked was staggering—it could almost have bought Lincoln County. The railroad men were flabbergasted. They mounted the stagecoach and returned to El Paso, sorry that no deal could be made with the Little Town of Heart's Desire.

White Oaks went into panic, from the mayor down to the veriest muckstick-heaver. "Good Lord, don't drive away the railroad! Give them the land for nothing!" So the council set a new price—nothing—an absolute gift from the adoring people of White Oaks. But the El Paso & Northeastern (as the line was called east of El Paso) had made up its mind. The rails would bypass the town about fifteen miles to the west, and a division point be established at Carrizozo.

White Oaks died with the loss of the railroad. The mines closed down and enterprise moved away. The surrounding plains and mountains seemed to take on an air of relief, for they didn't care to be part of a metropolis anyway. Vacant houses and rusting machinery, with the crude headstones in Cedarvale Cemetery, stayed on as fit memorials. The Old Abe, the greatest mine, went on producing until 1930—then quit.

The post office was lost in 1954. As late as 1928 some buildings remained cold and empty, among them the once-warm-and-boisterous Little Casino. The name was still there above the double doors, but slowly sandblasting away. And the doors hung crazy on their hinges. No click of roulette, no calls for "cash on the barrel," no more shots fired under the harp lamps. Madam Varnish didn't work there anymore.

17

THE YEARS OF LINCOLN TOWN

THEY FOUND the valley, the clean mountain valley, and they named their settlement *La Placita del Rio Bonito*—The Little Village of the Pretty River.

It was the early 1850s.

Some came in oxwagons, others drove packsaddled mules and burros, carriers of their worldly goods. And a herd of cattle, and a band of saddle ponies, each in the charge of mounted *vaqueros*. The men were strong, the bravest of the brave, their women likewise courageous and loyal. Together they were trail-blazers into the unknown, pioneers extraordinary.

They had come from the older settlements in the Rio Grande Valley—from Socorro, La Joya, Lemitar. Soon others would arrive from the Spanish villages to the north, from beyond Gran Quivira and the Salt Lakes, from Manzano and Chilili.

Deeply religious, they gave gratitude where gratitude was due for the safe journey and for their new-found wealth. Westward the white peak of Sierra Blanca shone with snowy promise, the source of irrigation for their fields and pastures. Here by the Pretty River they would build their mud-plastered *jacales*, lay their earthen floors, find shelter under pine-beamed roofs, get warmth from the pitchy piñon at their adobe hearths, and conduct with order their homespun lives. Their wood-breasted plows would cut ditches and furrows. They were men to match the mountains.

Today, The Little Village of the Pretty River is called Lincoln Town, but it still dreams a rustic dream midway between Roswell and Carrizozo on US 380, ten miles west of the Hondo junction and thirteen east of Capitan. It is a quiet place, uncommercialized, the air at 6,000 feet fresh with a high-altitude coolness.

118

A narrow one-street oasis, the town follows the Bonito between semiarid hills, and the atmosphere here is of long settlement and little change. Although the little Wortley Hotel carries a heavy guestload throughout the summer due to the racing season at Ruidoso Downs thirty-two miles away, it is the month of August that presents a hubbub. Then tourists invade the village, lured by the annual historical pageant, and the legend of Billy the Kid.

In 1869, almost two decades after the Spanish first settled the valley, the village name was changed to Lincoln. That was when the largest county in the United States was established by cutting off the eastern half of Socorro County, which had covered all southern New Mexico from Texas to the Arizona line. Fort Stanton, some 15 miles west of the village, had introduced the first Anglo Americans to the Bonito and Ruidoso valleys. The military was there because of "Indian troubles" and to deal with New Mexico's part in the Civil War.

Too, it was during the 60s that the first invasion by Texans took place, prompted by the cattle drives from Texas (to supply the military) particularly those of Charles Goodnight and Oliver Loving, who blazed the Goodnight-Loving Trail, a ribbon of hoof-pounded earth that entered the territory at the Horsehead Crossing of the Pecos, south of the site of Carlsbad, and ran north to the Bosque Redondo near Fort Sumner. This same route was followed by John S. Chisum, the cattle king of New Mexico, who settled at South Spring, near Roswell. Others would later claim the vast grasslands of Lincoln County.

Lincoln County contained 17 million acres and was as large as Connecticut, Delaware, Massachusetts, Rhode Island, and Vermont combined. The seat conducting its affairs was Lincoln Town. The early residents referred to Lincoln as "The Town," to distinguish it from "The County." And there is an anecdote that concerns its naming, not generally known to New Mexico historians.

The county commissioners in 1869 were hard pressed to find a name for their huge domain. Suggestions were offered, and finally the name of Captain Saturnino Baca was voted on unanimously—it would be Baca County. Saturnino Baca, a native of Valencia County, had come to Fort Stanton with the California Column, had distinguished himself in the Indian campaigns under Kit Carson and General Carleton, and had served valiantly in the Civil War, especially at the Battle of Valverde. Although but thirty-nine years old in 1869, he was to give his entire life to the service of New Mexico—in short, a great frontiersman and wise and honest leader.

120

When told that his name would be perpetuated, Captain Saturnino Baca protested, and most emphatically. He had done little, he insisted, to warrant the honor. And at such a time! There was but one name in all the American nation that should grace the nation's largest county, he said, that of the late martyred president. Saturnino Baca begged that the commissioners consider *his* choice. So Lincoln County came into being. But the officials were determined that something, somehow, would be named for Captain Saturnino Baca. Today a monument stands to his honor, one sculpted by Nature—10,025 feet above sea level, just north of Lincoln Town—the Capitan mountains. This story was told to me in 1941 by his daughter, the late Doña Sara Baca y Salazar—a beautiful and gracious lady.

Thanks to well-meaning authors—first Walter Noble Burns and his *Saga of Billy the Kid*, followed by a score or more nonfiction writers—the fame of Lincoln Town and Lincoln County has been carried to all continents of the globe. Millions of readers, moviegoers and TV viewers know all about Billy the Kid. And each is eager to know more. Substantial proof that it takes gunfire and bloodshed, handcuffs and shackles, pounding hoofs, and shouts of havoc to gather in such a wide audience. But the truth is that Lincoln's halcyon years have far outnumbered its days of violence.

Lincoln Town shares the Wild West limelight with places equally as raucous—Tombstone, Arizona, to name one, and Dodge City, Kansas for another. Tombstone mushroomed overnight, its fortune in Arizona silver. Dodge was favored by the commerce of the Kansas prairies. The town was a rail shipping point, the northern end of the Texas cattle trails and a division point on the new Santa Fe Railway. Both were noisy, vulgar, thoroughly Anglo-American. But Lincoln Town, then and throughout its years, never boomed but rather mellowed in Spanish dignity. To this day it still becomes its original name, the Little Village of the Pretty River.

From its mid-nineteenth century birth until 1881, the early settlement and surrounding area were wracked by every conceivable hardship. First were the constant Indian raids, then came the badmen and outlaws, particularly the Harrell gang from Texas who were a threat to every household and every life. Then, finally, came the feud to end all feuds—the Lincoln County War.

Nature alone was kind and generous. The settlers reaped the gifts of the soil watered by the Pretty River; theirs were the unspoiled grasslands and mountain forests, and theirs the sublime climate. At their elbows lay an abundance of raw material for the work of their hands. The coin of the realm mattered little. Left alone they prospered, but when the alien arrived to exploit the land and all resources within, including lives, the Hispanos were deprived of much of their simple wealth. They had to fight to survive.

The Apaches fought for their rights, honestly and bravely. Their raids on La Placita del Rio Bonito were part of a warfare covering the entire West, the Indian's endeavor to hold his own. His method was use of weapons and tactics of battle. But the Texan versus the Hispano, and the Anglo Military against the Indian, was stuff of a different fiber. The trash of Texas, probably rejects in their own homeland, pushed westward with the cattlemen; hence, the sound of the name *Tejano*, the very presence of the boastful, ignorant cowboy, was held in revulsion by the original settlers of Lincoln Town.

The Lincoln County War was not a cattle feud as most people suppose. It was a fight for supremacy between two rival merchants in Lincoln Town. One was the Murphy-Dolan-Riley combine, whose store was at the west end of town; the other was the Tunstall-McSween faction with a smaller business halfway along the one long street. John Tunstall was a young Englishman who operated a ranch on the Rio Feliz, some distance south of the Bonito. But distance meant little on the frontier. He took a partner, Alexander McSween, for operation of his mercantile interests. Although Lawrence Murphy had gone into semiretirement before the war, he was still involved in it along with his partners—John H. Riley and James J. Dolan. Another partner, Col. Emil Fritz, died in Germany in 1874. In 1877, when the fracas commenced, the Murphy firm was known as J.J. Dolan & Company.

Oddly, the leaders in the Lincoln County War were born outside the United States. Lawrence Murphy was a native of Ireland, as were his partners Dolan and Riley. Colonel Emil Fritz came from Germany. John Tunstall was from England and his partner, Alexander McSween, a Scots Canadian, was from Prince Edward Island. Not quite so foreign was Billy the Kid, an Irish American from New York City. Tom O'Folliard, the Kid's most cherished pal, was from Uvalde, Texas, of Irish parentage. The rest of the gang were mostly outlaw Texans of assorted ancestries.

Lincoln County was sparsely populated then. Other than Lincoln and White Oaks, there were no towns of consequence. Roswell was a shack or two, the site of Carlsbad a cow camp. Seven Rivers, near the future Carlsbad, was carousing ground for cowboys, gamblers, and outlaws. But the county contained some of the largest ranches in the United States, east and west of the Pecos. One was the vast holdings of John S. Chisum, with headquarters at South Spring near Roswell, whose cattle were said to number somewhere near 100,000 head. These baronies of grassy magnitude were patrons of the Murphy-Dolan-Riley enterprise in Lincoln Town. The profits earned were enormous. And it stood to good reason that Murphy & Company asked for no competition.

Too, there were dirty politics involved. Murphy was a henchman of the Santa Fe Ring, a clique of Republican lawyers in the Territorial capital. Their specialties were buying the Spanish-American vote and favoring moneyed interests in the Territory—money in Lincoln County being John Chisum and the bowlegged brotherhood whose wealth grazed the wide pampas. The Ring needed Murphy and Murphy needed the Ring. Not until July, 1879, did Las Vegas—145 buzzard-flight miles due north of Lincoln Town—become a railhead supply base for merchandise shipped in from the "States." Before that time all Murphy wares for sale and barter came west over the Santa Fe Trail by wagon train, then southward from either Las Vegas or Santa Fe by the same slow conveyance. Murphy's price tags, therefore, were damnable to behold, but the customers readily paid.

John Tunstall's concern was minding his own business—the ranch on the Feliz, and the store in Lincoln. His partner, McSween, was somehow involved with a $10,000 insurance policy left by Murphy's deceased partner, Colonel Emil Fritz. Things were getting hot around town in 1877, but hotter they'd be the following year. In January of 1878 a young cowboy found a job on Tunstall's ranch—a cowboy who rode around wearing several names. William Bonney was one, Kid Antrim for another, as well as Henry McCarty (which was probably his real name), Austin Antrim, and always The Kid. Later, however, the world would know him as Billy the Kid.

From his first day on the job—he was 19 at the time—he took a liking to Tunstall, who was comparatively young, jovial, kind, and, above all, honest. Never before had The Kid known all such qualities wrapped up in one person. Tunstall was the exact opposite of Lawrence Murphy.

Tunstall had no hand in politics, nor did he lead the social activities, which were considerable in Lincoln Town. Murphy was the helmsman there, due to his connections in Santa Fe. What with politics, the whirl of gaiety, and the complete monopoly of commerce, Murphy wanted no thorn of an Englishman to fester in his Hibernian side.

John Tunstall was found shot to death on the trail south of Lincoln Town that led to the Feliz ranch. The body was found on February 13. Billy the Kid was there to view it, and vow revenge.

The Kid had come out from New York with his mother at a very early age, to wind up in New Mexico via Coffeeville, Kansas, and Pueblo, Colorado—thence to Santa Fe, Silver City, and Lincoln. He is said to have killed a blacksmith in Silver City at age 12, but probably didn't. The blacksmith had insulted The Kid's mother. If so, it was the only justifiable killing he committed. All others, and there were many, were done in cold blood.

As a result of Tunstall's murder the Lincoln County War broke out in flame. It was accepted beyond suspicion that Murphy agents had committed the crime. Furthermore, it was suspected that the Lincoln County sheriff, William Brady, was among the killers. To Billy the Kid's way of thinking, it was Brady who had fired the shot.

Men took sides. One faction was led by McSween with The Kid as his ready gunslinger. The opposing party was made up of Murphy-Dolan-Riley sympathizers, or hired fighters. From February to July 1878, Lincoln Town was the scene of constant battle. Riflefire and slugs from six-shooters took over the one long street as 200 marksmen, each for his own cause, fired at anything that moved. Killings became a matter of course. The Reverend T.F. Ealy, a Presbyterian minister, claimed that during his five-month residence in Lincoln he conducted 30 funerals, and only one of the deceased had died a natural death. There were, of course, others who did not enjoy the dignity of a funeral.

On April 1, Billy the Kid avenged Tunstall's murder by killing Sheriff Brady and his deputy, Hindman, as the two walked down the street unsuspecting any danger. The ambush took place from behind an adobe wall beside the Tunstall-McSween store. Ironically, Tunstall's grave is said to be against the same wall.

The Kid kept clear of Lincoln after Brady's ambush, but the feud continued its noisy course. He was on hand, however, for the Three Day Battle the following July. This was the reprisal for the sheriff's murder. It was the fight to end all fights. And it finished the Lincoln County War. The battleground was in front of and around the McSween store. McSween was killed and his house burned to the ground. Billy the Kid and his gang took to the flat country north of the Capitan Mountains to earn a sorry living at rustling cattle. They preyed on ranches large and small, and especially on the Long Rail and Jinglebob herds of John S. Chisum.

Meanwhile, the county commissioners had brought in Pat Garrett, a tall Texan, to be their sheriff and clean up the thievery. This Garrett did, capturing The Kid at Stinking Spring near Fort Sumner in December 1880. The young outlaw spent two months in the Santa Fe jail, until his trial at Mesilla in March 1881. He was charged with the murder of Sheriff Brady, although he also boasted of taking nineteen lives. There were two more killings yet to come. Judge Bristol sentenced him to be hanged, the execution set for May 13, 1881, a Friday. He was taken to Lincoln Town in the custody of Deputy Bob Olinger, to be jailed there until his execution.

But, of course, he didn't die there. Any Billy the Kid expert will supply all the details. These experts reside the world over, from Carrizozo to Rotterdam, from Zanzibar to Walla Walla. Ask the readers of Walter Noble Burns, George Coe, Frazier Hunt, Maurice Fulton, George Curry, and a dozen more writers who knew the ways of the hoodlum as they did the keyboards of their gunsmoking typewriters. Ask the members of the National Association of Outlaw and Lawman History, of Logan, Utah; the Western Writers of America; the pistol-packing Cowboy Club of Munich, Germany; the Stetsoned gents in the Corral of the London (England) Westerners; even Egypt's President Sadat, a self-confessed enthusiast for all things Western, including cowboys and Indians.

But above all, attend the annual Last Escape of Billy the Kid pageant held every August in Lincoln Town, three days of historic reenactment, dancing, eating and fun. There you will learn that the Murphy-Dolan store building was acquired by the county in 1880 for a new courthouse. That in an upstairs room in March of the following year Billy the Kid arrived to be shackled and handcuffed, constantly guarded as he awaited execution. That on April 28 by a clever ruse he overpowered his guard and shot him on the stairway, and from a corner window shot and killed his other persecutor, Bob Olinger, as the deputy came across the street from the Wortley Hotel. "Hullo, Bob," called The Kid, shotgun pointed out the window. The shot rang out, the guard fell. By sundown, after acquiring a horse, Billy the Kid was loping across Capitan Gap to temporary freedom; two months and a half of it, until Sheriff Pat Garrett fired the shot in Pete Maxwell's house at Fort Sumner on July 14, 1881. The Kid died with twenty-one dead men to his record, one for each year of his life.

If you enjoy pageants and tourists, go to Lincoln Town in August. But for the sheer peace and beauty of it, go any other time, for the quiet months will display Lincoln's true character—clean and rural, shy of the rat race, of harsh concrete and reinforcing iron, of small hearts, and the commercial mind. If it were not for US 380 that runs east to west along the single thoroughfare, blessing would be complete.

The old Murphy-Dolan store (Lincoln County Courthouse) is now a state museum. The county seat was moved to Carrizozo in 1913, and the building became a school. The state of New Mexico bought it in 1936 for restoration.

Today other buildings of historic significance have been purchased by the state. All are restored and maintained, their preservation assured. The old Wortley Hotel, which had burned to the ground sometime in the past, is a hostelry with an atmosphere of the quiet, unhurried long ago. There is the *torreon*, the watchtower built by the earliest Spanish settlers as a defense against Apache raids. The old Tunstall-McSween store is state-owned, a museum. And the Sheriff Brent house, Watson house, Fresquez house, site of the McSween house are all in the safekeeping of the State of New Mexico. And there are other grand old houses of the Territorial period waiting to be bought, restored, and lived in. The whole town is a museum.

Lincoln itself is classed as Historical Zone A, protected from exploitation. A master plan has been drawn for controlled growth, restoration, and preservation. There is even a possibility that the highway could be moved south against the hills, to bypass the town.

It is only natural that Billy the Kid and the Lincoln County War will spring alive in the mind of the tourist and casual visitor, for to such sound and fury the very ground is a memorial. But to those who look beyond violence and sensation, the quieter years are the essence of Lincoln—the earthy, rough-hewn, sunburnt West of yesterday after Billy the Kid had been put in his grave, the gun returned to its holster, and greed succeeded by the friendliness and hospitality peculiar to the American West. That West is still there. Only the clocks and calendars are changed.

Alive in memory is the frontier spirit, and the people who lived it. The hush of the dark hours when the harp lamps gave their easy flame, and the windows glowed with a soft yellow light for saddled Spanish ponies at the hitching racks along the street. The gentle pat of equine hoofs on the unpaved earth, the creak of saddle leather. And always the sound of the Bonito, the vein that kept the valley alive. The lifeblood of the Little Village of the Pretty River.

Aerial view of Kuaua Pueblo ruins, Coronado State Monument, looking east toward the Rio Grande, Santa Ana Indian farmlands, and the foothills of the Sandias. *New Mexico State Tourist Bureau*

Ground floor walls, Kuaua Pueblo ruins, and the Museum
at Coronado State Monument before a backdrop of Sandia
Mountain. *New Mexico State Tourist Bureau*

Pueblo deities, murals in The Painted Kiva, Kuaua. *Eloy Blea*

A close-up of the Stone Lions of Yapashi. Note antler
offering. *National Park Service*

Relaxing on the plaza in Old Town, Albuquerque, with the Bandstand and the church of San Felipe de Neri in the background. *Dick Kent*

Ruins of the old mission at Taos Pueblo below the snowcapped Sacred Mountain. *Photographer unknown*

Timeless: a Taos Pueblo Indian beside the straw-flecked ado walls of the ancient pueblo. *New Mexico State Tourist Bure*

The irrigated Valley of Chimayó, about a mile upstream from *El Santuario.* Here, according to legend,
the Christ Child walks by night—healing the sick,
comforting the bereaved, and wearing out His shoes.
John L. Sinclair

Chimayó weaver. Generations of Chimayeños living in the mountains of
northern New Mexico have produced some of the most distinctive and
durable textiles in America. *New Mexico State Tourist Bureau*

Chimayó weaver at his loom in the shop of the
Ortegas. *New Mexico State Tourist Bureau*

El Santuario de Chimayó, one of the best known shrines in the Southwest, visited by pilgrims for the cure of its healing earth. *New Mexico
State Tourist Bureau*

Main altar, El Santuario, an excellent example of
religious folk art. *New Mexico State Tourist Bureau*

This small crucifix of Our Lord of Esquípulas looks over the *tierra bendita,* the
Blessed Earth in the Chapel of El Posito. *John L. Sinclair*

Crutches and braces hang on the wall in the Chapel of the Holy Child,
left there by people who claim to have been healed by *tierra bendita.*
John L. Sinclair

This iron lock and hasp on the front gate of El Santuario de Chimayó were probably hand-forged by a local artisan when the church was erected early in the nineteenth century. *New Mexico State Tourist Bureau*

Mudhead Kachinas dancing at Shalako
ceremonies, 1897. *Museum of New Mexico
Ben Wittick Collection*

Shalako dancers "crossing to south side of the river to dance on
the plain." *Museum of New Mexico Ben Wittick Collection*

White Oaks "gone ghost": when the nearby gold fields played out, the settlers drifted away, leaving sturdy stone buildings as monuments to the past. *New Mexico State Tourist Bureau*

The late Señor Daniel Carabajal, of Lincoln, in 1941 at 70. As a boy of 10, while playing in front of the courthouse and jail, he watched Billy the Kid make his famous escape on the evening of April 28, 1881.
John L. Sinclair

YGINIO SALAZAR   ISABEL SALAZAR
BORN   BORN
FEB. 14, 1863   SEPT. 3, 1868
DIED   DIED
JAN. 7, 1936   MAY 15, 1935
PAL OF BILLY THE KID

HERE LIES SHEBA HURST — the wit of the Black Range boom town at Kingston. *New Mexico State Tourist Bureau*

The fabulous Bridal Chamber silver mine at Lake Valley produced about three million dollars in horn, or free silver. *Historical Society of New Mexico*

During the "Three Day Battle" at the McSween store in Lincoln, Yginio Salazar fell to the ground as he fled and pretended he was shot. He lay "as a deadman" until the battle was over, then got up and walked away. *John L. Sinclair*

Through the portals of the old assay office at Hillsboro
passed hopeful hearts and hands toting samples of
ore. *New Mexico State Tourist Bureau*

Stagecoaches on exhibit in the patio of the Pala
of the Governors, Santa Fe. At right is Sad
Orchard's *Mountain Pride. Museum of Ne
Mexico*

Crumbling rock walls, a barred window and door, all that remain of the jail at Hillsboro. *New Mexico State Tourist Bureau*

A ranch near Rodeo with the Peloncillo Mountains in the background. *John L. Sinclair*

18

MESILLA:
THE PLACE AT THE CROSSROADS

THERE ARE IN THIS WORLD certain bits of geography, God-created or manmade, that hold themselves aloof, demand to be noticed above their more commonplace neighbors. An island of the sea, for instance, surf-pounded, remote. Or an oasis in the desert, a haven of green amid the abounding wasteland. A mountain in the Indian country, known to be sacred to pagan gods. A venerable inn, associated with men of greatness. Or a place at the crossroads, ripened with age, serene under the sun, garnished with the spice of history, with the flavor of the sunburnt West of yesterday... Mesilla, New Mexico, is a monument of this kind.

To find Mesilla drive to rapidly expanding Las Cruces, seat of Doña Ana county. There Highway 70, running east and west from Alamogordo across the Organ mountains, meets Highway 85 (now Interstate 25, Pan American Highway), the Albuquerque to El Paso artery. Mesilla lies two miles south of the heart of town, toward the Rio Grande. That's a short distance by foot or car, but as long as its distinctive atmosphere is allowed to remain the span is immense in time and difference.

Las Cruces is a booming trade center for nearby military bases. From a green-bordered agricultural town of 12,000 in 1950, it has spread block by block, street by street, into one of New Mexico's largest cities. Everything is built to pattern and the straight line, loaded with efficiency and hygiene, the bigger-and-better ideal, the forward look. It's an urbanite-suburbanite's dream. Its only color is highly polished glass. But in spite of it all, Las Cruces contains some very nice people and must be an extremely comfortable place for living.

At the town's eastern skyline the dramatically scenic Organ mountains range north to south abreast of the Rio Grande Valley—peaks barren and rock-capped, spires and pinnacles, sheer drop-off walls of sun-burnished granite, a world of desert magnificence, painted with colors that vary according to the time of day. There are hazy reds, pinks and lavenders, grey and cobalt blue—and a sunset extravaganza. Most conspicuous are the organ pipe spires nested together that give this spectacular range its name.

To the west of the mountains lies the river valley, wide, irrigated, fertile, flat, green against the arid desert. Corn, alfalfa, watered pastures; here world-famous chile peppers are grown, harvested, and even canned in this strip of bounty. And here is spread the largest pecan orchard in the world. The fields are a patchwork of green. Squat adobe houses are shaded by leafy cottonwood and box elders, a checkerboard of ditches carrying the vital water from artery canals. And hard against this ribbon of fertility, at the edge of "big town," lies Mesilla Plaza, a naturally sleepy place if Las Cruces would permit, a village more Mexican-American than Spanish-American, a child of the blood of two republics.

Mesilla has a long and varied history, suffering under and triumphing over men of assorted colors, creeds, and political views, all selecting the ancient plaza for their special purposes. And the effect is there today in the atmosphere, in the leisurely movement of the people. The shadow of the Spaniard is every-where, though not so pervasive as in Rio Grande plazas north of Albuquerque. Because the Mexican Americans of Mesilla are familiar with El Paso and beyond the border, they look southward with extreme respect for the motherland.

A bandstand centers the plaza, of course. And there is the shade of trees. Good taste and the use of adobe is everywhere evident. The sunbright feeling of *southern* New Mexico, in contrast with the cool blue sky of the *northern* half of the state, is definitely here—being less lofty in altitude with none of that certain chill of winter. The Mexican flavor hints strongly that Chihuahua is just over the south horizon.

The plaza was designated one of New Mexico's state monuments a few years ago, by act of legislature. For that reason alone it may be hoped that experts in gimcrackery will be given the cold shoulder should they try to in-vade—and try they will. For in spots where tourists gather the ring of the cash register more often than not takes precedence over tradition, cheapens the homespun works of centuries past, and pollutes God-given natural beauty. A hope and a prayer that the custodians of Mesilla Plaza will stand against any who seek to blemish their prize.

Prehistoric sites found in the vicinity indicate that pioneer Indian occupation occurred about A.D. 900. The first Europeans to tread this ground were Alvar Nuñez Cabeza de Vaca and his three companions. They were making the long trek from the Texas Gulf coast, where they had been shipwrecked, to Mexico City to report to the Spanish viceroy all they had been told by the Indians concerning the fabled Golden Cities of Cíbola somewhere to the north. They were survivors of the ill-fated Narvaez expedition to Florida. The year was 1536. Alvar Nuñez had once been appointed by the King of Spain to be Treasurer of the *Rio de las Palmas*, a stream later to be called the *Rio Grande Bravo del Norte*, the "Great Bold River of the North." The party crossed this river close to where Mesilla Plaza was to be. The Spaniard was no doubt unaware that just then he was wading through his "Treasury."

Antonio de Espejo, first explorer to follow the Rio Grande northward, passed the site of Mesilla in 1582. It was Espejo who named this region *Nuevo Mejico*, or "New Mexico," a province of New Spain. Sixteen years later the same route was followed by Juan de Oñate and his long train of colonists. They had come up from Zacatecas to establish the first seat of government in what is now the United States. For that they chose the Tewa pueblo of Yuque Yunque, far upstream near the present Española.

With Oñate came the first mention of Mesilla in the archives. His chronicler wrote of a Piros Indian pueblo, one called Tzenaquel. This was officially named *Trenaquel da la Mesilla*, or "Trenaquel of the Little Tableland." When later the Franciscan missions were established, Trenaqual and other lower river pueblos were given to the care of the missionary priest Fray Juan de Clara. This most southerly pueblo lay just west of the Rio Grande.

Mesilla had not yet become a "Place at the Crossroads." But it was soon to be an important station on the Camino Real that carried exports of New Mexico down to Mexico City, by oxcart, muleback and lackeyback, a distance of 1,500 miles. The cargoes were mostly hides, grains, textiles, as well the assorted gains of Indian exploitation by the Spaniards. Apache slaves wore price tags. Northbound merchandise were things that the northern frontier could make use of— ironwork, farm tools and such, and supplies for the Franciscan missions such as clerical vestments and necessities for the altars. And some really prize paintings

129

that had reached Vera Cruz from Spain. If Willa Cather is correct in her novel, *Death Comes For The Archbishop*, even a genuine El Greco came up the *Camino*, camped briefly at Mesilla, then found a dusty home in the mission church at the Indian pueblo of Zia, near Bernalillo—although no sign of it appears there today.

By 1680 the Pueblo Indians had swallowed enough of Spanish exploitation. Under Popé, their Tewa medicine man and leader, they rose in bands and killed four hundred of their tormentors, including twenty-one priests. They desecrated and burned the northern missions. About nineteen hundred Spaniards—men, women and children, led southward by the angry governor Antonio de Otermín—found sanctuary near Mesilla. There they quartered for twelve years, were supplied with provisions by Father Ayeta who founded the mission at Guadalupe del Paso—now El Paso, Texas. . . . Or, rather, Juarez, Chihuahua, across the bend of the Rio Grande. . . . The refugees returned to the north with the reconquest of Santa Fe by Don Diego de Vargas in 1692. That colorful army made camp at Mesilla on its long march to victory.

Traffic on the Camino Real resumed when peace, such as it was, came to New Mexico. But the Apache menace was everywhere. The corrals and hovels that comprised Mesilla were especially vulnerable. It was a place where oxdriver and muleteer met, to chat awhile and rest the weary foot, to water and nourish the traction between Mexico City and Santa Fe when only Paso del Norte, Chihuahua City, Durango, Zacatecas, were the larger towns between. Far to the west of Mesilla lay California, to the east the region later to be called Texas. Both were dangerous to penetrate, and at that time were of no consequence whatsoever.

With the turn of the nineteenth century came Spanish bluebloods who received land grants from the Spanish Crown. Among them was the legendary Doña Ana de Cordova—for whom it is said Doña Ana County is named—and who maintained vast herds and cultivated extensive orchards and irrigated fields on her hacienda eight miles upriver. It was then that Mesilla took true village form and ceased to be a mere stopover convenience on the Chihuahua Trail. Around the plaza were built the *chozas*, the homes of her many field workers, herders and *vaqueros*. The fields of today adjacent to Mesilla first felt the plough when they became the *ranchitos* of the servants of the great *patrona*.

But it took the nineteenth century to establish the importance of Mesilla, then whittle it down to the sleepy plaza it is today. Mexico won her independence from Spain in 1821 when New Mexico became a province of the new republic. The first wagon trains on the Santa Fe Trail brought huge cargoes of American merchandise down from Missouri, unloading on Santa Fe Plaza, and the Chihuahua Trail that served Mesilla was a southern extension of that trade route. At midcentury, in 1848, General Stephen Watts Kearny and his Army of the West arrived to banish the Mexican governor from Santa Fe and claim New Mexico as a Territory of the United States. That is, all New Mexico except for Mesilla.

131

The Treaty of Guadalupe Hidalgo, written that same year, established the Rio Grande as the boundary line between the two republics—the United States on the east, Mexico to the west. As Mesilla was on the west side, the switch in geography gave it the status of a Mexican border town. Colonists from Chihuahua began to move in, with sixty families led by Rafael Ruelas. They were joined in 1850 by Father Ramon Ortiz, who became the first commissioner of the La Mesilla Colony Grant. His application for land was approved the next year and the Church of San Albino was built. Another three years, then the Gadsden Treaty was ratified—the purchase by the United States of all lands west of the Rio Grande, which included most of southern Arizona. The price was ten million dollars. The American flag was raised on Mesilla Plaza November 16, 1854.

Mesilla's population reached its peak in 1857. It was the largest town between San Antonio, Texas, and San Francisco, California. The Butterfield Trail and its famous stage line made Mesilla an important horse-change and supply station. Connections were made at Mesilla with the north-to-south Santa Fe-Chihuahua stages. And at last the plaza became the Place at the Crossroads.

But it took the Civil War to put Mesilla truly on the map. The years that followed the Blue and Gray strife were hectic for the old town. As the seat of Doña Ana County, its authority covered all southern New Mexico and the south half of Arizona. The *Mesilla Times* became one of the Territory's leading newspapers. The trial of the outlaw Billy the Kid was held in its courthouse. The United States Land Office was established there, charged with business pertaining to all public lands in southern New Mexico. It was a key station on the first military telegraph. Also, it was the first capital of the Territory of Arizona.

Brief as it was, the distinction came about when on July 26, 1861, Col. J.R. Baylor led his Confederate troops to Mesilla where he routed the Union force under Major Lynde. A few days later, on August 1, Baylor proclaimed Mesilla the capital of Arizona, a territory of the Confederate States of America. He put himself at the helm as governor. Baylor's army held the town for one year, until General Carleton and the California Column retook it for the Union on August 15, 1862. Six months later Congress separated Arizona from New Mexico, creating an independent territory. The Rio Grande changed its course that same year, putting Mesilla on the east bank. The railroad arrived in 1881 and the county seat was moved to Las Cruces. And with so much history behind it, Mesilla promptly dozed off to a well-earned rest.

19

TRAIL OF THE MOUNTAIN PRIDE

SADIE ORCHARD made a boast, and lived by it, right to the end of the line. Her boast was that in all of her years of stagedriving, almost daily in the Apache-ridden, bandit-infested Black Range, her coach had not once met a holdup; that is, so long as *she* was mistress of the teams. Her coach has been on exhibit in the Museum of New Mexico since 1935, with a label stating that it was in use from 1878 into the 1900s, and was operated by the Kingston, Hillsboro and Lake Valley stage line. On a panel over the coach doors is painted the name that smacks of trail dust and rawhide:

MOUNTAIN PRIDE

Sadie is a legend in southwestern New Mexico, one as boisterously dramatic as the times in which she lived, serene on occasion but never dull. Her story is as unpredictable as the mountain peaks that loomed about her chosen home.

Toughened by the environment, she was not beautiful, yet physically attractive. She is said to have been slender with small hands and feet. But those who remember her speak of her magnificent courage and of the rough stuff of which she was made. She met and survived the rigors of the Wild West, first as a young "parlor girl," with all the tender attributes of the proverbial whore. Then, after surviving some fifty-seven years of ways and methods of the times, she passed from this world as a highly respected frontier matron.

Sadie Orchard came to the Black Range in 1886, one among many professionals imported for stocking the cribs and parlors along Hillsboro's Shady Lane. Hillsboro, then, was a gold-mining camp, shouting the Bonanza Call on every street corner at every hour of the day and night. The excitement started in May of

1877 when two prospectors, Dan Dugan and Dave Stitzel, braved the hostile Apache country to hunt for gold. They found "sign" on Percha Creek, a canyon on the east slope of the Mimbres Mountains.

134

At first, on examining the "float," they decided their find was of little worth. Dugan threw his handful back to the ground, but Stitzel slipped his "rocks" into the burro packbag. Secretly, he was taking no chances. They whacked their jackasses westward over the Black Range to the Rio Mimbres, where, at an ore mill, Stitzel had his sample assayed. The report gave an estimate of $160 to the ton. The pair had apparently separated somewhere along the trail, so Stitzel headed his burro, or burros, back to the lucky spot on Percha Creek. He staked two claims, the Opportunity and the Ready Pay mines. He sank a shaft and brought out five tons of gold ore, which after milling brought him $400.

Dugan, hearing of Stitzel's luck, returned in late June with another partner—one Frank Pitcher. They scouted around for a likely claim, stopped to kill a rattlesnake in the brush, then sat down to rest. The rock they sat on contained the glorious sight and feel of gold ore. They staked a claim there on the spot and named it the Rattlesnake Mine.

Now the Black Range is far from just an ordinary range of mountains. It extends its dark verdure for sixty-five miles on a north to south course, from Wahoo Peak to Thompson Cone, west and abreast of the Rio Grande Valley. Viewed from a distance it is appropriately named—its skyline somber, forbidding. Today its heights look eastward and downward on the huge reservoir of Elephant Butte Lake, and on the town once sensibly named Hot Springs—Sierra County seat—now officially and unfortunately called Truth or Consequences.

The Black Range summits elevate to more than ten thousand feet above sea level, to feed on cloud and blaze with glorious sunsets, to tempt the snows and thunderheads. It is a world of deep canyons and rockslides, lush meadows and a dense growth of pine, fir, oak, juniper, spruce, and aspen. Game abounds—deer, bear, wild turkey—and always the stealthy pad of the mountain lion. The silence of clear starlit nights is broken by the yip-yap of the never-satisfied coyote. The streams are the fulfillment of an angler's dream, the canyons sanctuary for those who seek solitude. The Range is a botanist's paradise, a herpetologist's laboratory, and for the enthusiast of things mineral the absolute rainbow's end.

There is no record of Sadie Orchard's whereabouts at the time of the Dugan-Stitzel strike in 1877, and no one seemed to have known her maiden name. All we know is that she was English, born and probably raised in the Stepney district of London. She was far from the manor born, for Stepney contains Limehouse and Whitechapel, two of London's seamier sections.

She possessed a natural fondness for horses and a high seat on a vehicle, with a handful of whip and lines. This she no doubt attained by familiarity with the huge Shire dray horses that tractioned the carts and wagons down cobbled streets from docks and warehouses. Where she learned the art of whoredom can easily be determined, for the natural propensities of mariners in dockside pubs are somewhat similar to those of miners "gophering" in the Black Range.

It took no time at all for news of the Percha gold strike to hit the "muckstick and jackass" fraternity, and they flocked in from all directions. Nick Galles who built the first store was an early relative of the family that today operates one of the largest automobile dealerships in New Mexico. The first home of any distinction went up the following August, out of a hodgepodge of shacks and tents. Soon a town took shape—a quantity of saloons for the relief of cotton-spitting miners, dance halls for the frolicksome, gambling rooms for the adventurers, and sweet havens of tenderness for relief of the overly virile. Assay offices, livery stables, wagon yards, general stores, a church. But a town yet without a semblance of a name.

By December, just six months after Dugan and Stitzel killed the lucky rattlesnake, a name was provided—Hillsborough. A man transplanted from Ohio thought to honor his home town by suggesting it. Lady Luck played a hand and "Hillsborough" was drawn on the town lottery. However, being sticklers, the miners objected to the "ugh," and the name was shortened to Hillsboro. Sure enough, there is a town in Ohio once called Hillsborough, now shortened to Hillsboro. Soon after, when the newly formed Sierra County required a seat for its government, Hillsboro won the honor. Later, the seat was shifted to Hot Springs on the Rio Grande, today known as Truth or Consequences. Hillsboro's population in 1878 was 250 souls, 700 by 1882.

Whatever the tally was in 1886, when Sadie Orchard arrived, the population contained a hearty number of enterprising citizens, gents bent on profit from the shafts under the gallows frames, giving joyfully the sweat of the brow and the heave of the muckstick, the miners themselves and all and sundry who sought to reap fortune from their toil. And among the most ambitious of opportunists was Sadie, tender in the bloom of twenty-three (no one knows exactly), humbled in the shadow of Shady Lane, ambitious to stand erect as a tinseled

"Madam of the House." And while Sadie dreamed the dreams sublime, a new and equally boisterous "boom camp" had grown on the high trail against the Black Range—Kingston, with a comfortable altitude of 6,000 feet, lush and green with the scent of pine sweeping down from the mountain bulwark to the west.

136

Today, Kingston is a place of memories, of landmarks and monuments, of blissful repose after decades of riotous bonanza and slow decay. Once the acidy fragrance of giant cottonwoods along the main street was evident in the thin air. Today the old Victorio Hotel, named for the Apache chief who once terrorized the district, stands lonely and forlorn. There are wrecks and hulks of miners' cabins, the remains of the newspaper office, and the old graveyard lush with tumbleweed and thistle. Here is the resting place of Sheba Hurst, the humorous character Mark Twain wrote into his *Roughing It*. Sheba the wit and critic of old Kingston days and ways. A plain slab with the inscription "Sheba" identifies the clay.

The old firebell, once used to call willing volunteers, has rung in modern days to hail the arrival of the mail car and summon the scant population to pick up their letters. The Percha Bank, a large stone building built in 1882, is now a museum and art gallery, still offering a hint of financial business in the presence of the donation box. Deposits only, no withdrawals. Mr. and Mrs. Paul Vetter are the curators, each equipped with that special sense of humor it takes to bring a ghost town alive. And with all they have to offer "once upon a time" Kingston is humorously alive. On exhibit is the walk-in safe, a relic of this very building, and rooms filled with all manner of frontier memorabilia—from ox yokes to mining tools, newspapers, and photographs; and old bottles, empty today but once alive with the vintage.

Kingston was a silver camp that came to being with the discovery of the Empire and Iron King lodes in 1880. The town won its name from the latter mine, when the cry of "Eureka!" echoed in the mountains and the klondike horde swarmed in. Silver float was everywhere around, and in 1882 a townsite was laid out. They blazed a wagon road eastward down the slope to Hillsboro, to become the thoroughfare of bearded hopefuls and their understanding burros. Town lots sold for $500, the price of everything was exorbitant. There was a brick kiln and stone quarry and buildings grew as thick as lambsquarters.

A butcher shop sold beef and pork and goat's meat, as well as venison, bear, antelope, and wild turkey. There was a Dr. Guthrie, always too drunk for serious practice. And one fine day of that boisterous year found a grizzled old "prospect-man" whacking two heavily laden burros into town from over the hill. He appeared to be "hunting for color." But instead his rawhide *alforjas*, hitched to his packsaddle prongs, contained no miner's gear at all—but three hundred cigars, six bottles of champagne, five gallons of whiskey, and eighteen bottles of beer. He sold the cargo on the street as fast as he could hand out the items and pocket the cash. Legend has it that the street was so crowded it required ninety minutes to walk a half-mile.

Kingston was the center of toil and entertainment, of shrewd commerce, and a repository for the fruits of the shaft. Round about were the mighty producers, among them The Solitaire, The Blackie, The Lady Franklin, The Bullion, The Comstock, and—fatefully—The Miner's Dream. This last was operated by a certain Edward L. Doheny, teammate of Albert Bacon Fall, silver miners both who met each other in Kingston and formed an alliance resulting in Teapot Dome, the scandal that besmirched the Harding administration. By 1893, thirteen years since the discovery, the Empire and Iron King lodes had produced seven million dollars in silver and related ores.

Pastime enterprise was tailored to masculine taste. There were twenty-two saloons going full rackety-blast; gambling and dance halls were bright and noisy under the harp lamps. There was Big Anne's Orpheum, competing with Pretty Sam's Casino. Shady Lane was kept well stocked, offering love at bargain prices. And a theatre where, it is said, the silvery voice and heavenly looks of Lillian Russell charmed all and sundry at the oil footlights. There is some dispute about that, however, in the probable fact that Lillian spent a short time as a guest at the Horseshoe Ranch up the Black Range, and never saw the stage in Kingston. But her troupe performed. Sadie said so herself.

In Sadie Orchard's time there were three newspapers that kept the populace informed, while the Percha Bank was the camp's beating heart. And a G.A.R. post, a Masonic Temple, never to forget the Knights of Pythias and Odd Fellows halls. Fourteen general merchandise stores dealt everything from calico to potatoes along the main street, three hotels took care of the constant stream of travelers, and seven sawmills ran day and night to satisfy the demand for lumber . . . . But there was no jail, merely a snubbing post where prisoners were tied and gagged.

Paydays called for nights of gladness. Then the streets and Shady Lane throbbed with humanity, sounding off and smelling of dusty bachelors. There were arguments over the felt-topped poker tables, resulting sometimes in gunfire but more often the thud of clenched fists—and all the while the roulette wheel went clickety-click. . . . And just as sure as the camp was without a jail, likewise it was shy of a church.

In fact, not a soul had thought one necessary—not even the godly, or rather the half-godly. Until one pious night, just for the hell of it, a small group carried a hat from gambling casino to dance hall, on to the red-lighted doorways of Shady Lane. They asked for contributions to a good cause. The gamblers, the harlots, the sinners in general—all the low-down riffraff that leached upon the fleshpots—gladly dropped cartwheel dollars in the upturned hat, until it heaped itself above the brim with fifteen hundred round beauties, the amount needed for building a "meeting house." The walls went up and a tested preacher took charge; tested, that is, for his ability to deliver loud and entertaining religion. Behind the preacher's stand blazoned the consoling words: THE GOLDEN GATE.

Whatever trail Sadie followed from Stepney Green to the Mountain Pride, a girl of her caliber could be assured a better one stretched ahead. First, the slimy cobblestones could be improved on for the profession of streetwalking. And somewhere beyond the sunset was relief from the smell of docks at Limehouse Reach. The Atlantic was to be crossed, and the prairies of North America, then sanctuary found in the brand-new boom town of Hillsboro, where silver dollars were plenty in supply and generous free-spending hearts abounded. Soon, very soon, sweet petite Sadie would graduate to a full-fledged "madam," with a "house" of her own and the opportunity to be motherly to a bevy of calloused hookers, most of them older than herself.

Up the ladder toward respectability.

And, bless Pat, that's exactly what happened!

As an aid to Sadie's prosperity, a new and fabulous silver camp was enjoying wealth equal to the vaults of Croesus seventeen miles south of Hillsboro, along the road that led to the deserts of the New Mexico-Chihuahua border. End of the line for stagecoach and wagon traffic was the healthy town of Lake Valley, small in everything except for the enormous profits it provided its very lively population.

Lake Valley's story begins in 1878 when a cowboy named George Lufkin, after saving up some "grub money," staked out claims covering a hundred acres south of Berrenda Creek and east of the Mimbres Mountains. Lufkin was always short of cash, because his method was to "just cowboy around some." Try as he might he could never garner enough to develop his holdings. But there was something about this particular stretch of earth that indicated silver deposits under the grass. A man has a right to his suspicions, and Lufkin was "superstitious aplenty."

So he let his claims lie while he chased around with the cows. Two years passed, when in 1880 two veteran prospectors staked out a checkerboard of claims around those held by Lufkin. Then, a year later, a syndicate of Easterners bought out all the claims, paying $450,000. This enterprise was known as the Sierra Grande Company.

Then another prospect-man stepped into the scenery. John Leavett was a blacksmith by trade. He liked his metals in the form of horseshoes and miners' drills and the heavy weight of an anvil. But a man has the right to go scouting for raw stuff down below if he thinks it might be there. That's his privilege. Leavett leased a piece of ground from the Sierra Grande Company and got to "poking around." He found the tidiest nest of hornsilver a man could lay eyes on, a bonanza strike for any prospector worthy of the name. But Leavitt wasn't a prospector, neither the "single-blanket" nor the "double" variety. He was a blacksmith and loved it. So rather than work his lease, he turned it back to the Sierra Grande folks in exchange for several thousand dollars.

The company got its mucksticks out and went to work, dug a little deeper and struck a pocket of pure silver that seemed to go on and on forever. Here was a mine that deserved a tender, loving name, so they recorded it as *The Bridal Chamber*. Tramload after tramload, the bounty was hauled to the surface until a room walled, floored, and roofed of pure unalloyed silver was chiseled out. The space was about the size of a small dining room, about ten feet long by seven wide. In the first six months of operation *The Bridal Chamber* delivered one million dollars worth—not ore, but the pure horn stuff. The next six months yielded $750,000 in bullion. Water was brought into the area and Lake Valley took shape.

So lucrative was the industry of mining in the camps of Kingston, Hillsboro, and up and down the Black Range that the Santa Fe Railway laid branch tracks up from Rincón on the Albuquerque-El Paso line to Lake Valley, called Daly in railroader's language. The trains started rumbling in 1884.

Here's a question: how far along the bonanza road was the Percha District traveling toward ultimate prosperity? Toward the riches of Solomon, the gems of Cleopatra, the diamonds of the Rand, the renderings unto Caesar, the stocks and bonds and securities of the Rockefellers and the Mellons?

140

Well, the *Solitaire Mine* was reaping an outcrop that assayed sixty percent silver—with one solid specimen weighing a hundred pounds. Jefferson Reynolds, the banker, was part owner of the *Brilliant Mine*, the hole that assayed in Denver at from $153 to $1,700 to the ton. Word of the bountiful Percha reached California, and there Governor Perkins and Senator George Hearst, father of William Randolph Hearst, formed a company and opened the *Superior Mine:* one vein gave out $5,000 dollars in silver in a single day. And from Lake Valley a piece of solid silver, straight from *The Bridal Chamber* and worth $7,000, was sent to the Denver Exposition in 1882.

Until recent times, the ruins of an old adobe building and fallen down corral marked the site of the Orchard Stage Line station, located at the edge of Hillsboro where the road turns south to Lake Valley. Massive cottonwoods spread their leafy limbs thereabout, but the forlorn spot is now open to the bountiful ever-therapeutic New Mexican sun. There is something clean and wholesome about it—just the right memorial, as long as it lasted, to a body and soul that was good and gallant and a symbol of the wild and reckless frontier.

In 1886, when Sadie began it all, there were two hotels operating in Kingston: the Victorio, catering to the middle classes of mining society—commercial travelers, itinerant medical personalities—and The Mountain Pride Hotel, a place of elegance that matched the prosperity of the town, fashionable with those who had coin to spend, lawyers, judges, politicians, mining tycoons down from Denver or out from the Coast or on a business visit west from New York.

Do you like oysters served on the half-shell, shipped from the Texas Gulf in iced barrels? Or shrimp from Sonora, wines from Europe, and every delicacy imaginable popular in New York or San Francisco? Do you love to wallow in hotel luxury possible in the nineteenth-century boomtowns of the West, such as blessed Central City and Denver, Virginia City and Santa Fe, wherever the rich and powerful congregate? You do? Then you would have stayed at the Mountain Pride.

To top the luxuries, this grand hotel ran a special stagecoach service for its patrons, an early day version of the courtesy cars offered by the better motels of today. The route from Kingston was to and from the railhead at Lake Valley, or down Percha Creek past Hillsboro to its confluence with the Rio Grande abreast of the Caballo Mountains, where the Santa Fe-Albuquerque-El Paso stage line was met, passengers picked up or unloaded. This special courtesy coach was one of the finest ever to roll over the American West—the most comfortable, durable and safe—namely, the Concord. And, too, this particular vehicle had the name of its owner painted on a panel above the doors.

MOUNTAIN PRIDE

Little has been written and published about the life and days of Sadie Orchard, but countless anecdotes concerning her hotelkeeping and stagecoach driving are recounted by men who knew her, with a twinkle and grin when her primrose career is discussed. Most stories are creatively stretched with adventure when told over and over again. One English writer has her arriving in Hillsboro in 1886 as a young prostitute of eighteen years, another at twenty-three, yet another at twenty-eight. Most folks agree on twenty-three. Some have her practicing on Shady Lane, which was probably so, and graduating to a house of her own. Then, in time, taking up the virtuous pursuit of running a boarding house. But her claim to driving the stagecoach for fourteen years is probably not so.

There is no record of the year Sadie married J.A. Orchard, operator of a freighting business in Kingston and a silver mine in the mountains. There is a strong probability he was one of her star boarders.

The late Adlai Feather of Mesilla Park, writer-historian, whose researches concerned southern New Mexico, had this to say about Sadie in a letter dated May 5, 1961:

> The story of Sadie's stage-driving rests entirely upon her own authority, and is perhaps of her own manufacture. Though Orchard was part owner of a stage line, once had a freighting outfit and built a toll road through the Box Canyon, there is no record that he operated the stage after his marriage. But whether truth or fiction, the story has been so often repeated that it probably deserves historical status. There is no record of the date on which she married Orchard—licenses were not required until 1905 and few J.P.'s bothered to report their activities. The marriage was short and stormy and ended in 1900—in action in the civil, criminal, and divorce section of the courts. She took a couple shots at him when he came to take away a team and carriage which she had in her possesion. He was primarily a miner and worked the

Dude Mine on Macho Creek. Apparently the hard feelings between the two continued, for in 1910 she brought action against the miners at the *Dude* who came to Hillsboro and demolished her place. She did not return to Kingson to live after 1900, but had a place in Hillsboro, more of a boarding house than a hotel.

142

Long after bonanza days, bearded and stubbled miners sang the song of Sadie at the Gold Pan Restaurant, where they lived again the joys and sorrows of men and jackasses, long gone to memory, and in their imagination let the delicious feel of first-sight-gold-bearing-float tingle the fanciful mind, all to the tune of whittling knife and discharge of tobacco juice. Much mining, said the wags, was done on the plank bench at the entrance to the restaurant, where the proprietor was forced to stud this furniture with nails to keep it from being whittled away.

But Sadie had her own version of her life's tale, given an interviewer in 1936 at her Orchard Hotel in Hillsboro:

> I came to Kingston, famous mining town in the Black Range Mining District in Sierra County in 1886. At that time Kingston had a population of about 5,000, with a big silver boom going full sway. Dance halls and saloons did a rushing business almost day and night. Fortunes were made, and in some cases lost overnight. Mr. Orchard and I drove the stage line for 14 years. We had two Concord coaches and an express wagon.
>
> I drove four and six horses every day from Kingston to Lake Valley, and sometimes as far as Nutt Station. In those days we did not have roads we can justly boast of in New Mexico today, and my trips were surely trying—especially through picturesque Box Canyon between Kingston and Hillsboro. Many times I had for passengers some very famous people. Lillian Russell, stage star, as far as I know was never in Kingston, but members of her troupe were, and I had occasion to meet the actress.

She made no mention of Shady Lane, however, but duly confessed, "I'm a product of the Old West, and you know in those days we didn't have much chance to practice the niceties and refinements of high society."

The Orchards, bride and groom, probably took their vows while the hotel was in operation and primrose days things of the past. J.A. Orchard, himself, operated a freight line across the Black Range to Silver City, and on to Piños Altos and Mogollon. When Sadie came into the business two stagecoaches were added to the fleet. Passenger service was from Kingston to the railhead at Lake

Valley. It was a twenty-five mile run, with a horse-change stop at the Hillsboro corral. One Concord coach was a veteran of this same trail, that with the name *Mountain Pride* painted on the upper door panels, obviously retired from courtesy service by the luxury hotel in Kingston and purchased by the Orchards. The records have it that this particular vehicle was Sadie's own "pride." Roundtrip passage from Lake Valley to Kingston was $5.50, with fifty pounds of baggage free, ten cents for every excess pound.

143

Now-a-days, for those who voice legends, the mind might flash to small gloved hands holding lines that control the teams of four, to dust clouding the Kingston to Lake Valley road, via Hillsboro, to a coach bucking and swaying through the Box Canyon, speeding on with all the strength and courage of pioneer womanhood high on the driver's seat—whistling, cracking the whip as the spinning wheel throws rocks on contact and the harness creaks and the horses bleed the sweat of loyalty and passengers ride their seats outbound to the waiting train at Lake Valley. The mails are safe, sacked in the "treasure chest" under the driver's seat, along with a probable silver shipment from the Percha Bank. The great stagecoach of the American West is on the trail—the nine-passenger Concord, the finest of them all.

More than that—*much* more than that—*The Mountain Pride*.

Kingston, Hillsboro, Lake Valley—like neighboring Chloride, Grafton, and Gold Dust—roared with the pangs of wealth as men of metals poured in from all directions; lured by the Black Range, throne of the seductive Goddess of Luck, glorious against the sundown skies. Trail's end it was for seekers of gain, honest or otherwise. Silver bounty was spent in town or hauled out by the waiting Lake Valley train. The Percha District was home-sweet-home for gambler, rustler, thug and bunco-steerer, shelter for outlaws "on the dodge." Eureka's hymn was sung to the skies as Sadie and her *Mountain Pride* pitched and swayed along the dusty trails.

Armed bandits ranged the stagecoach routes, but passengers felt secure with Sadie boss of the teams. Bankers and brokers trusted their most precious shipments to her care. One day Bill Holt, an Orchard driver who sometimes relieved Sadie on the Lake Valley run, had a hunch that he would be waylaid before reaching the end of the line. His coach was carrying $75,000 from the Percha Bank for delivery to the train in Lake Valley. So with a splendid idea snug in his head, he cut open four horse collars, selected that day for the traction harness, and placed the divided bounty into the cavities. He then sewed up the gashes and took off in confidence. He was stopped by masked men south of Hillsboro, who searched the coach in every cranny, but were rewarded with a waste of time.

144

"Hell, boys," said Holt, dangling the lines as he sat his high seat, "Mistress Sadie took the money shipment down yesterday. All I got is a load of bank-busted passengers and a mail sack full of love letters."

He drove on to deliver into the hands of a flabbergasted express agent four pieces of harness worth $75,000.

Holdups did happen, but not on the Orchard line. They were made dramatic by gunfire, shots from the bandits and volleys from the coachtop guards. Both sides took equal chances, and the Territorial newspapers were constantly reporting the robberies.

Chloride, a thirty-mile crowflight up the Black Range from Kingston on the Continental Divide, enjoyed prosperity along with the Percha towns, and had its own stagecoach line to the lower and outer world. One day in the 1880s the Pioneer Line that operated from Chloride to Engle, a railroad station on the Rio Grande, was involved in a typically Wild West incident.

Newspaper readers of Cimarron, in northern New Mexico, read about it three days later in their local *News and Press*.

> San Marcial, N.M.—May 16. The outward bound stage of the Pioneer Stage Line was stopped by two masked men about 20 miles southwest of here, about noon yesterday. They advanced with guns aimed at the driver, Pete Donnell, and both shot as they called him to halt. Chas. McConkey, one of the proprietors of the stage line, and W.H. Berry, a passenger, were on top of the stage near the driver. On seeing the desperadoes they drew their Winchesters and fired, downing both robbers. One laid still, but the other raised three times, trying to shoot the driver, but was quieted by a second ball from McConkey's gun. McConkey then fastened a paper on one of them, on which was written, "A failure on the part of the stage robbers." The stage being full, the robbers were left where they fell, and the stage was driven on to Black Range today.

The Orchards ran their stage line until 1900, when the always-stormy marriage was dissolved in the courts. The business went with the marriage, but Orchard, as expert a miner as he was teamster, continued working his *Dude*

Mine on Macho Creek. Then, in 1910, the Saga of Sadie ended with her operating a boarding house and small hotel in Hillsboro. For thirty-three years, from then to her death, she lived a quiet life catering to the kind of people she loved—the stubble-chinned miner still gophering with tall tales of raucous times, sitting and whittling on the bench in front of the Gold Pan Restaurant, to prospectors in search of "color"—ever-hopeful of another bonanza strike in the Black Range, the genuine kind, the stringers along with their packed burros, the "single blanket jackass" variety—cowboys in town from the foothills and flats. Old ones particularly, folk who lived with her in dreams of the wild and glorious years gone forever.

The following notice appeared in *The Sierra County Advocate,* the Hillsboro newspaper that had been moved to Hot Springs (Truth or Consequences) with the change of the county seat. The notice was dated April 9, 1943.

> Mrs. Sadie Orchard, said to be between 80 and 90 years old, died in the weatherbeaten remains of her old hotel in Hillsboro. She came to Kingston about 1880. She married J.A. Orchard and took turns at driving the stage. She has been ill several years. A sister lives in California. A brother lives in Omaha. She was buried in Hot Springs, as no one could be found to dig a grave in the rocky cemetery in Hillsboro.

There you have her, Sadie Orchard—*"a product of the Old West, and you know in those days we didn't have much chance to practice the niceties and refinements of high society."*

But the Black Range looks down on Hot Springs. Nineteen miles up the slope Hillsboro rests lovely in the sun, and Kingston is clean in the scent of pines—and if the ghost of a strong, brave woman walks at night, her course is up that way. Because after all, it would have taken dynamite to bury Sadie on her Trail of the Mountain Pride.

20

THE FARTHEST SOUTHWEST

AN ARIZONAN and I looked eastward across the San Simon Valley from the mouth of Cave Creek Canyon in the Chiricahua mountains, a high point that offered an uninterrupted view of this far southwestern corner of New Mexico. What we saw was the immense flatlands bordered on the east by the Peloncillo mountains, a world of mighty distances, abrupt contrasts, pinnacled summits, grassy pampas, upthrusts of black basalt, rich earth and precious subterranean waters.

"Build a town of ten thousand on the floor of that valley," said my friend, "and it will appear from here as insignificant as a pimple on the back of Goliath." Goliath is legend, the San Simon is real, from the Arizona side of the state line a truth was spoken.

Towns and villages, even wayside stores and filling stations, are scarce along waterless San Simon Creek. Ranch houses stand alone, mostly remote from the roads. The only town of consequence, Safford, Arizona, is at the northern end of the San Simon Valley, on the Gila river. In fact, all the wide flatlands between the Peloncillo and Chiricahua ranges belong to Arizona, other than a crescent-shaped portion that intrudes across the state line into New Mexico. And center of the crescent, midway between Steins Peak and Outlaw Mountain, lies the small town of Rodeo, a place as western as its name.

Rodeo, on Highway 80 almost equidistant between Lordsburg and Douglas, was established by cattlemen as a shipping point soon after the turn of the century, when the El Paso & Southwestern Railroad was built through the San Simon Valley to connect El Paso with Tucson, via Douglas and points along the Mexican border. This was a rail convenience for some of the nation's largest livestock enterprises, especially so the San Simon Cattle Company. It served as

146

trail's end for stagecoaches down from Paradise, a boom camp high in the Chiricahuas, iniquitous, rude amid some of the loveliest landscapes in the world, now entirely "gone ghost." The rollicking Concords met with such crack passenger trains as the *Golden State Limited*, pride of the Chicago to Los Angeles run; and with the less-elegant (though pungently picturesque) *Drummers' Special*, affectionately dubbed the *"Drunkards' Special."*

Here in the valley's halcyon days the locomotives sent black smoke into the clearest of skies, as they pulled their clattery burdens over the Antelope Pass. They strained at the upgrade on the hump between the San Simon and San Bernardino valleys. Their whistles moaned, they wailed, they echoed to the wayside peaks. Here at Rodeo sounded the pound of hoofs as great bovine herds were driven from their native grass to the corrals and loading chutes. The cattle's anguished bellowing, the shrill nickering of horses, the shouts and whistles of the attending cowboys gave Rodeo the substance of its name. When the dust settled and the bedlam stilled, it was from Rodeo that the mile-long freight trains left.

People have used the valley resources for a long, long time. Ranch homes are veritable museums of amateur archaeology. Displays are framed on the walls, shoe boxes overflow with pot sherds, projectile points and bone and stone implements. Grinding stones of coarse and fine textures are built into rock fireplaces. The collections grow as men ride the range, or cultivate the field, when keen eyes catch the presence of artifacts on the desert earth. Ancient life here was ancient indeed. Such eminent scientists as Emil Haury, Paul Martin, and Joe Ben Wheat classify the earliest inhabitants of this section as belongig to the Chiricahua phase of the Cochise complex—from about 2,500 to 300 B.C.

This is "Apache Country." From the earliest years of the nineteenth century to almost the end, bands of hostile nomads ranged the San Simon and its adjacent mountains. Settlers' lives were constantly threatened by such able leaders as Cochise, Natchez, Chihuahua, and *Gokliya*, better known as Geronimo. To the north lay the tribal range of the Warm Springs Apaches, whose most noted chief was Mangas Coloradas; while due east across the Animas and Playas valleys ranchers and miners kept their weapons ever primed to combat marauding bands led by Victorio and Nana. It was in Skeleton Canyon, in the Peloncillo mountains south of Rodeo, that Geronimo in 1886 surrendered to American troops—after five years of constant raids and massacre in New Mexico, Arizona, Sonora and Chihuahua.

From the mid-1870s to 1886, both Apaches and outlaws played havoc in the San Simon. Skeleton Canyon gets its name from the grisly event of 1882 when Curly Bill and allied badmen ambushed a company of Mexican smugglers who had plundered north of the border and were driving the laden mule train homeward to Sonora. It was a rich haul. Fifteen smugglers were killed and the loot distributed among the American outlaws. The bodies were left for the coyotes and buzzards, the bones to bleach in the sun. Bits of human anatomy littered the canyon for years thereafter, scattered by winds and rains. Cowboys picked up the souvenir skulls, the crowns of which made ash trays and soap dishes for San Simon and San Bernardino valley ranch houses.

High in the Chiricahuas west of Rodeo lies the rocky rubble that was once the "hell town" of Galeyville. Prospectors found "color" in the area during the late 1870s and John Galey established the camp that was to honor his name—honor such as it was. But the klondike was short-lived. As the miners packed out the outlaws moved in, for the site was a superb brigands' lair. Saloons, gambling casinos, dance halls, and brothels rendered their fickle services, corrals and warehouses for bandit plunder maintained a roaring trade. Curly Bill, Johnny Ringo, the Clanton family, and others of lesser repute, strutted Galeyville as cocks of the roost—and a "robbers' roost" it truly was.

Though Galeyville menaced solid society for a couple hundred surrounding miles its raucous days and nights were seldom disturbed by the law. Stolen goods kept flowing in, rustled beef was constantly driven to the corrals. But like the honest bonanza of a couple years previous, the hard-case regime was not to hold on for very long. The mistake was made when Galeyville rustlers purloined cattle in the San Bernardino Valley belonging to John Slaughter, the most celebrated of Cochise County sheriffs. Slaughter had been named to the office on strength of his fearlessness and staunch ability to deal with badmen. Aided by cowboys of the San Simon Cattle Company, Slaughter made a thorough cleanup. Once emptied of the reckless element, Galeyville's buildings, barns and corrals were dismantled and hauled a mile south to the new and law-abiding town of Paradise, on East Turkey Creek. In other words, the rocks and timbers of "hell" were used to build "Paradise."

Prior to 1880 all southwestern New Mexico was given to the freegoing ways of miners, the military, freighters and stage company employees, roaming

148

bands of Apache Indians and equally predatory outlaws, most of whom were wanted by sundry hangmen in Texas. A mighty land lay open to the sun: valley after valley ran north to south along the border, with sufficient summer rains, scant winter snows, thousands of grass-carpeted square miles, abundant surface water in springs and *cienegas* (marshlands), an inexhaustible supply of wild game, a sweet moderation of year round temperatures—and empires there for the taking by any cattle baron with the will and energy to claim them.

As one Texan who had seen the San Simon said to another Texan who hadn't, "There's a paradise in Arizona with nothing on it but grass, game, and outlaws." Which excited the less-traveled Texan to go see for himself. So in 1883 J.H. Parramore, of Abilene, along with Clabe Merchant of the same city, formed the San Simon Cattle Company and drove somewhere between 10,000 and 12,000 head westward to the Gila, turning south and crossing the Peloncillos north of the Steins Pass area. They kept driving south until they came to the Cienega west of Granite Peak, some twelve miles north of what was to be the town of Rodeo.

Families of Mormons were settled at the Cienega by squatters' rights. The Parramore and Merchant interests bought them out and took a hundred-year lease from the government on the lands. They established a headquarters and the huge San Simon Cattle Company was in business. Parramore held properties east of Carlsbad that were profiting him little. These he turned over to the Merchants in exchange for their share in the company, and Parramore became sole lord of the San Simon. The Merchant ranges covered an immense chunk of the Llano Estacado, shown on today's maps as the San Simon Swale and the San Simon Sink, southwest of Eunice.

Characters rich in rustic color have brightened the frontier scene, and Rodeo and its environs have had their share. But none could match for a lively personality the Reverend J.A. Chenowith who homesteaded at the Cienega long before the San Simon Cattle Company arrived, and who remained after the mogul firm was established. Born in Tennessee in 1813, the parson moved west to Texas in 1854. Despite living amid the West's most callous outlaws, neighboring with so-called law-abiding range barons who would kill to attain their selfish goals, and making a home and fireside on land that was tribal range of the most hostile Indians in the West's history, the Reverend Chenowith actually lived to be a hundred years old.

The Reverend's business was his and the Lord's, and he let all and sundry know it. He was as good with a gun as he was with Leviticus. He asked nothing of anybody but to be left alone. He sent a note to the villainous Black Jack Ketchum, warning that if he should ever steal a horse from him he'd kill him "as sure as hell." He obliged the Apaches with the same threat. But he was considerate, for he once killed a man in Galeyville and afterward preached his funeral.

His wife had also answered The Call. She preached long sermons in the Rodeo church, remembered to this day as "damn good religion, even if a little noisy."

For the first twenty years—from 1883 to 1903—cattle were shipped from San Simon Siding on the Southern Pacific, twenty miles north of the Cienega headquarters. Then, in 1902, the El Paso & Southwestern Railroad was laid across the Antelope Pass and up the valley to the San Bernardino, across to Douglas in the Sulphur Springs. The track was built and maintained by the Phelps Dodge mining interests to haul coal from Dawson, in Colfax County, to Douglas for smelting copper ores brought down from the Bisbee pit. The San Simon Cattle Company put corrals and loading pens at a trackside point for their own convenience. Then the first houses in Rodeo went up, the start of a "cow town" if one ever deserved the name.

Rodeo's shining years commenced in 1915, when Arizona went as dry as her alkali flats. Because of Prohibition, Arizonans "spat cotton" while they dreamed of bygone names, names such as Old Thompson and Budweiser, and of nectar flavors like Jack Daniels Tennessee Sour Mash. Rodeo, New Mexico, a scant half-mile from the state line, wept sympathetic tears for a beloved neighbor's predicament. Nor would Rodeo sit idle while a good friend suffered. She'd help if she could.

Arizona's Prohibition years lasted until the Volstead Act put the nation to drought in 1918; and gloomy years they were for "The Grand Canyon State." Yet all the while New Mexico dripped with choice brands of alcoholic dewdrops. Then Rodeo, cognizant of her God-given place on the map, schemed mercenary schemes coupled with tender compassion. Immediately "the stuff that cheers" was given priority over cattle. Seventeen wholesale liquor establishments went into trade, thirty-five saloons prospered in the beery ozone. Pilgrims with parched appetites put up at the three hotels, while the overflow camped contentedly along the street.

Every day "The Drunkards' Special" deposited its load of pleasure-bent Arizonans at the little depot while from eastern points the barreled liquors came to supply the demand. Bands blared their horrible renditions at the frequent dances held in Threlkeld's Hotel, and the dining room catered sumptuously to the enormous patronage. As for the unattached male, whose proclivities waxed tender in the blue of twilight, there was a cozy enterprise near the mouth of Mouser Canyon, about a half-mile northeast of town, called by the wags "The Goat Ranch."

Roads, trails, and dry creek beds came alive with wagon and packhorse traffic—with contraband out of the realm of the blessed, into the secret caches of the parched and damned. The Smuggler's Trail across Skeleton Canyon was revived; southward down the San Bernardino, northward through the San Simon, across the high passes of the Chiricahuas moved the clandestine freight. One sweet old lady in a wagon wore out a load of hay she kept hauling to Douglas, never bothering to change the cover cargo that concealed the more lucrative consignment hidden within. Arizona agents raided a liquor cache in Pirtleville, near Douglas, said to have had a wholesale value of $110,000. Sold by the shot, the retail profit would have figured into the millions. It required three days to carry it out into official custody. Its point of origin, of course, was Rodeo.

When the nation went dry, Rodeo ceased to boom. From 1918 on, post-World War I prosperity seemed to give the town a shrug out of the way. The San Simon Cattle Company went out of business, its vast territory broken up into lesser ranches. Homesteaders moved in to claim their lawful legacies from the government. They were Texans, for the most part, with an abundance of stamina but lacking in the uproarious humor possessed by the frontiersmen who had passed on. Paradise, high in the Chiricahuas, had gone ghost. The stage-coaches no longer kicked up dust as they rollicked along to Rodeo's depot. Commercial concerns along the street sold off their stock, the hotels closed shop. The vacated saloons lost their riotous animation, to become roadside mementos of "the days that were." The town turned dark of nights, quiet in sunlight—pristine of morals, calvinistic of temperament, unspeakably dull. "The Goat Ranch," naturally, went with the springtime winds.

In 1924 the El Paso & Southwestern became the "South Line" of the Southern Pacific. The *Golden State Limited* stopped at Rodeo only on flag. Mesquite thrived in the vacant lots amid rolling tumbleweeds and ugly bits of household litter. Dwellings were (and still are) boxlike affairs, practical and sufficient. Beauty was rampant in the surrounding landscape; nowhere was it evident in the works of men.

152   Highway 80 ran parallel with the railroad from Rodeo southwestward to Douglas. In time it was treated to a coat of asphalt, to increase truck and tourist traffic. Some new life was kindled, but not too much. There was a definite hostility toward any *new* idea offered by "*new* blood," should such invade the thoroughly Texanized community. The presence of "foreigners" would blemish the serenity. Gossip, bickering, and feuding were the sports enjoyed.

Had ideas of progress been accepted then, Rodeo today could be a worthwhile place on the map. It is the only wayside point of consequence between Lordsburg and Douglas, with little now to offer the highway traveler other than gas, oil, snacks, and a stop at the tavern. Huge semi-trailer trucks speed through at forty miles per hour, the lawful limit. Tourists approach town, consult their fuel gauges, and thankfully keep going.

In the late forties a change came to the flat sweep of the valley, one that resulted in brown earth appearing where green mesquite and dusty creosote brush had thrived before. As the years passed on into the fifties the clean, cultivated fields spread more and more over the face of the San Simon. Some time before, a stab at experimental farming had begun in the Animas Valley, which lies to the east beyond the Antelope Pass. There test wells had brought water in mighty volume to the surface—one flowed two thousand gallons a minute from a paltry depth of sixty feet. The climate was found to be congenial to cotton growing and a wide variety of feed crops giving rise to brand-new Cotton City, a farm center about ten miles north of old Animas village. A fresh breed of Texan answered the call of the virgin earth. He was not the dusty, bowlegged horseback man of days gone by, but an overalled, straw-hatted gent riding a tractor's metal seat.

Rodeo of the San Simon, not to be outdone by Animas of the Animas, put down a test well just west of town on the ranch of Jack Hoggett, the gamble underwritten by a number of ranchmen in the district. The work was given to the Morrison Brothers, well drillers of Rodeo. If successful, the San Simon would rival the Animas Valley as a producer of field crops. Anticipation was terrific. And a gusher of a well it proved to be. At a 1000-foot depth it delivered between 2,200 and 4,200 gallons a minute. Most of the cattlemen continued loyal to the

God-given grass, but some invested in heavy machinery and took to cultivating the good soil, with well after well giving generously from the underground water level—until too many demands on the supply began to lower the table. The State Engineer included the Rodeo area in the Animas Soil Conservation District and a control on well drilling for irrigation was enforced. The Morrison Brothers, and other drillers, still keep busy with their rigs, but the work is to deepen existing wells—as the underground water table lowers steadily—rather than to bring in new ones.

Crops flourish today. Up and down the valley the greasewood flats of a couple decades ago show rich brown as the earth is tilled, or neat rows sprouting green between channels of water, eventually becoming spreads of fluffy cotton and vast acres of lush alfalfa, corn, milo maize, barley and irrigated pasture. The growing of sugar beet seed is successful. Corn reaches twelve feet. Cotton averages two bales to the acre.

Rodeo and its San Simon Valley go for moderation rather than extremes—the moderate pace of living in a climate not too hot, or too cold, or too windy, or too humid, and just dry enough. The only extremes are sunshine and blue skies, and the fact that here is the chosen domicile of extremely nice people. Only Nature is flamboyant. Here wildlife abounds, with 224 species of bird recorded in the area, 74 varieties of mammal, 31 different kinds of snake, and 37 other reptiles including the formidable Gila monster. Coyotes prowl the valley and border wolves invade the mountains out of Mexico. High among the rocky Peloncillo pinnacles the javalina roots the ground in packs, and the mountain lion comes in a generous quantity. Rattlesnakes grow old and huge, and are packed with venom.

Altitudes range from the Lower Sonoran life zone (4,000 feet) at Rodeo to the Hudsonian (nearly 10,000 feet) at the summit of Chiricahua Peak. The region offers a feast for the ornithologist, zoologist, herpetologist, botanist, entemologist, climatologist, and astronomer—for here can be found such rare wildlife as the trogon and the Chiricahua parrot, the coati-mundi, and the Sonoran coral snake. Out of Arizona's 3,200 known species of plants 2,000 are identified here. And there are 25,000 species of insects. Lightning storms in the months of rain put on a show fascinating, sometimes frightening to watch—and when the night skies are clear, as generally they are, star and planet enthusiasts have a field open to them between the widest horizons in the world.

154

But things wonderful, beautiful, or strange are not put here solely for the scientist, or for professional research or probings. Here is a banquet for those who love the wild, the clean, the open, and the free. Behold the San Simon when the sunsets glow fiery over the Chiricahuas, and the world below is all somber in a deep mauve, ever darkening as the sky turns in a flash from one violently beautiful color extravaganza to another, and night moves in and all the creatures of Nature come awake. Watch the sunrise, and the blaze of noon. View the San Simon from the heights to the north, or the south, or the east, or the west—for it is surrounded by mountains. From the mouth of Cave Creek, from the Granite Gap, from the Antelope Pass or the slope of Steins Peak, before you will be spread a wonderworld so immense that, as the feller says, a town of ten thousand will appear as "a pimple on the back of Goliath."

21

THE BRAVE MEN
OF DOUBTFUL CANYON

THE COUNTRY SURROUNDING Steins Peak, New Mexico, is eerie even in bright daylight. By dark of night, or quiet moonlight, it is no place for those sensitive to scenes where tragic happenings of the past hold fast to the atmosphere, to linger on seemingly forever. In Doubtful Canyon, of which Steins Peak marks the east entrance, the noise of havoc is silenced a hundred years, the once-bloodstained earth is cleansed by so many seasons of wind, rain, and piercing sun.

But the eeriness is there—weird, cruel. It is there on the arid slopes, on the painted buttes, amid the pinnacled crags, in the harshly eroded gullies, in the lifeless shale; it is there to be heard in the sad call of the birds, in the whirr of the rattlesnake, in the wail of the suffering coyote. It is there in the very name—Doubtful Canyon—once the most vicious ten miles anywhere to be met on the long Butterfield Stage Line Trail.

Here was a death trap in the very heart of Apache country, a terrain of natural ramparts along most of the canyon's length that offered cover for painted warrior bands or lone snipers whose purpose was to terrorize and destroy any white man arrogant enough to trespass on the tribal domain. Doubtful Canyon is narrow, deep, meandering; the trail is boulder-strewn, washed and eroded by infrequent but sometimes torrential rains. There is gloom and shadow here, and always the feeling of "someone present"—always the haunting thought that here, on this very earth, human beings were subjected to torture and to deaths too horrible for the imagination.

Yet up and down Doubtful Canyon, eastward and westward across Steins Pass, the rollicking coaches of the Butterfield Stage Line once made their

155

ways driven by men who were paid high bounties in return for their defiance of the dangers lurking on this section of the Trail. As they approached Steins Peak from the east, drivers took a firm grip on the lines that controlled their four-horse teams; the armed "messengers" who lolled atop the coaches sat erect, fondled their guns, and kept ammunition within easy reach. The passengers below had been warned to prepare for the worst. The E. Garrison Relay Station lay ahead and, beyond, the gauntlet of Doubtful Canyon. Most made it through alive, but the feat was always "doubtful" until the run was over.

The Southern Overland Mail and Stagecoach Line began operations in September, 1858, under contract awarded the year before to John Butterfield and Associates. It called for a twice-weekly mail-coach service between St. Louis and San Francisco, by way of Missouri, Arkansas, the Indian Territory, Texas, New Mexico, Arizona, and southern California. The government agreed on paying $600,000 a year for six years of service. Two coaches were to leave each week, eastbound from San Francisco and westbound from St. Louis, to meet on schedule somewhere along the 2,795-mile route, with each "run" to be completed in twenty-five days. Passengers paid a $200 fare between St. Louis and San Francisco. A letter cost 10¢.

John Butterfield's company invested a million dollars in the project. Eight hundred men were hired, and 1,000 horses and 500 mules purchased in addition to 250 coaches, wagons, and a mountain of harness and livery. The relay stations were about twenty miles apart. Those in the arid Southwest were serviced by tank wagons that kept the water supply ample. In the Indian country, a force of armed men at every station a resident defense. Coaches were not of the familiar Concord type, but rather the canvas-superstructured Jersey Wagons, each with three seats to accommodate ten persons. A good driver kept the coach moving at an average speed of four and a quarter miles an hour. The plan called for mounted, heavily armed guards to accompany the coaches— *especially through the Apache country.*

The first westbound mail-passenger coach left St. Louis on September 16, 1858, when the eastbound out of San Francisco was already two days along the road. The meeting of the coaches took place at night in Guadalupe Pass, about a hundred miles east of El Paso. The eastbound coach was driven at intervals on this maiden run by John Butterfield, Jr., son of the company president, who completed the "voyage" in twenty-three days and four hours. The average time thereafter, in the three-year life of the Butterfield Trail, was twenty-one days and fifteen hours.

Danger spots along the Trail were the horse-change stations on the lonely 320-mile stretch between Mesilla and Tucson, for there were no towns or settlements anywhere between the two points. There were fourteen relay stations—among them Cooke's Spring and Cow Springs (both north of today's Deming, New Mexico), Soldier's Farewell (near present Lordsburg), the E. Garrison Relay Station in Steins Pass, San Simon, Apache Pass, Dragoon Springs, and the crossing of the San Pedro—all adjacent to Apache strongholds, and vulnerable. But the section most feared by travelers was the E. Garrison, the New Mexico entrance to Doubtful Canyon.

North and east of Steins Peak lay the tribal range of the Mimbrenõs, or Warm Springs Apaches, whose leader was Mangas Coloradas—"Red Sleeves"—named for the pretty habit of smearing his arms with the blood of his slain enemies. To the south and southwest the Chiricahua Apaches held dominion from a central stronghold in the Dragoon mountains. This division of the far-spreading tribe was especially powerful. The commanding word for every member came from the mouth of Cochise, the greatest of all chiefs.

Little trouble had been given the surveyors who mapped the Butterfield Trail. During 1857–58, though evermindful of the cowardly murder by white men of the chieftain Juan José several years before, Cochise kept to his stronghold in the Dragoons and left the Empire Builders pretty much alone. But this happy state of affairs terminated one night in 1859 when, in a lamp-lighted Sibley tent not far from Dragoon Springs, Cochise himself was dealt a blow of treachery.

A settler had complained to the military at Fort Bowie about a missing cow and suspected an Apache to be the thief. *But which Apache?*

So young, peach-complected Second Lieutenant Bascom had been sent with a squad of troopers to inquire among the Chiricahua chiefs and to ask their help in locating the culprit. Within the tent, Cochise faced the officer across the table; beside him sat five subchieftains, frowsy-haired, unwashed, stoic, contemptible in the eyes of the self-important young man so freshly arrived from West Point.

"Who stole the cow?" Bascom asked, through an interpreter.

"We do not know," was the Apaches' reply.

Bascom turned to the sergeant. "Arrest them," he said.

The sergeant—seasoned by years of grueling experience to Indian ways—the desert-hardened troopers—together they stood for a dozen seconds in unbelief, appalled that such a show of arrogance, coupled with ignorance, could happen in their presence. Cochise knew no English. Neither did his five chieftains. But they read the command on Bascom's lips. The soldiers moved forward. The lamp was knocked over. Commotion, shouting, a flow of profanity erupted in the darkness. And when the light was struck again, five Indians were pinioned to the floor by the overwhelming cavalrymen. One Indian had escaped.

By the time Bascom and his men could gather themselves to order, Cochise was mounted and riding fast toward his stronghold in the Dragoons. And as the little company of military made its way back to Fort Bowie, not so victorious with the five poor captives, the Indian-wise sergeant and the campaign-seasoned troopers pondered the situation, well aware that Apache hatred for all white men had been rekindled. Massacre, kill them, whenever and wherever encountered—exterminate the purveyors of treachery, broken promises, and worthless treaties. Revenge for all crimes committed against the Indian race was struck into flame by two thoughtless words: "Arrest them." Said by one small man on behalf of a nation.

Thereafter, for more than a quarter century, the Chiricahua, Warm Springs, and Mescalero Apaches scourged the Anglo intruders of the Southwest. In New Mexico, Arizona, Chihuahua, and Sonora, they let their wrath be felt with a vengeance upon wagon trains, stagecoaches, ranches, mines, and settlements. Deaths were inflicted, torture and mutilations too horrible to describe. Bands of warriors were led by the great chiefs, Cochise, Mangas Coloradas, Victorio, Nana, Loco, Chihuahua, and Natchez, all the great chiefs, in one long demonstration of savagery that would not be quelled until September 1886, when Geronimo surrendered to American authorities in Skeleton Canyon and so ended Apache hostilities in the Southwest for all time.

The Butterfield Line, however, was to enjoy a short but busy lifetime. Early in 1861, Washington decided that the United States mails should not be trusted to a line serving Arkansas, Texas, or any of the Confederate states. Orders were that the Southern Route should be abandoned and the Overland Mail to the Pacific Coast be routed over the old California Trail from

Independence, Missouri, westward, via the Platte, Fort Laramie, Fort Bridger, Great Salt Lake City, across Nevada into California by way of Truckee and Illinoistown (now Colfax) and on to Sacramento and San Francisco.

In April of that year, Butterfield agents traveled the line to transfer stock and equipment north. Accordingly, a realignment party left Mesilla by coach, destination Tucson. It consisted of Briggs, the driver, Sam Nealy, Michael Neiss, Anthony Elder, and John James Giddings of San Antonio, traffic manager of the Butterfield Texas division. Giddings had been ordered to sell any stock or equipment not transferable. Consequently, he carried $28,000 on his person.

The coach rumbled westward, leaving Soldier's Farewell behind. Soon the cone of Steins Peak was clear on the west horizon. They had traveled through the night, the sun had risen, and breakfast and rest at the E. Garrison Relay Station was pleasantly anticipated. But it was not to be. An Apache band under Cochise swept down from the canyonside, riddled the coach with bullets and arrows and killed the driver and Anthony Elder. The team stampeded with the driverless coach, tossing and pitching over the boulders, past the relay station to a point about half mile into Arizona, where it capsized. Giddings and Nealy prepared for a fight, to stand off the raiders and quite possibly survive. But Neiss claimed Cochise to be a friend of his, and suggested that they walk boldly up to the Chief and let Neiss identify himself. Once he was recognized, Neiss assured Giddings, they would not be molested; in fact, Cochise would most certainly bestow his blessing on the trio. The deaths of Briggs and Elder, apparently, were incidental to this meeting of "old friends."

Giddings and Nealy were persuaded, only to find that Cochise was to bestow his own kind of "blessing," one especially reserved for white men. Neiss had the "honor" of being dragged at a rope's end—by Cochise himself—up the wash toward Steins Peak; two ruthless warriors did likewise with Giddings and Nealy. The Apaches' hatred for all white men was expressed on that hillside. Torture and mutilation were dealt them before merciful death came to the rescue. Their bodies were later found by passing freighters and buried closer to the road. Giddings's daughter visited the grave in 1925 and had a stone erected where it may be seen today.

Cochise judged men by two attributes of character alone: integrity and valor. A man's honor was nothing at all unless backed by a show of bravery under the most grueling conditions. Tom Jeffords, a stage driver during the 1870s, was so replete with the two qualities in the eyes of Cochise that he was actually claimed a "blood brother." After the Giddings ambush, Cochise told it around Chihuahua that the three men killed on Steins Peak "died like sick women." Without a doubt, screams pierced the stillness of the canyon that day, for no man—honest, brave, or otherwise—could undergo the terrible methods of Apache torture and not shout to heaven for the agony of it. But if frontiersmen were not generally to the manor born, neither were they cowards. The first requirement for anyone who ventured into the west during the 60s, 70s, and 80s, was *valor*.

160

Shortly before the Southern Overland Mail Line was discontinued, at a time when Apache hatred for all white men was most intense, a Butterfield coach entered Doubtful Canyon California bound. The six passengers, atop the coach and below, included a man named Free Thompson, who acted as overseer of the others: history would record this fateful journey as "The Free Thompson Party."

At that time, both Cochise and Mangas Coloradas were in the vicinity, leading a double array of Apache warriors armed with rifles, ample ammunition, and bows and arrows. The men in the westbound stagecoach were supplied with several thousand rounds of cartridges looped in their belts, bags, and boxes, since the Butterfield people encouraged all travelers using the line to carry as many firearms as was physically possible.

The coach came to the relay station, changed teams, and drove on into Doubtful Canyon. High in the natural ramparts were concealed the two chiefs and six hundred warriors—waiting, ready to strike. This would be an easy kill, for the scouts had reported that the coach was without an armed escort.

The first shots, aimed at the horses, missed. The second volley struck the coach, yet left the passengers unscathed. The driver savvied the business and had the knack of handling such emergencies as this, for he was a Butterfield man, hardened even to the ways of Doubtful Canyon. One crack of the long coach whip sent the teams on a climb to the summit of a nearby knoll, where a few craggy rocks offered poor but welcome cover. When a third blast of fire felled the horses, the seven cool-headed men took positions behind their scanty barricade.

Now the Peloncillo Mountains, of which Steins Peak is a prominent height and Doubtful Canyon a rugged gash, is made of rocks and shale, coarse desert growth, treacherous footings, all drenched in a flood of the cruel sun. It is the habitat of America's most venomous reptiles. Yet it is beautiful in nature's splendor and desolation. The black of basalt—of hot lava gone cold; rock cliffs of somber gray, an ochre here, a brilliant yellow there; violently abrupt hillsides, orange gravel where torrential rains have washed the gulch. From such camouflage the painted warriors of Cochise and Mangas Coloradas let fly their bullets and their iron-pointed arrows. While the dying horses panted their final breaths, as the fine coachwork of the wrecked vehicle was peppered into splinters, the seven Free Thompson men gave shot back for shot. And the day wore on past noon.

Up and down and across Doubtful Canyon echoed the gunfire, until the sun had set and darkness overtook the West. The Apache gave no combat in the dark of night, because of "spirits" and sundry superstitions. It was a custom not to be offended. But come sunrise—

It would seem that night cover offered an easy escape for the Free Thompson Party but such was not the case. Although the Indians had ceased their fire it was certain they had formed a close cordon around the hill where the defenders were grouped under flimsy cover. A break for the canyonsides would spell suicide, as sure as there yet remained a small spark of hope. So they sat out the night, chatting, planning the next day's combat, chewing cud tobacco, smoking, passing the plugs back and forth, just "good ole boys" whiling away time. A couple napped while the others watched—then the light began to show behind Steins Peak.

Another day. Now the rifle cracks sounded again from the canyon's painted heights. Occasionally a brazen warrior would show himself above the rocks and a well-aimed slug from the open hilltop felled him for his folly. Smoke lifted from secluded arroyos to inform the hapless seven that the Indian hunters had killed deer, that venison was roasting above hot coals, that a nearby spring of clear water quenched their enemy thirsts. But on the barren knoll where the white men fought there was no water, no food to maintain strength—nothing there but to match seven against six hundred, to fire every cartridge in stock—

For three days the battle was waged. Three days and two nights of gnawing hunger and choking, parching thirst. And always after the quiet night came the fierce Southwestern sun, and never absent the moistureless heat. On the morning of the third day, when the ammunition supply atop the hill was nearing the last fifty rounds, the Apaches slithered down to the gullies and sought cover for moving toward the kill.

Sundown of that day fell on the Free Thompson Party, on seven whose deaths were valorous even by Indian standards. For three days, in spite of a weakened physical state brought on by hunger and dehydration, *seven men had fought off six hundred Indians to the last bullet, and killed between one hundred thirty-five and one hundred fifty of their enemy.*

In later years, in the old settlement of Janos, in Chihuahua, Cochise told of the battle. And while he spoke his eyes blazed with admiration for the memory of men whose likes are born to the world just once in awhile.

"They were the *brave* men!" he said. "They were the bravest men I ever saw. Give me five hundred warriors as brave as those men. Then all New Mexico. All Arizona. All Chihuahua. All Sonora will be mine!"

22

THE PLACE WHERE DE VARGAS DIED

I F HIS DIVINE MAJESTY shall be pleased to take me away from the present life, I desire and it is my will that a Mass be said while the corpse is present in the church of this town of Bernalillo...."

So read the last testament of Don Diego de Vargas Zapata Luján Ponce de León, conquistador and reconqueror of Spain's Kingdom of New Mexico after the Pueblo Rebellion of 1680 when he led a small army to a so-called bloodless victory and restored the Palace of the Governors in Santa Fe to the authority of the Spanish viceroy in Mexico City.

True it is that De Vargas died in Bernalillo; and, most unheroically for a warrior of such caliber, of an illness brought on by eating spoiled eggs.

Bernalillo, seat of Sandoval County, population about 6,000, is one of the important Rio Grande Valley towns adjacent to Albuquerque. The lights of Albuquerque, twenty miles to the south, nightly glow against Bernalillo's skyline. If it were not for an Indian reservation between the towns, Albuquerque and Bernalillo might share the same urban-suburban sprawl.

Bernalillo is one of America's very oldest Spanish-American towns. Before De Vargas, Bernalillo's history is clouded and vague. The soldier-settlers who colonized New Mexico after the Oñate entrada of 1598 had a way of laying out their farms and ranches adjacent to established Indian pueblos. Thus a number of hacendados claimed the fertile valley between the pueblos of *Katishtya* (San Felipe) to the north, and *Nanfiath* (Sandia) at the south. Sandia was, in fact, during early times, the Spanish seat of government for the Rio Abajo, the lower river, as Santa Fe served the Rio Arriba, upper river. But it was not until after the De Vargas reconquest of 1692 that Bernalillo took on any semblance of a town.

Bernalillo's riches are in its history, locked in coffers and stored away. Here was a rich Indian world long before the Spaniard made his appearance in 1540. High in the mountains east of town is Sandia Cave, beside the road a few miles above the village of Placitas. Here archeologists from the University of New Mexico discovered fossil remains of prehistoric animals, a manmade projectile point, and other stone tools that indicate that human life existed 22,000 years ago on this very ground.

Indian people have been in this part of the Rio Grande Valley for centuries. The Tiwa-speaking people of Sandia Pueblo may have been among the earliest occupants, possibly going back to 2,000 B.C.

The Keresan-speaking people of San Felipe, according to one theory, drifted down from Chaco Canyon and some may have been in the area before A.D. 900. Another theory, supported by San Felipe legend, suggests that the Chaco people settled the Pajarito Plateau area—Bandelier National Monument is one example of these settlements—before moving on down the Rio Grande. Both theories may be correct. At any rate, the Indian farms and villages in the vicinity of Bernalillo have been there a long, long time.

The Bernalillo area was the scene of many "firsts in America." Here the Spanish language was first spoken in a community for any length of time—for two years. Here on the lush grasses the first horses were grazed. From this point the first white men penetrated into what is now Kansas. And here the first trial for rape was conducted in Coronado's camp. Here, too, the first gunpowder north of Mexico was manufactured, when Coronado sent Captain Francisco Barrio Nuevo to the Soda Dam in the Jemez Mountains, to obtain sulphur from which a crude explosive was made.

Bernalillo was given the status of a town in 1696, and it was named a "town" in the De Vargas will of 1704. Naturally there was a church, which De Vargas mentioned. Great names of Spanish origin claimed vast holdings in the valley and across the high-rolling grasslands. These were the Montoyas, the Castillos, the Pereas, the Bacas and others—and their sprawling adobe haciendas occupied the lush valley floor. These *patrones* employed paisanos to work the fields and graze the herds. A section of town was given to them and their families—a servant *barrio* of squat adobe houses, known as Las Cocinitas, it may be seen today in ruins just west of the main business block.

Lieutenant James Harvey Simpson visited Bernalillo soon after the

American occupation of New Mexico in 1846, and reported the thick and nutritious range grasses and "some respectable looking *rancho* residences, surrounded by well cultivated grounds, which are fenced by adobe walls, some of them twelve feet high, and crowned with cactus, to prevent their being scaled."

Soil, climate and irrigation were found ideal for grape growing, and the vineyards gave bountiful harvests. This industry was encouraged by French and Belgian families settling in the valley, the earliest being the Mallets. Until recently many of the priests and brothers were French and Belgian, who conducted their own La Salle vineyard and winery.

In spite of Bernalillo's pastoral serenity, its frontier days were as full of havoc and hangings as any other outpost settlement. In 1775 a band of Indians made a successful raid, murdered some townsmen, and carried off a cargo of women and children. Hangings were so commonplace that most folks thought them boring, so, to teach a lesson, the lawmen staged the performances at midnight on Saturdays, leaving the culprits to sway in the breeze through Sunday morning. The reason: churchgoers could be taught a lesson on the wages of sin better than any voice from the pulpit. It was all too practical, and the hang tree stood beside the road between Las Cocinitas and Our Lady of Sorrows Church. It grew beside an irrigation ditch near the junction of the Camino del Pueblo and the street leading to the high school. The tree has long since been chopped down.

Bits of history remain in evidence in today's Bernalillo. There is Las Cocinitas, for one; and the Spooky Mill now in ruins, but once an adobe building three stories high—named because of a hanging that took place within its dark interior. There is the Baca house on the Camino del Pueblo, once the home of a noted hacendado, later a coach and horse-change stop on the Santa Fe-Albuquerque-El Paso stage line. There was, perhaps still is, a coat-of-arms painted on the ceiling, presumably that of the Baca family. The convent of the Sisters of Loretto who were installed in the days of Archbishop Lamy is now a place of business. And relics of vineyards and wineries, ghosts of the industry that once made Bernalillo famous, are everywhere. Now silent, the vines rooted out, the vintage without even a stain on the land. All past but the sadness.

Two historic monuments are readily visible—one, sturdy with age but no longer in use, is the Church of Our Lady of Sorrows, built in 1857. The old church, already a national historic site, was slated for permanent preservation. It is one of the truly beautiful churches in the Southwest. But a new church of modern style has been erected at its side, far from beautiful, and although revered is a cause of friction among the parishioners—one faction hopeful of preserving the ancient shrine and another determined to raze it, cart away the sacred rubble, and convert the site to an up-to-date residence for the local priest.

166

The second monument to the history of the town is the thriving enterprise known as the Bernalillo Mercantile Company. Operating for over a hundred years, the "Merc" was typical of such establishments in the Southwest, and until its sale in 1978 to a businessman without frontier background was unique in a colorful tradition.

The parking lot, then, was constantly filled with pickup trucks bearing customers from all over Sandoval County—from the pueblos of Santa Ana and Zia, from Jemez, Santo Domingo and Cochití, San Felipe and Sandia. Navajos from the "checkerboard" area near Cabezon, Jicarilla Apaches from beyond Cuba and La Jara, Spanish Americans come from near and far. All this was a memorial to its founder, Nathan Bibo, pioneer, frontiersman extraordinary.

The name Bibo is engraved in the history of every community in northern New Mexico from the extreme northeast westward to the Four Corners, and is marked as a village on the map north of Cubero and east of Mount Taylor. In fact, Cubero and the Grants area are the focal point of the far-reaching Territorial enterprise, where the Philip Bibo family operates a store today.

The great Jewish trading families—Spiegelberg, Seligman of Santa Fe, Staab, Ilfeld, Rosentein, Zeckendorf and numerous others—made their contributions to New Mexico's progress without taking the "New Mexican" out of the cultures. Harvey Fergusson's fictional Leo Mendes, in his novel *The Conquest of Don Pedro*, characterizes the veracity and stamina of these pioneers.

The first Bibo ancestor, Lucas Rosenstein, came to New Mexico in 1820. He was on his way to Mexico from his native Germany. Santa Fe was as far as he got, but the town so intrigued him that his decision was to sail back to his homeland and return at a later date. He did not return, but his descriptions of New Mexico were so forceful that other family members emigrated to the land of their "enchantment." Among the later venturers was Nathan Bibo, who remained in New York only long enough to master the English language before moving on to New Mexico.

Reaching Santa Fe in 1866, Nathan went to work for the Spiegelbergs, later for the Zeckendorfs in Albuquerque and Tucson. In 1867 he joined Willi Spiegelberg, who was post trader at Fort Wingate. So great was his ambition to found his own business that things happened speedily for the adventurous Nathan Bibo in the next six years. With his brothers he opened the trading posts at Cubero and Cebolleta, near Acoma and Laguna pueblos, and did a brisk business supplying Fort Wingate, Fort Defiance, and Fort Apache with Indian-grown corn and other grains, along with fruits and vegetables. In time every imaginable product that could be freighted in over a long distance was loaded on the wagon trains.

In 1873, the Bibo Brothers opened a store in Bernalillo. Under Nathan Bibo's management it operated as a true frontier trading post, with a patronage as rough as the times, a great part illiterate and superstitious. Although the valley was lush and cultivated, the mountains to the east and the rolling flatlands to the west were sparsely peopled.

As with all Spanish towns in nineteenth century New Mexico, Bernalillo had a patrón, a landed gentleman to look up to—"the boss." Generally these patrónes were very rich owners of extensive valley land and open ranges, sheep, cattle, horses—even human hirelings who couldn't survive without them. On the ground now occupied by El Charro Cafe, close by the post office, once stood the hacienda of Don José Leandro Perea. This huge adobe building had forty rooms, and in some of the rooms were entertained many of the frontier's most important dignitaries, Lieutenant W.H. Emory, for one, who dined in the great hall and later complained that the silverware was too heavy for comfort (hand-forged at Don José's private silver mine), and worse, that the food was too highly seasoned with onions. And, it is said, José Leandro Perea owned more sheep than any other man in America. He spoke no English. His nephew Don Francisco Perea, educated in St. Louis, acted as interpreter.

It was a sunny but dismal day, as Nathan Bibo told it, when the fate of New Mexico's commercial future and the prospect of a great metropolis was juggled in the hands of José Leandro Perea. The railroad that would honor the name of Santa Fe was in early 1878 building westward across the Kansas prairies, its terminal to be the California coast, its rails to serve New Mexico and Arizona on the way. Although the first locomotive would not cross Raton Pass until December, the company had plans for the route well in hand—and a very elaborate plan for Bernalillo.

An afternoon in February, that year, found a stagecoach of the Santa Fe-El Paso line halted before the entrance to the Bibo store, when five distinguished-looking, well-tailored gentlemen stepped out. They were high officials of the new railroad, among them Albert Alonzo Robinson, Chief Engineer, and Lewis Kingman, Chief Surveyor of the Atchison, Topeka & Santa Fe. They were met by Don Francisco Perea and escorted to the big house on the hacienda. Because of their importance, the stagecoach waited before moving on to Albuquerque, and it waited no longer than forty-five minutes.

Bernalillo, it seems, had been selected by the railroad as the site of the main offices and chief division point on the transcontinental line with roundhouse and extensive yards. From here the track, down from the northeast, would turn directly west and cross the Rio Grande one-half mile north of the center business block, or where the Bernalillo High School is located today. From here the jointly owned Atlantic & Pacific would beeline for California, and a down-valley line be built south to El Paso via Los Lunas, Belen, and Socorro. The main line west would go directly to the Laguna-Cubero area, bypassing the insignificant placita of Albuquerque. The plan was elaborate, expensive for the railroad, and a godsend for blossoming Bernalillo. Many acres of land would be required, so the representatives asked Don José for a price.

Four hundred and twenty-five dollars an acre!

That was the price and nothing less would do. He made his declaration—slyly, knowing the railroaders would refuse to pay. The land in question was valued at two, or possibly three dollars an acre.

So the tailored gentlemen returned to their coach. As Nathan Bibo described the departure, ". . . they left my place, and while Mr. Robinson never spoke a word, I could see on his pale face and also by the expression of contempt uttered by some of the party, that they must have met a most unexpected and unpleasant disappointment."

So the Atchison, Topeka & Santa Fe acquired land seventeen miles down the valley, about a mile east of the plaza of San Felipe de Neri de Albuquerque and made possible one of the largest and most important cities in the Southwest. For Bernalillo there would be merely a red painted frame depot, a railroad siding, and a grade crossing.

Little dreaming what he had wrought, Don José died far from being a rich potentate, but distinctive as one of America's first environmentalists, a man who didn't like clatter and smoke, or Anglos interfering in the affairs of a happy little Spanish village.

Siegfried Seligman and his brothers Julius and Carl bought out the Bibos in 1903. From then on the Bernalillo Mercantile Company extended its trade to branch stores. At sundry times these were at Grants, San Ysidro, Porter, and Paxton Springs, as well as the trading post at Thornton, now Domingo, which catered to the Santo Domingo and Cochití Indians.

All family members bore respectful Indian names, given with dignity and affection. Jack Seligman, manager of the Bernalillo store at the time of its sale in 1978, was distinguished with *Ah'tsinah,* meaning "tadpole" in the Keres tongue. And all the family spoke fluent Spanish.

Today, under the new owner, the "Merc" is a thriving business, but no longer a living museum of a way of life. In the days of the Seligmans there were horseshoes for sale and horseshoe nails, farriers' tools, trappers' supplies, old-style castiron pots for the camp pot rack, and dutch ovens for the old-time cowboy's sourdough biscuits. Most of the Indian patronage reject aluminum and stainless steel in favor of enamelware. What was good enough for their grandmothers is essential for them. And split leather for moccasins. The Seligmans were sympathetic to their needs.

The dry goods department displayed all manner of textiles for the Indian clientele, print goods, striped Pendleton blankets, denims, ticking and yarn for making mantas and dance kilts, fringe, and the special needles required; the makings for belts and sashes; sleighbells, beads, shells for ceremonial use, and the shells needed for cutting down into *heshi.* And shawls. The Bernalillo Mercantile was famed in the Indian country for a special shawl imported from Bohemia—the right decoration for dark and beautiful countenances, the true mate for silver, turquoise, coral, and shell.

There was blue corn meal, a very special product, which Joaquín Domingues so expertly roasted, ground and packaged. Chile, both ground and in *ristras.* And *cosas por la medica*—native herbs for home remedy: *azafran* (saffron) for the cure of measles and for reducing fever, *alhucema* (mint) for stomach trouble and the banishment of phlegm, *manzanilla* (camomile) for relief of neuralgia and baby colic—and *yerba mansa* (lizard's tail), the herb that combats every disease, plague, or infection imaginable.

When Julius Seligman operated the Indian crafts section across the street from the store proper in the 1940s, Bernalillo was treated to a fling of flamboyant Indian color. The shop workers were mostly Navajo, and a complete Navajo community was maintained between the store and railroad tracks.

170

It's reasonable to suppose that Bernalillo, being the important Indian trade center it is, would be a storehouse for Indian crafts of the genuine sort. And it is, especially for the amazingly popular silver jewelry and beads done at nearby Santo Domingo and the heavily turquoised articles from distant Zuni. As this is Indian country without tourist dressing, native craftsmen come to trade and barter their creations.

One of the oldest and best known trading posts is the Rose Store and Pottery House operated by James Silva. Directly opposite the Bernalillo Mercantile on the main block, the store displays every conceivable item of Indian art. The museum collection of pottery is renowned. Pots, from pieces fired last month at Zia to precious ollas used a thousand years ago at Chaco Canyon, line the shelves of this unusual private collection. Visitors are invited to come see the display.

In spite of the recent Anglo influx, mostly commuters to Albuquerque jobs, Bernalillo remains a town distinctive for its Hispanic flavor, its quiet friendliness, its love of politics, its earthiness, its pride of heritage. The lilting Spanish tongue, inherited from early times, is heard everywhere and the people who speak it are proud that the first and greatest conquistador made his base camp near here, and the illustrious reconqueror departed life in a ranch house that may or may not be part of Las Cocinitas. And nowhere is the Spanish heritage more apparent than at the annual fiesta held every August 10th, when the gente pay homage to San Lorenzo. Then the air comes alive with gaiety and with the rich aroma of Spanish cooking. Then the Matachines dancers perform the ritual so ancient that its origin is unknown, and do it to perfection. And visitors come from great distances to join the festivities.

The scythe of progress may be making its sweep, but the heart of Bernalillo remains Spanish—and thoroughly American. Because that's the way it beats.

23

SAINT OF THE HEAVY HEART

THE SISTERS OF LORETTO, that gallant little company whose convent lay at the western end of the Santa Fe Trail, were filled with joy and gratitude in 1878, in spite of the raw life that surrounded them. At that time New Mexico was making strides toward taming the wild frontier; progress was advancing in spite of many obstacles. The Lincoln County War was at its turbulent peak, Billy the Kid was riding high, wide and ugly, and the Apaches were still disturbing the nights and days of quiet citizens in the southwest corner of the territory; nevertheless the first railroad was pushing its tracks toward the summit of Raton Pass and men of worth were moving in to invest, and to suppress the law of the six-shooter by planting the seeds of decency and enterprise. In the midst of it all, the Sisters of Loretto walked in peace.

They had good reason for gratitude. The girls school they had founded, a full quarter century before, had proved successful and occupied a substantial building on the convent grounds. And now they had acquired the funds to enable them to build a chapel of their own, which they dedicated to Our Lady of Light.

Today, that chapel is one of Santa Fe's popular tourist attractions. Not only for its age, its severe Gothic beauty, and the golden figure of the Virgin—but also for the masterpiece of the woodworker's skill, a thing so lovely that it seems unearthly, the spiral access to the choir loft called the Miraculous Staircase.

Ironically, the architect who designed and supervised the building of the chapel had been stricken with blindness. The chapel was almost complete when sight failed him. All had been finished except the stairway that led to the choir loft. Funds were exhausted. Mother Mary Magdalen and her companion nuns were truly faced with a dilemma.

172

Legend has it that the nuns in their desperation appealed in prayer to their patron, Our Lady of Light, for a solution. They asked for some sudden windfall that would enable them to construct the final detail. Not long thereafter the solution arrived: he was an old man in paisano apparel, with twinkling eyes above a long white beard, carrying a crude boxful of carpenter's tools. He informed Mother Mary Magdalen that he had come to build the stairway to the choir loft.

"But we have no money," the nun explained. "You will require wages and the price of materials."

"You can pay me later," said the stranger. "Now show me the way to the chapel."

He asked to be left alone and gently closed the chapel door. It seemed strange that no materials were brought into the chapel—not a board or a keg of nails. Nor did they hear the sound of hammering or sawing while the carpenter went about his task. Then, in much too short a time, the stranger informed them that the stairs were complete. With great excitement they started for the chapel, but were told to wait—for the workman must be on his way.

"But we must pay you for your labor," Mother Mary Magdalen told him. "Give us your name; we will send you the money."

"*Soy El Carpintero*," was his reply in Spanish. And without another word he was gone, leaving the sisters bewildered and with a certain feeling of ecstasy—a feeling that comes once in a lifetime.

"He is Joseph," said Mother Mary Magdalen, "the Holy Carpenter of Nazareth."

Today, the Miraculous Staircase may be seen while making the tourist rounds of Santa Fe. It is a superb creation with thirty-two steps in five spirals, built without braces or nails. It is so perfectly balanced that no supports are necessary; the handrails descend from the choir loft in two complete and unbroken sweeps of exquisitely turned, highly polished wood. Yet the stranger who described himself to the Sisters of Loretto as El Carpintero was unknown in Santa Fe, and after his brief but mighty task was never seen again. Whoever he was, divine or otherwise, he built more than a staircase—he crafted a legend.

The community of *La Cienega*, (The Marshland) is situated some fifteen miles southwest of Santa Fe, about a mile north of U.S. 85. It sits serene in a lush valley, surrounded by grassy hills, mounds of winter caramel and summer verdure. The name is appropriate, for there is an abundance of spring water everywhere, and there are gardens, subirrigated pastures, orchards, fields of corn and alfalfa, and veteran cottonwoods.

The little church is not the familiar mission architecture; but still, it is clean and white and in tasteful harmony with the green of the valley. And it is very old. Its patron is San José de la Cienega—"Saint Joseph of the Marshland"—whose bulto stands above the altar.

As in most of the very old Spanish communities in New Mexico, the first houses of La Cienega were built adjacent to an Indian pueblo, one now long gone to ruin. But the Spanish houses still remain. And just as enduring as the simple homes is the legend concerning the bulto of San José that has stood for centuries in the church.

It seems that once, a couple of centuries ago, a young man who lived in the village took the Camino Real south to Durango, Mexico, where he was to study for the priesthood. While there he came upon the bulto, bought it and, after completing his studies, carried it by muleback to his native La Cienega. The bulky image was received with great joy by the devout paisanos who saw in their new patron a source of protection against physical maladies, witchcraft, blight on the crops, and other disasters. However, the church at that time was built on land owned by an arrogant and not very popular rico who also operated a large hacienda at Bernalillo.

In time the rico moved himself and his belongings to his Bernalillo holdings, and along with the freight went the cherished San José. The pleasure of the natives was great as they watched the long train of oxcarts lumber west. Until, of course, they discovered the richly garbed statue to be missing from the church. The cry was sounded and the entire village—man, woman and child—rallied for the rescue.

Armed men on horseback were followed on the road by a colorful regiment of paisanos of both sexes and all ages, irate and determined. A half-dozen miles brought them to the brink of the steep incline called *La Bajada* (The Descent), where stood the San José statue alone and abandoned in his collapsed oxcart, the golden crown glistening in the sunlight. The oxen lay dead beside their yoke. The crowd swarmed about. Groans of sorrow changed to songs of joy; men fired their guns into the air to salute the occasion.

But a serious problem confronted them. How could they carry San José back to La Cienega in the dignified manner he deserved?

174 By happy surprise, an old rawhide spring bedstead of the frontier type was found beside the road, apparently cast off or lost by a passing traveler on the Camino Real. Here was the ideal vehicle for a saint who deserved only the best. Four stalwart young men each took a corner, the image was placed in the center, and with singing and laughter and cries of gratitude the procession moved triumphantly home.

The bedstead, of course, was a necessary part of the miracle, and the reason for the broken-down cart and dead oxen is obvious. When the little saint found he was being kidnapped—away from his beloved pobres by a rico of the most abominable sort—his heart became so heavy with sorrow that it was too much for the cart and oxen. Under the mighty weight the axles cracked and the bulls expired. A new church on holier ground was built for San José, where he stands today, with golden crown and lavender robe, staff in hand and the happy Child in his arms. Every November 19, which is his special feast day, he is again carried in procession, but on a more compact platform. Whatever happened to the historic bedstead, legend has failed to record.

The Indian pueblos of Laguna and Ácoma lie twenty-one miles apart in the region of painted rocks and arid distances west of Albuquerque. Here the offended heart of San José made itself felt, and also involved one of the most unusual lawsuits ever to be brought to court in the United States. This San José was a painting that hung beside the altar and reredos in the Ácoma church—where it is today. It is said to have been given to Father Juan Ramírez by King Charles II of Spain and brought to Ácoma in 1629. From the earliest times to the present the Indians believe this painting to have miraculous powers. It is greatly venerated—without its help Ácoma could not possibly exist.

But the church at Ácoma is dedicated to Saint Stephen, not Saint Joseph, while neighboring Laguna's church has the patronage of the latter. In fact, a large painting of Saint Joseph done on elkskin hangs on the reredos behind the altar there—very beautiful but not so potent as the San José at Ácoma. When the nineteenth century reached the halfway mark, Ácoma was enjoying prosperity sublime; Laguna, on the other hand, was plagued with drought, floods, epidemics, and a general lack of fertility. The Laguna tribal council decided that the only effective medicine was the miraculous painting at Ácoma, and ordered a committee to go borrow it.

Ácoma complied and San José was taken to Laguna. But no sooner had the saint left the pueblo than the tables turned—good fortune came showering down on Laguna, and Ácoma fell into the rut of infertility. The months passed and San José remained at Laguna. A council was held and the decision made to "go get it." Laguna refused to surrender. So one Sunday, after Mass, as agreed by the governors of both pueblos, lots were drawn by shaking twelve slips of paper in a jar—eleven were blank and one bore a crude sketch of San José. Two little girls—one from Laguna, the other from Ácoma—were appointed to draw the slips from the jar. On the fifth try the San José was drawn, by the Ácoma child. And the painting was returned to its rightful home. "God has favored us," said the priest, "and the blessed San José."

Now good fortune descended on Ácoma in wholesale lots while Laguna slipped into its wretched old self again. Until one morning, when Ácoma went to church to pray, it was found that the beloved saint was gone!

Stolen, kidnapped, and only Laguna could be the culprit!

The Ácoma council decided on war, but Father Lopez urged something less drastic, such as taking the matter before the United States District Court in Santa Fe. In 1852, the court favored Ácoma, but Laguna appealed to the Supreme Court. After five years of fuss and feathers, the final decision favored Ácoma. With great rejoicing a delegation was sent from Ácoma to get the painting. The members had journeyed but halfway when they discovered San José sitting beside the trail, leaning against a scraggy juniper. Miracle of miracles! The little saint had already heard the Supreme Court's decision and without known human aid had set out for "home," only to become wearied, to sit by the juniper and wait to be received by his beloved people.

By the Miraculous Staircase in Santa Fe, in the little church at La Cienega, high on the rock of Ácoma, or mellowed with age in the elkskin painting in the old Laguna Mission, the little saint of the once-heavy heart now beams halo-bright for the success of his accomplishments.

24

DRY CLOUD
OVER BROKEN HEARTS VALLEY

I ONCE RODE HORSEBACK WITH *Milt Haymes atop Glorieta Mesa headed for Cow Springs. It was April 1934. It was Milt's own country, piney in patches, with the cleanest air in the world, open meadows, and juniper breaks. Sometimes we'd brush against a juniper when our ponies cut a trail among them. They were the blue gray silvery kind, with fernlike branches, not the "scrub cedar" of down below. You meet them only in the highest altitudes. No telling what they're called, but they're pretty. Right then we were riding at about 8,000 feet.*

But that day the silvery needles weren't so silvery. They were yellowish gray. Shake them and the dust would rise up, and if you didn't duck it would smack you in the eye.

"Milt, where in hell does that dirty stuff come from?"

Milt was a purebred philosopher; he knew everything. He said, "Well, it's hard to say. The wind ain't from the east, so the dust cain't come from Oklahoma. It's from the west. That way I reckon this yeller stuff is dust off them poor folks down below—that away. T'other side of Cow Springs."

He pointed while he talked, his hand aimed straight over our ponies' ears, ahead toward Cow Springs.

And southwest to White Lakes, to Stanley, further still to Moriarty and Estancia, to the Salt Lakes around Willard—way down south. He pointed full of sympathy to the long, wide stretch that was the prosperous, most fertile Estancia Valley.

Like I said, Milt was philosophic by nature. He'd come out of Arkansas in the early days, driving a wagon and team. That way, he knew everything.

176

Well, maybe not everything. Almost everything.

The poor dusty people Milt referred to were a special breed. They were people who tilled the land or grazed the herds, or both. And like Milt, they were hardy.

They had to be to match the terrain. Although many came to the valley for reasons of health, they regained their strength by bucking the hazards and the toil. And above all, they possessed honesty, and faith in the blessings of God.

This is the Estancia Valley—the place some have called the Valley of Broken Hearts.

The heart of the valley is the town of Estancia, also the seat of Torrance County. It lies at 6,093 feet altitude, some 54 miles southeast of Albuquerque via Moriarty. South of Moriarty is the Estancia Valley proper. Here was the true "pinto bean country" and here are the towns and remnants of towns like Willard, Mountainair, McIntosh, Lucy, Pedernal, El Progresso, Cedarvale, and Torrance. And, of course, Estancia—"the hub."

The Gallinas Mountains and Jumanes Mesa flank the south end of the valley. The Manzanos rise to form the skyline west of Estancia, while the Sandias range west of Stanley. Some geologists claim the valley was made eons ago by the settling of a huge lake measuring 20 by 35 miles north to south, which left a series of salt lakes dead center of a wide and fertile plain. The larger of these lakes are shown on today's map as Laguna del Perro and Laguna Pago, directly east of Estancia.

Nature gave man here a clean level sweep of fertile soil, abundant underground water, and a climate ideal for dry farming—just the right amount of summer rain, warm sunshine, winter snows, all dealt at the right interval. And a season between frosts ideal for raising the crops that spread the fame of the Estancia Valley far and wide.

All over the West, in the latter half of the nineteenth century and the first third of this, when a man made use of his homesteading rights and filed a 160-acre claim, his hope of success was strong in his mind but flimsy in reality. He found his desired land, learned its description, paid a filing fee at the U.S. Land Office in Santa Fe, signed the documents, located on the land, and made the improvements. He built a dwelling and lived in it for three years. Then there was the matter of cultivating a portion and putting down a well—in short, "proving up." After three years he obtained the deed signed by the President of the United States. He could then continue to live on his land or sell out to his neighbor. In this way was the Estancia Valley settled.

178   But the Good Book says that some blessings, as the lives of men, wither in the sun and fly away. Today, the valley is a graveyard of the prosperous times that were. Abandoned homes rot in the sun. And rusted farm machinery gives evidences that here, once upon a time, lived rollicking prosperity.

"Look yonder," said Milt, as we trotted our horses toward Cow Springs. "There's a mighty dry cloud hangin' over that valley. And right now we're lookin' at ruination prime grade."

And sure enough.

There it was—the no-good kind of cloud, full of dust and corruption, sickly to look at. The same kind of cloud that drove farmers westward from the Dust Bowl of Oklahoma, Kansas, and Texas. It wasn't the usual kind of dry dust cloud that the valley folks lived with, season after season.

In prehistoric times Pueblo Indian peoples tilled their fields in this area, at the foot of the Manzano Mountains, in the pueblos of Chilili, Tajique, and the present villages of Manzano, Torreon, and Punta de Agua at the threshold of the great Quarai. They, too, grew beans, as well as corn, both native to the New World.

Then came the Spanish to the valley, bringing the speckled pinto bean they'd found in Mexico. These were the hacendados, the sheep and cattle barons, who ruled their ranching empires with the gauntlet hand. Earliest was the Ortiz family, whose adobe mansion was at Galisteo but with lands extending southward to the Pedernal Hills near Lucy. Chilili, an outpost of defense in the Rio Abajo, brought in Bartolomé Baca, *jefe politico*, second governor of New Mexico in the Mexican period (1821–1846), who served from 1823 to 1825. Baca was granted a huge domain in the vicinity of the Salt Lakes east of Estancia in 1816.

The Texans arrived at a later date. Jim Stinson, manager of the New Mexico Land & Livestock Company, in 1882 brought in 20,000 head of cattle from Texas. The trail he blazed was extended westward into Arizona by other drovers from Texas. While trail-herding, they gave a friendly eye to grasslands available in the valley.

In 1902, when the New Mexico Central Railroad was ballasted from Kennedy on the Santa Fe's main line down the Estancia Valley to Torrance on the El Paso & Southwestern, a mighty land sales campaign exploded. Operating headquarters for the line was at Estancia, but it served many valley communities—Stanley, Moriarty, McIntosh, Willard, and Progresso. Farmland and town lots sold like bakery pies, and homestead rights were filed and proved up. Available homestead acreage was soon claimed, and prospective farmers began buying good tillable land adjacent to the old Spanish villages of Torreon and Manzano, and on the high cedar bench footing the Manzanos. Land in the first quarter of the century was cheap and good, and a nice level 160 acres could be bought for $800.

The October 10, 1935, issue of the *Estancia News-Herald* carried this advertisement:

> 155 acres of land in the cedars joining on the north the town of Torreon, drilled well with best water in the country, home pump, 42 acres in cultivation, and all fenced. $1,750.

Neal Jenson, Jr., a long-time Albuquerque resident, thinks that The Valley of Broken Hearts is a misnomer. Those who left sold out without tears, he says. Those who stayed were used to hard times, and didn't cry about it. Neal was born near Estancia, raised there, knows the valley and its days and ways. Agriculture, he maintains, is the industry for this geographical heart of New Mexico—as it always has been. Today the crops are corn, feed for livestock, potatoes, all under irrigation. But the little speckled bean that made the valley famous is gone.

Anyone of long-time acquaintance with the Estancia Valley can remember the Jenson Bean Company, with its headquarters plant and warehouse in Estancia. Out from its processing machinery the cleaned and sacked beans went first on the New Mexico Central, then via other railroads of the West to all points of the compass. The sacks bore an insignia—a diamond with a J in the center, which was also the Jenson cattle brand—that identified the Estancia Valley product to be the peak of quality.

Neal Jenson, Sr., arrived in the valley in 1906, alighting from an El Paso & Southwestern train at Torrance, southern terminus of Estancia's own New Mexico Central. He engaged himself in hotel and lumberyard activities in Torrance and Encino, and in real estate in Estancia, then married Judge Garvin's daughter in 1911 and homesteaded near Antelope Springs, six miles north of Estancia. Like many another settler with foresight in those days, he "blocked up" a ranch, buying out neighbors' homesteads. In 1912 the Jenson Bean Company started up business in Estancia. Throughout its years of operation the company received and processed Estancia Valley beans in plants at Estancia, Willard, Mountainair, Moriarty, Pedernal, McIntosh, and Cedarvale—with outposts to serve such faraway points as Pietown and Magdalena.

180

Today, Neal Jenson of Albuquerque recalls the days of his boyhood, the school days, when life was prime in the valley. That's when the rails were shiny on the "Central," and beans and livestock kept the traffic going. Carloads of sacked beans went off to Texas. The trains connected with the EP & SW main line at Torrance, from there to unload in El Paso. Others turned east at Willard on the Santa Fe to head for Amarillo and east. And by some quirk of geography, maybe natural as rain, the railroad tracks from Stanley to Willard marked a division. East of the line was the domain of the cattleman and the sheepman, the grazers and drovers; west lay the farmlands, the famed homeland of the pinto bean, stretching to the foothills of the Manzanos.

There in the days of glory farms occupied almost every quarter-section, with a windmill and house, and the brown cultivated earth that turned green in summer. And the sound of shiny new farm machinery. There was warmth and life in the homes, homes where folk were joyous and sad, where the newly married beamed from bright eyes on the prospects ahead, where babies were born, where friendships were firm, where the word "neighbor" carried the same meaning as "respect and consideration," where the Sears Roebuck catalog was the ultimate in literature—second, of course, to the Book that contained the Word of God.

That's when John McIntosh came out of Scotland and homesteaded near the community that today bears his family name, blocked up a sheep ranch and sent to Inverness for his relatives, the MacGillivrays—and in New Mexico the "Luck of the MacGillivrays" is legend. That's when young Will King came out of Texas with his pretty bride Mollie. Both with their belongings in a Tin Lizzie. They exchanged their vehicle for 160 acres at Stanley, from which was built the 40,000-acre King Brothers homeranch in the valley, spreading to another 400,000 acres in counties to the west. That's when. . .

Heaven help us, the success stories are endless!

That's when the bean fields yielded four 100-pound sacks to the acre, the beans selling at four cents a pound—for an average year. Plus a stack of bean hay for stock fodder. That, with income from supplemental crops and sales of cattle and hogs—not to forget home butchering and the family garden. And this at a time when Arbuckle's coffee cost 25 cents a pound, salt pork 10 cents a pound in 20-pound slabs, potatoes 2 cents, flour. . .

Then why the abandoned houses, the rusted machinery, the bean processing plants so silent and cold, the warehouses empty? Where now the New Mexico Central? Where the homes and windmills on every quarter-section?

Neal Jenson remembers 1929 as the valley's most prosperous year. Somehow, the valley weathered the Crash of 1929 and the depression. The people worked as hard through the dismal period as they did when they first built the valley to comfort and fame. They hauled wood from the Manzano foothills and sold it to supplement their incomes. Some took part-time jobs—in Albuquerque, Santa Fe, Belen—or on the highways nearer to home. Some even camped in the canyons of the Jicarilla Mountains, north of White Oaks, there to placer for gold.

Then in 1934 came the winds—the dry cloud overhead, the swirls of dust on the valley floor. But the winds had blown over the valley since time began, and the people were weathered to it. And it wasn't as bad as in Kansas and Oklahoma, whose refugees could be seen, blown and shriveled, making their way west along U.S. 66, by car, by truck, by mule, by foot, heading for the promised land of California.

The winds brought a blight on the valley. Things were not as good as they used to be, and folks came to the realization that 160 acres was no longer sufficient to afford a man a living. Times were changing and they did so with the winds.

Some left, to seek their fortune elsewhere, selling out to neighbors who decided to hang on. Then, as today, a high school diploma was a ticket to somewhere else.

Maybe it took World War II to start the unpeopling of the valley, when the young men were called to duty, some never to return.

And slowly, the climate was changing. The old steady weather pattern was migrating along with the youth—going somewhere else. The dirt farmer couldn't make it without irrigation. But the pinto bean wasn't made for irrigation. Without the heavy snows of winter to saturate the soil, without the dry spring when the fields were middle-busted and planted, without the blessed July rains, without the 80-day season, the irrigated pinto just didn't taste the same.

And the people left the valley.

"Them poor people, they're good folk, mighty clever," Milt said from his 8,000-foot piney perch. "But they're everlastin'ly livin' under a dry cloud. Maybe they like it."

They liked it then and those who stayed like it today. Theirs is not the "Pinto Bean Capital of the World" any longer. It's a land of big ranches, irrigated fields, and long reaches of dry, cactus-spotted land. Only an occasional ghostly farmhouse or rusting piece of machinery hints at the days that were, in what some still call the Valley of Broken Hearts—and others think of as the Valley of Heart's Desire.

182

25

SANDIA: THE SACRED MOUNTAIN

SANDIA MOUNTAIN, rising out of north-central New Mexico, has but half the elevation of Karakorum, a peak in the Himalaya upthrust of southern Tibet. The former has an altitude of 10,800 feet, the latter 24,000. The two are many thousands of miles apart; yet they are kindred peaks, spires to the heavens, sacred mountains, holy oracles upon the land. Toward their summits rise the pleading gaze and meditating mind of men whose every action is sprung, after long or short ceremony, from godly sanction and help. They are the altars of men who require a firm rock to support their stalwart faiths. Tibetan lama, Pueblo Indian—Karakorum, Sandia—one and the same spiritually.

Our New Mexican peak may be a mere earth blister when compared to greater American mountains such as Whitney or McKinley, Evans or the Grand Teton. But for folk who understand the reason for Sandia, in Indian mythology and religion, there is none mightier or more beautiful. For it has divine significance: to the trusting heart it is more than a pile of rock, timber and snow—it is the dwelling place, the watchtower of the gods.

Sandia is probably more widely known than any other mountain within our borders, for it rises just at the edge of Albuquerque, center of the most populous area in the State. Geologically, it has one of the most interesting faults, or breaks in the rock strata, on the continent; and its heavy mantle of pine, spruce, fir, and aspen provides a deep forest to contrast with the semi-arid plains and valley below.

Roads and trails lead to secluded spots where in the midst of summer crisp air may be enjoyed, where clear water flavored by fallen pine needles, soft as velvet, flows from hidden springs. And where quiet reigns—that most blessed of all currency out of the mint of heaven. A short drive from Albuquerque will take one to the deepest seclusion of the Sandias. But leave the two-toned job at some spot along its accustomed ruts, and yourself take Shanks' pony up the narrow, steeper trails. Exhaust vapors do not mix well with forest ozone, and God made knee action before men invented high torque power.

I, personally, am a man of great wealth. And my wife helps me spend it. Ours is not wealth of the material sort that dries as grass and flits with the wind, but we are recipients of a geographical legacy, dwellers in a house that affords an unobstructed view of the sacred mountain every daylight hour of the year. Seen from our home, on the west bank of the Rio Grande a few miles north of Bernalillo, the mountain lifts itself to a regal peak, crowned with Arctic-alpine rock and tundra above its richly timbered bulk—and the dawns and sunsets that attend the majesty are glorious to behold.

Seen from Albuquerque, twenty miles south, or at an equal distance to the north, the range is flat yet no less beautiful. But the panorama viewed from Coronado Monument, with river, bosque, and foothill for a base—the great peak has a quality all its own, as though the show lingers on after the final curtain when it performed for the highly spiritual long-ago folk who made these crumbled ruins their home. It is a feast for the inspiration, sometimes gay, sometimes sober, at all times dramatic. Like a Roerich painting that depicts some faraway, forbidden landscape. Cobalt earth against turquoise sky, according to the mood, or soft pink against cold steel. On moonlight nights it becomes silver-mounted under a diamond aura of stars.

Sandia. . .Oku Piñ. . .Sivya. . . .

Name it as you wish, for in all tongues it remains the sacred mountain of the Indians, the people who knew it first. It is their instrument to maintain survival, the mighty bulwark against the white man's progress that seeks to weaken their beautiful lives. To look upon Sandia is good medicine. But a man, any man, does not require Indian blood to look upon a mountain, any mountain, and in so doing find pasture for concentration and solace for his soul. He just needs the will power to turn away from material opportunities, just long enough to respond in kind to the twinkling of a star. Watch hands may move toward Nirvana but the *Wall Street Journal* never delivered a message of love.

Sandia is a Spanish word meaning "watermelon." But why the conquistadors should choose to identify lofty grandeur with such low significance is a puzzle in itself. Perhaps the strange aboriginal melons they found growing at the Pueblo of Nanfiath in the valley west of the mountains—the familiar Sandia Pueblo of today—attracted them so much that the village won the honor of a mistaken name; and in due course the mountains found themselves namesaked for the village. Persons with a fondness for Fourth of July picnics are inclined to believe that the name sprang from the "watermelon pink" glow the slopes take at certain sunsets. Quite possible. But I maintain that Sandia is a corruption of the name *Santiago*, St. James. A glance at the map will show that not a major range of mountains in all New Mexico is named for Santiago, a saint revered by all Spaniards. So to the abandoned picnic grounds with the watermelon theory, along with the rinds and seeds! The early Franciscans were the name givers, devout men concerned more with the rewards of heaven than with the fruits of the soil. . . . And why name a mountain for a vegetable when a saint is available?

From their pueblos north of Santa Fe, the Tewa Indians look upon Sandia as The South World Mountain—or *Oku Piñ*, Turtle Mountain. It is most sacred to war, for there dwelt Oku-wa-piñ, who fathered the Twin War Heroes. The twins were good boys, wise and brave and loyal, and they set off from the big cloud that drapes the summit to do wondrous and gallant deeds for their people, such as slaying giants. To this day they have remained a symbol, in spirit ever counseling the War Chiefs with their sublime wisdom, helping the councils to overcome the Big White Giant from beyond the East World Mountain—Bureaucracy. Also on the peak of Sandia dwelt *Wa-kwijo*, Wind Old Woman, a lady adept at raising the dust—and the reason for the grit in your eye. But, mostly, Sandia rises as the gateway to the south, to *The Everlasting Summerland*, from whence comes the warmth of spring and the rains of summer, the blessing of corn and sustenance, the gift of the very breath of life.

To the Keres Indians, whose villages lie westward as far as Ácoma, Sandia Mountain is known as *Sivya*. For these sincere people it is the altar of the sacred east, out from behind which comes the light of day, the rise of the moon, and the promise of the morning star. These three, as all the other goodnesses of life, come from the earth to bless the people—born of the Earth, the Mother, the tender benefactress of the Indian . . . Sivya, the mighty oracle whose crest is more than two miles above the level of the white man's distant sea.

186

Sacred to war, and how ironic the symbol has become! Over twenty thousand years ago Sandia Man, from his cave in the mountain, emerged with intent to club down or drive a dart into wild creatures now as extinct as himself; and, being human, at times engaged himself in battle with fellow flesh as part of the process of keeping life in his own. He found cold stone against the enemy cranium effective to his purpose. He was old-fashioned about his use of weapons, never dreaming in his *north* cave what effect weapons would ultimately have on the *south* end of the mountain. Pre-Folsom Sandia Cave, Ultra-Atomic Sandia Base, a few miles between.

In the shadow of Sandia, through the centuries, the warrior has held his own, demonstrating his prowess, his valor, and sometimes his fall. Wild nomad tribes invading the peaceful pueblos, the conquistadors bent upon and accomplishing their motives, conflict of church and state, one man working his inhumanity on another, exploitation of the Indians, revolt and retaliation, plunder, bloodshed, havoc and reconquest—then peace, such as peace was.

Mexican revolution, the Camino Real, then General Stephen Watts Kearny and his Army of the West—and New Mexico became a part of the United States. The settling and growth of Albuquerque, the coming of the Santa Fe Railway, the arrival of the merchants and the prosperity thereof, a change in the Indian pueblos and the start of a dwindling away of an ancient way of life. Then war and the boom and supermodern, push-button living. . . .

Throughout the world there are shrines built of a people's faith, some famed, others not too well-known, all sacred to thoughtful minds and living confidence. In the past there was the oracle at Delphi, and another at Patrae; and today there are the Grotto at Lourdes, the Hill of Tepeyac, the Temple of Kali. They were all made classic by the hand of time, maintained by the heart of trust. But are the people of New Mexico's largest city aware that an oracle to the gods looms at their northeast skyline?

Three thousand years ago the great King Solomon built a mighty Temple to the Lord. It was one of the greatest structures of all time; and though it has long since fallen to ruin, the faith and greatness of Solomon's people remain. And so it is with the Pueblo Indians who from the valley below raise voice and eye to the clouds that canopy the summit of Sandia, who for centuries have tended the most secret holies of holies deep in the most inaccessible fastnesses. Let them continue, and they'll never lose their identity as a people and always retain their souls, no matter how tall the skyscraper in the adjacent city. The Pueblo Indian has survived four centuries of the white man's interference, and with the mountain at his elbow his future is measured in terms of forever. His past, present and future depended and depend on a *rock*—and there is no more solid a foundation in all the world than the oracle of Sandia reaching to pierce our own blue sky.